# 'I want to be a Dolphin Trainer...'

## an autobiography

Siân Banks

authorHOUSE®

*AuthorHouse™ UK Ltd.*
*500 Avebury Boulevard*
*Central Milton Keynes, MK9 2BE*
*www.authorhouse.co.uk*
*Phone: 08001974150*

*First published by AuthorHouse  7/8/2010*

*ISBN: 978-1-4490-9777-6 (sc)*

# Acknowledgements

I would like to send heartfelt thanks to John Goodman, my good friend who without his encouragement and editorial skills this book would never have seen the light of day. Thanks also to Ellen, John's wife who laughed so much reading the early chapters that I felt it was worth carrying on with. Many thanks go to all the people who have over the years said 'You should write an autobiography'. Without all of you I wouldn't have put pen to paper, or fingers to keyboard.

Special thanks to Jim Marshall for putting some 'celebrity' into my book, that'll make it sell!

Lots of love and thanks go to Lynne Morris from www. lynnemorrisphotography.co.uk who has featured in one of my stories and has laughed and cried at my calamities, but more than that has been a wonderful friend and talented photographer who made me look 'not half bad' in the photo on the back of the book. Grateful thanks to Geoff my brilliant boss who has not only supported but put up with me when I have encountered some of my calamities. I would also like to send generous thanks to my colleague Ian Horton who designed the fabulous book cover.

I would also like to thank most deeply the charity Women's Aid who helped me in my darkest hours.

But most of all love and thanks go to my wonderful Mum Pat for encouraging me to read so many books and also for buying most of them for me, this has inspired me to write this in the first place and to John my step-dad for being the Dad we always wanted.

Love to you all xx

# Dedication

For my sister Sue. My very dearest friend, whose humour, love and friendship have made this book the funny read I hope it is. I love you.

Feel the fear... and do it anyway

*(Susan Jeffers)*

# Prologue

We sat in the 'spare office' normally reserved for in-jections, nit inspections and meetings with parents, it was a grubby uninviting room but in those day 'careers advice' was a relatively new concept so the interviews were held anywhere, I was lucky we had chairs. It was a hot sticky day and there was an odd smell coming from Mr Boyer, the school careers advisor.

He was an oldish man with a moustache, slightly stooped but a quintessential English gentleman, his tie always seemed to be over one shoulder as if he was facing a gale force wind, he was the stereotypical geography teacher, with leather arm patches on his jacket sleeves and what appeared to be hundreds of pens and pencils in the top pocket of his jacket. I used to wonder how he got them all in there, did he put them all in at once or squeeze them in one at a time. Perhaps there was a hole in the lining and he lost a few never to be seen again. It was the graveyard session after lunch so everyone knew that he was feeling relaxed and at peace with the world. The last thing he wanted to do was spend the afternoon learning about the hopes and dreams of twelve school leavers. And to be honest we were not that keen either as it all seemed a waste of time. It was common knowledge that the careers scheme had only ever helped one person get a job and that was one teacher's son, Nick, he was an odd lad with a slightly worrying grin. The careers team had taken finding a job for Nick as a personal challenge and were quite pleased when they found him a job stacking shelves in Kwik Save. He was quite good at it until they had to let him go because he was spending all his time staring into space.

'Now Shawn, (no-one ever pronounced my name correctly 'Sharn') what would you like to do when you leave school?' He leaned across the desk with his practiced 'care in the community', I'm here to help smile.

I already knew what I wanted to do but I thought a delay for thinking time would make sure that he took me seriously.

'I want to work with animals', I said, 'I want to be a dolphin trainer'. Silence!

'Have you thought about being a hairdresser or a nursery nurse', he replied, or you could be a secretary, according to your teachers you should get some good grades'. He completely ignored my answer as he suggested the only three jobs I had ever heard careers officers talk about.

I repeated my answer,

'I want to be a Dolphin Trainer, I have always been interested in dolphins and I think I would be good at it'.

He was visibly confused and tried to pull a pen out of his top pocket causing a cascade of pens and pencils to hit the desk, he selected one and I tried not to laugh as he tried to cram the rest back in his pocket. He then scribbled something in his pad and I strained to read upside down – 'Dolphin Trainer, no common sense, a dreamer'. I listened as he continued.

'I'm sure you would like to do that but it's only a short term job and it won't pay the bills when you get married and have a family and a nice house of your own'. He had adopted that condescending 'don't be stupid' voice and he was on a roll. 'And it's not that easy to find jobs like that, you need to have suitable qualifications to work with animals it can take five years to train to be a vet'.

'I don't want to be a vet I want to be a Dolphin Trainer and it doesn't matter what you say because I've already got the job'.

That stopped him. He sat there with his mouth open trying to think of something to say......

'OK, that's great news'. He wrote something on his pad, I think it said 'liar'.

'You have obviously been thinking of this for some time and I wish you every success, please send in the next pupil'.

I left the room pleased to escape the smell of stale tobacco. The next victim was sitting outside the door, I'm sure she had been listening but I didn't care – I was free. I told Sarah Tasker it was her turn, she looked as enthusiastic as I had been.

So that's it. I had officially told the school that I was to become a Dolphin Trainer and that I had already got the job. It was almost true, I used to visit Knowsley Safari Park whenever I could and after watching the Dolphins I went to the office and asked if they had any vacancies for a Dolphin trainer. I now realise that the staff in the office were taking the p@*s because they made me fill out a form listing all my relevant qualifications, none, and my previous experience, none, but they could see I was keen and they did have a vacancy on the ticket barrier. They told me to apply. I thought it would be a start and at least I would be on site for when the Dolphin Trainers job become vacant.

So as I walked home from school I thought I had better get on with it. How was I to know that my life was to include many careers, three marriages, three children, a change of identity, going out with a millionaire and finding my secret family........

So this is the story of my life. It's all true but I have been selective about what has been included as there are some bits that even I don't want to remember. Don't expect an exposé full of revelations, scandal and sex, where possible, I have obtained permission before using names and details.

I hope this book will amuse and entertain and hopefully take you along the emotional rollercoaster that has been my life. Perhaps it may help explain why I do the things I do and why I am happy with my 'lot'. Of course there are things I would have changed or done differently but it's all part of who I am and what makes me Sian Banks or Sian Williams? – You will have to read the book to find out about the name change, and it wasn't due to one of my marriages......

# Chapter 1

## 1982 - Don't look back

My last day at school was 11th June 1982. It wasn't an ordinary day as I was there to take my English 'O'level. It had all the makings of a lovely summer's day as 93 of us were nervously waiting to be let into the main sports hall where they always held the examinations. The doors opened and we surged forward past the miserable looking invigilator. She was a religious education teacher who appeared to have had any personality removed a number of years ago. As you can imagine she was very unpopular and some of us thought her first job was at a dairy where she was employed to turn the milk into sour cream by staring at it.

We settled at the rows of single desks and waited for her to tell us to turn over the paper and get started. The exam was as expected and I spent the last half an hour looking out the window at the sun beating down on the playing field. The papers were collected and we headed for the doors. As it was my last exam I was free, in those days they were keen for you to leave as soon as possible so with my careers interview completed and my last exam taken it was all over. I collected my things from my form room and walked through the school gates for the last time.

I was relieved to be leaving. Although I'd had lots of friends, and was fairly bright, I actually hated school.

I was unhappy there and I had also been unhappy at my old school before we moved to Rainhill. I don't know why I didn't like school but I didn't. The only thing I would miss was my form teacher Mr Kedge, he was a great laugh and I really liked his tutor group lessons.

It was more that 25 years later when I drove past the end of 'Two Butt Lane' and I was telling my children that the new housing estate on the right was where my old school had stood before it had been set on fire and they knocked it down. They then became hysterical when they saw the name of the road on the sign. I didn't get it, didn't see what was so funny 'Two butts, Two butts' they all chanted laughing their heads off. In my day it was your bottom or bum, never your butt. However they'd grown up in the world of American cartoon TV and Bart Simpson, so the road name had a brand new meaning, at last I got it and drove on laughing along with them.

Back to 1982 – as I walked down the lane, I thought 'Don't look back' you'll never ever have to go there again. It was a gorgeous afternoon and as I walked along I loosened my tie, that thing was coming off, never to be worn again. Who on earth had decided on Black and yellow diagonal stripes.  As I walked I was thinking about all the things that had happened in the year that I was at Rainhill High. A girl was murdered on the school playing field by her brother and he did it with a hammer – how horrific.

Rainhill was an interesting place, and some of its history was quite gruesome, must have been the lunatic asylum situated there that attracted the nutters!

The history of Rainhill goes back to Norman times and it is written in the Doomsday Book that Rainhill

2

was originally part of Widnes. Around 1246, Roger of Rainhill died and the township was divided into two parts for each of his daughters. One half was centred on the site of the Rainhill Manor Public House, in the Stoops area, and the other on Rainhill Hall, just off Blundell's Lane.

At the end of the 18th century, four sons of a farmer, who came from the area around Stonyhurst, decided to make their fortunes in Liverpool. The brother's family name was Bretherton. In 1800, they decided to move into the coaching business. The business quickly built up and by 1820, they had the bulk of the coaching trade of Liverpool, running Coaches to and from Manchester fourteen times a day from Saracen's Head in Dale Street. Rainhill became one of the major staging places and facilities were built on the land alongside the Ship Inn - originally called the New Inn owned by Henry Parr 1780. They had stabling for 240 coach horses and facilities for, farriers, and coach builders. We actually lived on Rainhill Road, next door to a pub called the Coach & Horses, a hang-over from the old days.

Later Rainhill was the site of the 1829 Rainhill Trials, in which a number of railway locomotives were entered into a competition to decide on a design for the new Liverpool and Manchester Railway. The winner was The Rocket, designed by George Stephenson. When we were kids in 1979 the 150th anniversary of the trials was celebrated by hundreds of trains of all ages, including replicas of the trials winner and runners-up, all travelling through Rainhill.

During the Victorian times, Rainhill was the home of a notorious mass murderer; Frederick Bailey Deeming. In March 1892, the bodies of a woman and her four children were discovered buried under the concrete floor of Dinham Villa, Lawton Road in Rainhill.

So it's all happened here, I was even involved in a murder myself, and as I walked home on that sunny day, my mind was taken back a year and a bit ago....

# Chapter 2

## 1981- Rainhill Murder

Mum's friend June was a make-up artist and she had her own model agency. Her other claim to fame was that she had been the girlfriend of Radio's City's Phil Easton. Phil was a fantastic guy who joined the original Radio City when it started in 1975. Recently he suffered a brain haemorrhage just a few hours after presenting his breakfast show on Liverpool's City Talk radio station and is a sad loss.

June was really busy at the time and asked me to join her model agency but I'd never fancied it. Don't get me wrong, I could have done it, I was nearly 15 and, although I say it myself, I was quite good looking but I liked my food and the thought of having to live on a stick of celery and fresh air didn't appeal to me.

Mum and June were going to have one of those 'Tupperware' type parties, where you invite a load of your mates; they come round, drink gallons of wine, and buy various things. Sometimes it was actually Tupperware, but more often it was jewellery or candles. These days it would be adult entertainment items from Ann Summers! Mum and June's 'do' was a make-up party, and the idea was that June would 'make-up the ladies with her professional make up products and then she would try to sell the cosmetics to the guests. It was all a bit of a con because even with the high quality cosmetics these ladies would never be able to re-create the professional look without years of training. It was all going very well, the wine was flowing and everyone was getting merry. Although I wasn't directly involved I was hanging around watching June transform Mum's old mates into gorgeous sophisticated women that were unrecognisable from the ladies that had arrived earlier in the evening.

'Do you want a go Siân?' June asked. 'I've finished with all the ladies and I still have lots of samples left'. I glanced at Mum to see if it would be ok, she knew I was going to the 'Scouts disco' and she wasn't over keen on me getting too made up. Mum smiled and said, 'OK June but don't go mad, we don't want her getting into any trouble later.' When June had finished I looked in the mirror and couldn't believe my eyes. Where was Siân, that 14 year old gawky looking school girl? All I could see was a beautiful young woman in her early twenties, it was fantastic, I couldn't actually recognise my own face. Mum looked stunned but had to admit that I looked lovely. 'Can I keep it on for the disco Mum?' I pleaded.

'Go on Pat, don't make her wash it off' one of Mum's mates piped up.

'Go on then love, but don't you be home too late, and make sure you look after our Sue'. Great! I looked like a million dollars and I was being allowed out. The only downside was that I had to take our Sue along with me. Sue was only 11 and to be honest she was never any bother but I was convinced that having a younger sister hanging around seriously damaged my street cred as I was a sophisticated young lady and didn't need to have children tagging along with me. But I had a plan, Sue knew more people than I did at the Scouts so I was hoping that I would soon be able to leave her with her mates.

As we walked to the Scout Hut I told Sue that I was going to the off licence on the way to buy some alcohol.

I had been saving up so I had a few quid in my pocket and as I walked along I was trying to decide what a sophisticated young lady like me would be drinking. Sue looked at me and said 'You'll never get served, you're not old enough'.

I laughed, 'You just watch me, looking like this I will get served, no bother'.

I was convinced that I would be served, that wouldn't be any problem. My big problem was deciding what to buy? I'd never really drunk alcohol before, and there were no alco-pops back then. I had to decide before I went inside so that I would look confident, as though I had done it before. Sue's voice broke into my thoughts 'I like a medium sherry'. I stared at her in amazement, she'd tried Nan's sherry before but I could hardly go in asking for a bottle of Harvey's Bristol Cream, they'd think I was mad. 'No way' I shouted at her.

Then I had a brainwave I would ask for a bottle of Cinzano! I had seen Mum drink Cinzano and lemonade in the evenings so it can't be that strong, I'll get a bottle of that. We arrived at Ashe & Nephew, the local off licence and I looked in making sure there was no one in there that knew me. It was all clear to I stood up straight, puffed out my chest and went in. Sue was left waiting for me around the corner; she was convinced that I would come out with a bottle of lemonade. How wrong she was, I walked out with my head held high holding a bottle of Cinzano wrapped in tissue paper.

'Told ya' I said to Sue and we sat round the back of the 'offie' and opened the bottle. We both took a swig and our faces creased up, my God, it was rank. How the hell did Mum drink this stuff, perhaps we needed the lemonade to go with it. But needs must so we both had another swig from the bottle and headed off to the Scout's disco, down at the stoops. Rainhill Stoops is the area of the village known affectionately as 'the stoops' but no one seems to know the origin of the name 'stoops'. It could relate to a stone column set in the ground, a stone frame for a door or gate or it could be of Dutch origin relating to a group of seats or steps.

Well it was a good night, the disco hosted by 'Shapes Disco' was packed, and I'd successfully lost Sue, and found my 'friend' Rob, who I was desperately hoping was going to be my 'boyfriend'. The only trouble was that he already had a girlfriend, Steph, and she already had her eye on me as the potential competition. But I didn't care as I had all the confidence that my new make-up had given me together with the effect of half a bottle of neat Cinzano. I thought I was invincible and I was flirting outrageously with Rob.

The next thing I knew I was under attack. Steph had come out of the shadows and was on me like a tiger, clawing, biting and scratching. Rob managed to pull her off me but not before the damage was done. My lip was bleeding, my lovely new Spandau Ballet frilly blouse was ripped and my make-up was ruined, I was leaving. I left Rob to it; after all it was his problem for getting involved with such a rough unrefined girl in the first place. I had no idea where Sue was and I staggered around for a while looking for her, I could barely up stand by now and as she was no-where to be seen I headed off home.

It must have been past 11.30pm when I walked past the Coach and Horses. It was our local and they always let my step Dad, Peter, stay behind after last orders. They would sit and finish their drinks playing dominos or cards in the snug I could see them laughing, warm and cosy through the window as I passed. It was getting very cold and I remember that a few flakes of snow were falling.

I couldn't find my key and as I didn't have Sue with me and I knew Mum was going to go mental. Should I wait for Peter to come home and let me in or should I knock on the door and face Mum? I didn't have a choice as the snow was getting heavier and I was shivering from the cold, I braced myself and knocked on the door. Mum opened the door and I could see from her face that she wasn't happy. I staggered past her into the back room where she had been watching the telly waiting for us. Then it started. 'Have you been bloody drinking? What's happened to your face?' she yelled, 'Where's Sue, and what time do you call this?' I don't remember if I actually managed to say anything, but the next thing I remember was a punch in the eye. She almost knocked me over but I recovered and made a grab for the door to escape. I ran towards the front door but Mum was soon after me and she managed to grab my lilac cardigan. She was beginning to pull me back so I let the cardigan slide from my arms as I escaped through the door. I can't remember what was being said but I do remember we were both shouting as I escaped into the road. Mum didn't seem to be chasing me but I wasn't taking any chances so I fled down the main road, and ran towards the pub. I needed my Dad. The pub door had a huge old ring door knocker and I slammed it into the door as hard as I could. In the quiet of the night the noise seemed so loud but no one came. I tried again, hitting the door with my fists and screaming at the top of my voice, I needed safety, I needed Dad. I could see my Dad and his mates through the little panes of glass and was frantically waving to him; eventually the door was finally opened. I barged in past the startled barmaid and ran into the snug towards my Dad. I was screaming at the top of my voice 'She's trying to kill me; she's trying to kill me'. Everyone was stunned into silence and they all looked at me as ran to Dad still shouting, 'She's trying to kill me!'

Dad looked up at me and saw my face covered in scratches from my fight with Steph, he took me into one of the little alcoves and between my sobbing I explained what had happened. Dad laughed and told me not to worry as he cleaned up my face with his handkerchief. He calmed me down and took me home before going out again to look for Sue. He quickly found Sue as she was almost home with my friends Sarah and Gill who had seen me leave the disco and thought they should look after Sue, so about 10 minutes later we were all in bed. It took me a long time to fall asleep as my bruises were beginning to hurt and my head was spinning from the neat Cinzano. I fell asleep hoping that Mum would have forgotten all about it in the morning and that I would never have to think about that terrible evening again.

Bang, Bang, Bang! What was the noise was it in my head? No it was the front door. I was first to get up so I staggered down the stairs and saw the uniforms though the glass in the front door. It was police. I glanced in the mirror on the back of the living room door, Oh hell, look at my face, I thought. I had a massive shiner from my Mum and scratches down my cheeks and a fat lip from my fight with Steph at the Scout disco.

'Mum, Dad, the police need to speak to you' I shrieked up the stairs, Dad came down with Mum just behind in her dressing gown.

It was only 7am on Saturday morning. 'What's all this about?' asked Dad.

The police didn't tell us anything but kept looking at my face. After the usual questions, name, age, etc., they asked how I had got my injuries. I explained about the trouble and the disco and with my Mum when I came home. They eventually explained that at the same time that I'd been running into the pub screaming 'she's trying to kill me', a young girl of 16, Janet Cheetham from my school was actually being murdered in the alley opposite the pub. When the pub customers heard about the murder the next morning they all assumed that I was involved.

I had the injuries and there had been lots of witnesses to my screaming session in the pub. It didn't look good. I don't think the police thought I had actually murdered the girl but they thought I was involved and that I knew more than I was telling them. They were there for hours and over the next couple of weeks we had 20 odd visits from the police and had to make numerous statements, in which my Mum, Rob and Steph had to account for my injuries. Thankfully they believed us in the end but it was a scary time. It took 10 years to capture that poor girl's killer, and it was only when the killer's Mum could no longer live with the guilt that she shopped him to the police.

I haven't drunk Cinzano since and just the smell of it brings back memories of that awful night.

# Chapter 4

## 1982 - First Job

I didn't take the job at the Safari Park so I will never know if I would have made it as a Dolphin Trainer, I am still convinced I would have been good at it and I've always wondered where my life would have ended up if I had taken the job on the ticket barrier. For the first, and to be honest one of the few times in my life I actually listened to my Mums advice. 'Get yourself off to typing college, if you can type you'll always have a job' sound advice from Mum and Mums always know best. I had 10 GCE O'level passes and I had no idea what I wanted to do. I decided to please Mum and headed to college. Dad's friend knew the principal of a secretarial college so he got me in. It was the Sight & Sound Secretarial College in Liverpool, now it's part of the Liverpool Community College and they don't offer any Secretarial courses anymore, it's now all media based studies. Unlike school I loved every day I spent at college. Everyone was 'grown up', we were there by choice and we were treated like adults, it was great.

I attended the enrolment afternoon at the college and as soon as they heard about my exam passes I was offered the full range of courses. This didn't help, there was too much choice so I followed Mums advice and signed up for the General Secretarial course. I also joined the Youth Opportunities Scheme that was run by the Government to get school leavers into work by paying their wages and finding job training placements. I earned £25 a week and I spent the first 3 months at the college learning how to type and carry out lots of general office skills. The most enjoyable thing about college was the friends I made there they were a great group of people, we were all about the same age and we all had the same interests.

The next 3 months was spent at a company called Heywood & Partners where I was a trainee Receptionist. The college found the placements and some of the students ended up being used as cheap labour. I was lucky as Heywood & Partners was a good place to work. It was an old family business and some of the family were still in charge. Most of the staff had worked there for years and as a result there was a wonderful friendly atmosphere. They were based on Tythbarne Street in Liverpool's city centre quite near to John Moore's university. I had no idea what the company did, but my role involved greeting visitors, issuing passes, typing letters, photocopying and sorting the post.

I had a brand new IBM golf ball electric typewriter and I thought it was the bee's knees, as you could change the typeface by changing the golf ball and using the internal erasing tape it would even remove mistakes, it lifted any mistakes right off the paper! It was fantastic. Everything was done in triplicate and I also had pink and yellow Tippex in case of errors, but as my typing speed was 55 wpm with 99% accuracy I made very few mistakes.

At 16 I felt extremely sophisticated commuting to work on the train from Rainhill. Liverpool has an underground very much like London's Tube system but much smaller, consisting of just 3 lines, the Northern, the Central and the Wirral. I used to take the Northern Line from Lime Street up to Moorfields it was then a short walk to the office. When I was invited to a colleague's birthday drink I was really excited. It was to be held in the evening at one of the local pubs in Dale Street so we could change into our party frocks and walk to the pub.

There were few affordable alcoholic drinks for young ladies in 1982. There was no such thing as alcho-pops and cocktails were far too expensive. The answer was to add blackcurrant into everything we drank, mostly lager or cider. So being a sophisticated 'girl about town', I was drinking cider and black, I was cheap to take out in those days. The Rose & Crown on Dale Street was a mock Tudor-style building with a large open plan bar and right in the middle of the main room was a huge staircase leading down to the ladies and gents toilets. For a young lady from Rainhill it was an exciting night out. We had taken over a few tables and there were about 15 of us celebrating Julie's birthday. I'd been sitting there talking and quietly sipping my cider and blackcurrant , when I decided it was time to go to the ladies, I felt decidedly unsteady as I headed for the staircase. I had been sipping my drink but I had been doing it non-stop for a couple of hours.

The next few minutes are a bit of a blur and I don't know how I tripped. I do remember that I cart-wheeled down the stairs and into a door which flew open as I tumbled through and it then slammed shut leaving me in complete darkness .

I took a moment or two to get my bearings, I had no idea where I was but I soon realised that the strong smell was beer so I guessed I was in the cellar! My head was now clear and all I could think of was that there would be rats in the cellar with me – I used to watch too many films.  I sat on the floor trying to decide what to do. My head hurt and I could feel a serious bump developing on my head but everything else seemed to be OK, quite surprising when I remembered the cartwheel down the stairs. I could feel the cold concrete on one of my feet so I realised I had lost a shoe in the tumble but I couldn't find it. It was freezing cold and noises from the pumps started sounding very human and I was sure that they were whispering something to me, I was petrified. I couldn't even see where the door was so I crawled until I felt a wall and worked my way around it until I felt what seemed to be crates of bottles, then beer barrels and eventually I found the door. I felt to the left and right of the door looking for a light switch, I could feel thick cobwebs coating my hands and arms but I couldn't find a switch. I couldn't even feel a handle or any way of opening the door, so I banged as hard as I could and shouted. I must have been shouting and banging for a few minutes before the light was turned on and the door was opened by a surprised looking bar man.

'What are you doing in here?' he asked.

'I've lost my shoe' I said

'What are you doing in here?' he asked again.

I was trying to appear as sober as possible and was trying to think on my feet. 'I was looking for the toilet and I came through the wrong door' I replied.

He raised his eyebrows and we started to look around the cellar for my shoe.

'It's up there' he said. I followed his gaze and right on top of pile of bottle crates was my red shoe!

'How did it get up there?' he asked

'I don't know, I just fell down the step when I came through the door and I realised I'd lost my shoe'.

He looked doubtful but it was true so the only thing I could think of. I couldn't tell him I was drunk and had fallen down the stairs from the pub; after all I was only sixteen. He climbed up and retrieved my shoe before showing me out and locking the door. He turned off the cellar light using a switch in the hall, no wonder I couldn't find it. I rushed to the toilets and threw up the pinkest vomit I'd ever seen. That was the blackcurrant!

I washed my face and returned to my friends. They were too busy enjoying themselves to notice I had been gone and luckily the developing bruise was hidden under my hair. I refused any more drinks and excused myself before the party had finished which is something would I never do now. I sobered up as I walked to the station and I decided that I was definitely too young to be out drinking after work.

# Chapter 5

## 1983 - Youth Club

I've always like taking part in sports so I volunteered to help out at the Sutton High Sports Centre Youth club. In those days Youth Clubs were great places, we played pool, badminton and table tennis with the kids and we supervised them to try and keep them under control. It was easy and they were a good group of kids so we often organised trips to the local roller skating rink in Warrington. It was good fun and even though I didn't get paid I loved it. I used to go on Tuesday and Thursday evenings and I had become good friends with Kieran, one of the other helpers. Kieran helped with the sports and specialised in karate.

We'd been helping at the Youth Club for about 6 weeks when Kieran and I saw a sign up on the notice board. The Leisure Centre were advertising for 3 part-time Leisure Assistants, they had to be keen on sports and enjoy working with children and teenagers – we were made for it, those jobs had our names against them. We applied for the jobs and after a couple of weeks we were both called for interviews.

Because the jobs were working with children we had to be interviewed by a panel and the letter included details of the panel. There would be the Leisure Centre Superviser, someone from the Personnel Department, a town councillor from the Leisure Department and a chap called Chez Parker who was the Leisure Centre

Manager. I couldn't believe my luck when I saw his name on the letter inviting me for the interview. He had been my scuba instructor when I took a course at Parr Baths. It had all been part of my master plan to become a Dolphin trainer and I had decided that being able to scuba would be one of the essential qualifications. I'm not sure if Chez was his real name but that's what everyone called him and here he is on the interview panel. The town councillor from the Leisure Department was called Mel Ennis – and strangely enough I ended up working for him years later when he got together with Mum's friend Julia and they ran the Nag's Head.

So this illustrious panel was going to interview me for an 18 hour a week Leisure Assistant's role paying £2.50 an hour! It seemed a bit extreme but that's the way it works in Local Government.

A couple of weeks later both Kieran and I received letters from the Council to say that we'd been successful and would be starting sometime in April as that was the start of the new financial year.

I went into work the next day and handed in my notice telling them I wasn't cut out to be a Receptionist. They were very nice about it and arranged a little farewell ceremony and a collection. They even said I could come back anytime if it didn't work out for me. I made a little speech and said that I was sorry to be leaving but the Leisure Centre was closer to home. I didn't tell them it was just one step towards my master plan of becoming a Dolphin trainer.

I had decided to have a holiday and had agreed to start my new job in 2 weeks time. The day before I was due to start I received a call from Chez explaining that Kieran and I had applied jobs that were internal which meant that they were only for existing staff to apply for. He apologised and explained that it was due to an internal error on the advertisement.

Oh hell. I'd quit my other job, I couldn't go back now, we'd had a leaving party and they'd bought me a gift. What on earth was I going to do now?

Well basically nothing. I sat round for about 6 weeks doing not very much. My friend Jackie was a part time model and a part time hairdresser so I spent some time in the hairdressers and some time going with her on modelling assignments.

Then out of the blue came another call from Chez. He'd been on to the union to fight our case for us, we had no idea. Because the job advert hadn't stated that it was only for internal applicants there was some kind of loop hole and we were going to be offered the jobs after all.  So at the beginning of April 1983 I started my ten year career as a Leisure Centre Assistant and although I was never going to reek of success, perhaps there would be a faint whiff of chlorine.

# Chapter 6

## 1983 - April Fool

My sister Sue has always been one for practical jokes so everyone was always on their guard when we were children. I remember she had a squirting flower in her lapel once when we were kids and she nearly had my eye out. I can't blame Sue because we were just as bad as each other, it could have all gone terribly wrong with a butter knife when I lost my temper, but as fate would have it I controlled myself in the end so no harm done. Although I think she was mentally if not physically scarred by the attack.

It was the 1st April and Sue planned to make it an April fool's day to remember. Sue had set her alarm clock for 5 am and a few minutes later she was trying to wake me up to help her set up the April fool jokes she intended to play on Mum. We were to carry out the TV, video recorder and other assorted electrical items and hide them in Mum's car. Mum was to come downstairs and think that we had been burgled! Yes it was going to hysterical, Mum would laugh, we all would laugh.

Not only that, Sue had stretched cling film over the toilet as another prank which would mean an awful mess on the bathroom floor, if peeing wasn't the only thing the first unfortunate bathroom user was doing that fateful 1st April. Suffice to say it all went horribly wrong. Because when 5am came and Sue was desperately trying but was unable to rouse me, apparently I turned over snoring loudly, which meant Sue had to carry the TV out to the car on her own and back in 1982 this was no mean feat for a 6 stone 12 year old. Our TV probably weighed as much as she did, I'm sure it had a block of concrete in it like a washing machine. The future slim-line LCD models mounted on the wall were 30 years away. Even the video recorder was huge and almost required the front window to be taken out just to get the damn thing out of the house; Lord knows how burglars actually stole anything. Anyway Sue had managed the whole debacle alone, and had gone back to bed. Waking a couple of hours later she'd almost forgotten what she'd done. We were awoken by a hysterical screaming from the bathroom – oh hell, the cling film. Mum obviously didn't find it funny. And now she is charging down the stairs at full speed like a raging bull in her dressing gown........

The rest is a bit of a blur, but it featured me and Sue, desperately trying to get Mum off the phone, she'd dialled 999 to report a burglary... Sue was screaming April fool at the top of her voice and I was wrestling Mum for the phone. You won't be surprised to know we both got a 'scutch' (Mum's favourite word for her slapping) and we were both laughing on the other sides of our faces - NOT!

There were lots of 'Jeremy Beadle' type shows on the TV at that time even 'Candid Camera' was back and we saw a sketch that we thought was hilarious so we decided to play the same trick on Granddad after Mum had gone to work.

We had recovered from the trick we played on Mum and she had eventually gone off to work in a stinking mood. Sue and I were laughing so hard at the prospect of trying out this April fool's joke we were having trouble composing ourselves to phone Granddad.

Sue finally composed herself, she was much better at keeping a straight face so she picked up the phone. Our Granddad was a bit hard of hearing, but that made the April fool joke all the funnier.

Sue dialled him and pretended to be a BT engineer – picture the scene. Sue is 12, and is putting on the voice of a burly telecoms engineer. We were already giggling hysterically and I was desperately trying to eat my sleeve so Granddad wouldn't hear me. This is how it went...

Sue – 'Is that Mr Elliott?'

Granddad – 'yes this is Mr Elliott speaking'

Sue – 'This is the BT engineer; we've had a report of a fault on your line'

Granddad – 'Pardon?'

Sue – 'There's a fault?

Granddad – 'A fruit?

Sue – 'A FAULT!'

Granddad – 'Oh a fault? It all seems fine this end'

Sue – 'Yes a fault and we need to do some testing would you have a couple of minutes to carry out a test for us please?'

Granddad – 'Pardon?'

Sue – 'WE NEED TO TEST'

Sue was raising her voice louder and louder as the call went on, and I was wondering if this was a good idea after all.

Granddad – 'Yes OK, but will it take very long? I'm just about to leave for my bus to the YM for lunch'.

Our Nan had died in 1980 and every week day since, Granddad had gone to the YMCA with his pensioner pals to get a hot meal which was a service available for a small weekly subscription to all ex-Pilkington Glass staff. Granddad called the YMCA the YM for short.

Sue went on… 'Not long. Now this test involves whistling down the line'

Granddad – 'Pardon?'

Sue – 'Can you whistle?'

Granddad' – 'Pardon?'

Sue – 'WHISTLE!'

By this time I'm barely able to keep myself quiet and am rolling around the floor laughing hysterically, even though I can only hear Sue's side of the conversation. She is now virtually screaming down the phone to our hard of hearing Granddad.

Sue was almost choked trying to keep up the voice of the BT engineer and was trying to indicate to me that he was actually whistling down the line. It was all too much for me, I almost peed my pants and at last Sue shouted 'April Fool Granddad – it's me Sue'

Granddad – 'Who?'

Sue – 'Me, it's Sue and Siân; we're doing an April fool'

Granddad – 'Where's the BT Engineer gone? Is he at your house? Has he fixed the fault?'

Sue – 'Oh it doesn't matter Granddad, happy April Fool's day'

We have all been the target of Sue's wicked sense of humour at one time or another and long may it last – you can always rely on Sue for a laugh.

# Chapter 7

## 1984 – The lost false teeth

If you ever meet my Mum you would never realise that she has false teeth. Her teeth look perfectly natural which is incredible when you realise that she has a full, complete set of upper and lower dentures. One of the reasons they look so real is that she never takes them out and never mentions not being able to eat nuts or anything with seeds that will 'get under my teeth' and there is no evidence of a glass by bed or a tube of 'Sterident' in the bathroom. Her dentures are definitely not like the stars – they DO NOT come out at night. She is completely different to many pensioners who have badly fitting dentures that drop or whistle when they talk. She didn't ever take them out to pull silly faces to amuse the grandchildren and sometimes she even cleans them like normal teeth with a brush and toothpaste only taking them out in the privacy of the bathroom and only then if she has too.

Mum had all her teeth removed back in the 60s when she was little more than 23 years of age. She'd always had a fear of the dentist and had always been unhappy with her teeth since she was a child. After one very unpleasant visit to her dentist where she had to have several fillings, she just went completely mad and said 'Take the lot out'. The dentist was stunned and couldn't understand why, they weren't that bad and the fillings had all gone to plan but there was no stopping her. She's never looked back and loves her false teeth, saying 'It's the best thing I ever did'.

Because her false teeth are so good few people know that she has them – until they read this book, Sorry Mum. I can't even remember when I found out and Dad has certainly never seen her without her teeth. I can remember as a child that if she was in the bathroom cleaning her teeth and you tried to go in you were bloody for it. 'Get out, Get out', she would scream 'I'm cleaning my teeth'. She was fine if she was in the bath or on the loo – it was just her teeth that were private and she would not allow anyone to see her cleaning her teeth.

Family legend says that only the dentist, who removed her teeth, and an anaesthetist and surgeon, when she has a minor operation a few years later, are the only people to have ever seen her without her teeth. I assume the nurses had to wear blindfolds. She says that she had her false teeth fitted when her gums were still bleeding from the extractions so that no-one ever saw her without teeth. She'd had the same set of falsies for over 20 years and they still looked natural because they were custom made to look slightly crooked so that she didn't have the standard NHS Hollywood smile so familiar with many pensioners.

It was her first holiday abroad since having us kids and it was to be to Salou in Spain. I was 18 and looking forward to being left 'home alone' while Mum and Sue went off for 2 weeks in the sun. They were going with a big group including some of Mums friends from the local pool where she worked part-time as a swimming teacher.

It was the days before mobile phones so people still sent 'wish you were here' cards that usually arrived a few days after you got home. I had been having a great time on my own with my mates and I was in the process of planning yet another party when the phone rang – I thought it was one of my mates asking what time we were due to meet at the pub. I picked up the phone and heard lots of crackles and pops before hearing my Mum ringing from Spain, I immediately thought there was something wrong as it cost a fortune to ring from Spain in those days. Mum said hello but she sounded different and not her usual happy self. 'How's the holiday?' I asked 'Are you having a nice time?' The next thing I heard was Mum in floods of tears and it was difficult to understand what she was saying but I caught some of it, 'holiday... ruined... wave... teeth' and then she started crying again mumbling something about teeth. I could hardly understand a word she was saying and I soon realised it wasn't because of a bad line it was because I couldn't understand my Mum's voice. She sounded strange but not just because she was crying, there was something else, it just didn't sound like my Mum. I asked her to put Sue on and then it all became clear.

Sue didn't sound very happy either and I soon realised she was working from an agreed script, telling me what had happened, I could still hear Mum in the background prompting her and telling her not to forget to tell me this or that. When I heard the complete story I was struggling not to laugh, it was like a story off the television. Mum and Sue were having a great day on the beach. Mum was diving into the surf and messing around when she was hit quite hard on the back of the head by a huge rogue wave. The wave knocked her over and although she is a good swimmer Sue was worried as Mum surfaced gasping for breath.  The wave had hit her so hard that she couldn't breathe but worst of all it was so powerful it had knocked her false teeth out of her mouth and into the sea. Mum and Sue had spent the rest of the day searching for them but the heavy sea had either washed them out to sea or further along the beach. Anyway they were lost and Sue said that Mum had seemed to age in front of her. She'd gone from an attractive lady of 40 to a little old dear of 80. I couldn't even picture my Mum without her teeth but I knew she'd rather die than be seen without them, even now in her mid 60s she still won't take them out for the grandchildren even though we've pleaded many times.

The reason for the phone call was to ask me to contact her dentist to arrange for a new set to be made ready for her return. I spoke to Mum again and she said that she wasn't going back to work at the Council without teeth. Between the sobs she went on to say that all she could eat was spaghetti and everyone at the hotel was laughing at her. I knew her friends and I tried to reassure her they wouldn't do that as they are a nice group of people. But as I was saying it I was imaging Sue's face when Mum arose from the surf without her teeth. The more I imagined the scene the more difficult it was not to laugh. I promised to ring the dentist straight away and Sue said that they would ring again the following evening.

I spent the next few hours looking through Mums old phone book trying to track down her original dentist from twenty years before when she first had her dentures. Mum remembered his name but he had changed premises a couple of times, our only hope was that he had kept all his patient records and the gum impressions so that he could make another set ready for Mums return. After trawling through the local phone books and directories I finally found him and relayed the tale of woe. All credit to him he didn't laugh but he didn't have good news.

He was very apologetic and explained that it wouldn't be possible to make another set because the gums and mouth change over the years. Mum would have to come to his office as soon as she returned to be fitted for a new set and this would take approximately two weeks.

Oh hell, how was I going to tell Mum, she'd be without teeth for another two weeks?

I broke the news when she rang the following evening. Understandably she was even more upset; losing her teeth was bad enough but having to live without them for another two weeks was worse. She didn't want to face work and her colleagues without her teeth but she didn't have any more annual leave left, and as a principled person, certainly wouldn't go off sick, so there was nothing else for it, she'd have to front it out.

I thought I would try and help so I called Jules, her best friend at work, to explain what had happened to Mum, I asked her to tell everyone in the office so they could all have a good laugh about it before Mum returned. She told me not to worry and that she would make sure that everyone would be aware of the problem before Mum returned. I had done all I could, we just now had to wait for the return of my toothless Mum.

It's a day I'll never forget, I was keen to see Sue and Mum again but I couldn't wait to see Mum without her teeth for the first time ever. I heard the coach stop outside our house and rushed to the door to welcome them home. Sue was smiling and sporting a lovely tan and beside her was this little old lady, it was Mum. She had her hand across her mouth and it looked like she'd aged an awful lot. Sue rushed to the door and said, 'For God's sake don't laugh'. She was struggling not to laugh and this only made it harder for me to keep a straight face. I could see that Mum was really upset and although my heart went out to her, it was the one of the funniest things I had ever seen in my life. I had to turn away and pretend to be helping Sue with her case. Mum must have felt awful and I felt for her too, but she looked so funny it was impossible not to howl out laughing.

Once we had all composed ourselves things got back to normal and Mum went to the Dentist on the Saturday to organise her new dentures. We had a quiet Sunday and Sue and I answered the door and the phone so that Mum didn't have to appear in public. It was Monday the next day and you could tell that Mum was dreading going into the office that was going to be a hard day for her.

Jules and Mum worked in the Leisure department of the local council and in their team was a Graphic Designer affectionately known as 'Little Les'. Les was a great artist, with a very strong Scouse accent and the typical humour of a Liverpudlian. Apparently the whole office had been in stitches for over a week and they were all looking forward to the toothless Pat arriving for work.

Les had done a massive A1 size cartoon drawing like a seaside postcard. In was in the style of Donald McGill who did all those famous saucy postcards. It showed a lady, with the look of an OAP, with no teeth and a shocked expression on her face. She was in a boat and coming out of the sea behind her there was a gigantic shark spitting out Mum's false teeth!

It all had a happy ending. Everyone at the office was very polite and understanding and the dentures were even ready a few days early which cheered up Mum no end.

# Chapter 8

## 1984 – Eighteenth birthday
## on the back of a camel

'Would you like to go on holiday to visit your cousins in Cyprus for your 18th birthday Siân?' That was my Nana Beth's question to me. Well of course I would, I'd never even been abroad before, and was absolutely thrilled at the prospect of a foreign holiday. So it was all arranged. We were to have two weeks in Akrotiri on the British Air Force base in Cyprus with our Aunt and Uncle and 2 cousins Michael and Peter who lived out there in the Air Force married quarters. Then we would have a week in Limasol staying in a nice hotel. Nana informed me that the big surprise was that we were going on a cruise from Cyprus to Egypt for a three day trip to see the pyramids and a few other sites in Cairo. What a wonderful birthday I was going to have I was very excited.

And wonderful it was. We had a fantastic time seeing our cousins, we had never seen much of them over the years as they were constantly travelling with their parents to far flung places around the world, but we did spend a few summers together in Anglesey with our Nana. My sister Sue came along too, it was just the three of us. Nana, me and our Sue, I'll never forget the cruise to Egypt. If you've never visited it, from what we saw Egypt is a dirty smelly land and I don't think I've ever experienced anything like the heat of the Sahara Desert in August since. Seeing the pyramids and the gold of Tutankhamen's treasure in the Museum of Cairo was an experience I'll never forget. But something I'll remember even more than that was the so called 'cruise' that took us there.

The trip consisted of a seventeen hour 'cruise' on what looked like an ocean going liner in the brochure photograph that Nana had shown us. We would be travelling across the Mediterranean Sea from Cyprus to Alexandria in Egypt. The ship called the Oceanos turned out to be more like the ferry across the Mersey when we arrived at the docks but it was very large so we were going to be quite safe aboard. I had no fear of the sea or ships however it turned out that a mere 7 years later on 4th August 1991 the Greek cruise liner Oceanos would sink with 581 passengers and crew, thank goodness we couldn't see into the future. Anyway I had never experienced sea sickness either so was pretty confident.

So we trouped onboard and had to hand in our passport to the Arabian staff. We were then handed a ticket, much like a raffle ticket with a number on it in return. We hadn't booked a cabin, and were just walk on passengers, we would be allotted a seat and they all had numbers on them, like on an aeroplane and would travel the seventeen hours in it. So off we went in search of our seat that corresponded with the ticket number we clutched. Off we headed, upstairs, along corridors, downstairs, we must have travelled along about a dozen decks in search of the seats. The lower we went, the more the rooms looked like engine rooms with pipes running round. Every seat had a number but none corresponded to the tickets we had. By this time I had definitely got my sea legs although it hardly felt as if we were moving, Sue seemed fine too, but a closer inspection of Nana revealed she looked decidedly green around the gills. I wondered what was wrong. So up more stairs along more corridors, this place was like the Titanic an endless rabbit warren of doors leading to more doors, stairs and corridors, we seemed to be going around in circles and still no seat. We had been on the move with our bags and belongings for what seemed like a few hours now every door and wall was a creamy magnolia colour and as I glanced back at nana she looked even worse. Perhaps she was tired and we should just find a restaurant and allow her to rest. As luck would have it the next flight of stairs took us to a cafeteria type area and we eventually found a seat. So we sat down relieved, I realised that something was blocking my legs from getting under the table and I discovered 3 Chinese people lying across the floor under the dining table. As we looked around the whole ship appeared to be full of what looked like market traders with massive bags full of clothes and other items, there was hardly room to move. Some 'cruise' this was.

All of a sudden Nana fled the room, I'd never seen her move so quickly, Sue looked pretty fed up too she didn't even have a seat and was squashing onto mine. 'I wonder what's up with Nana' I asked Sue, 'Probably sea sick' she replied. I headed off in the general direction Nana had fled and found a ladies rest room and walked in. Well the stench hit me as soon as I opened the door, obviously a good few people felt like Nana and the sound of retching was almost deafening in the small lavatory.

'Nana, are you in here' I yelled. Out came Nana looking even worse, her balance was completely gone as was the colour from her face. I grabbed her arm and led her back to our table.

We spent the next 14 or so hours slumped at a table desperately trying to sleep in the hope that when we woke we would be in the next part of our adventure. Cairo – here we come!

At last we were docking and it turned out that the raffle tickets we'd been issued were just like a cloak room ticket for coats. This ticket got you your passport back after disembarking from the ship. The number bore no reference to a seat number and it was a free for all! 'Just run as fast as you can and grab a seat' the Arabian ticket clerk advised. It appeared they oversold the seats to make sure they filled the ship. I'd certainly know what to do on the way back!

Next we all boarded a coach in the most severe heat I'd ever experienced; thank God it appeared to have air-conditioning. Cyprus had been hot in August, but Alexandria where we had docked was even hotter like a furnace, I could actually see the sweat pumping out of my skin and I wondered how people actually lived and worked in this heat. Our tour guide warned us that by the time we reached Cairo and went into the Sahara to see the pyramids it would be well up in the 40 degrees and that we should wear a hat at all times. I really don't mind the heat the hotter the better for me, but this was something completely different.

We boarded the tour bus for Cairo and the guide started his talk. 'Ladies and Gentlemen, if you look to your right you'll see the university, and on the left is the hospital, the largest in Cairo'. 'Jeez I could see all this in Liverpool' I thought. Cairo as a city looked very much like any major city in the UK, the cars were beat up but the buildings were all huge monstrosities that you could see anywhere, had we just come 17 hours in the bowels of the titanic just to see this I wondered? So far the only difference I'd seen was a dead horse at the side of the road, and a Mercedes taxi with a coffin hanging out of the boot – bizarre!

'Now ladies and gentlemen, if you look straight ahead you'll see the pyramids in the distance' the tour guide yelled in broken English. There was a gasp from the passengers and I squinted into the sunshine in the distance and all I saw were more sky scrapers and office blocks. I was peering between the buildings looking for the pyramids but saw nothing.

'I can't see a thing' I said to our Sue 'Can you?' 'Look there in front' Sue retorted, I still couldn't see anything, and gave her a blank look. 'Up, Up, look up you idiot' she yelled back.

'OH MY GOD!' I gasped. I had never seen anything like it in my life. I had to blink a few times to focus my eyes, I'd see the pyramids many times on TV and expected them to be big; I thought they would be like a four story building, twice the size of my house. Was I shocked or what? In the distance were skyscrapers and massive buildings but what I had failed to notice purely because of the sheer size, was that towering above the skyscrapers and office blocks were the pyramids which were absolutely dwarfing the city buildings. I couldn't believe what I was seeing; I had to blink a few times to get it in focus, the giant one must have been 500 feet high, that's 50 stories high!

When we arrived the tour guide went on to tell us all the things we had learned at school; that the pyramids are over 6000 years old and are constructed from over 25 million tonnes of limestone. The pyramids were built as tombs for the pharaohs. The giant pyramid was originally 481 feet high, but has since lost 30 feet due to erosion. It was fascinating stuff and we had experienced nothing like it before. There were 2 smaller ones which were still massive and a chap who was dressed only in a loin cloth was proceeding to run up and down the side of one. They're not smooth as you would imagine, but built out of massive blocks and have a step like structure to them, and it was up and down these huge steps the skinny local was climbing and then collecting funds thrown to him at the bottom. He must have been bloody fit!

To the east of the pyramids is the Great Sphinx, the largest single-stone statue in the world. The Sphinx has the face of a man and the body of a lion. Just like the pyramids the nose has also been eroded by sand storms but I was in awe of the whole place and it's a sight I'll never forget. The tour guide offered us the opportunity to follow her into one of the pyramids which was now open for viewing, but I'd remembered my history classes about Howard Carter and Lord Carnarvon and how they had all been cursed after breaking the seals on the tombs. The whole place had a funny feeling about it, I can't describe it but I decided not to go in. I don't think Nan and Sue were very keen either and looked relieved when I told them I didn't want to enter.

'Can we have a ride on a camel instead Nan?' our Sue asked. 'Yes of course' our Nan replied. And we headed off towards one of the herds of camels who were adorned in brightly coloured pom-poms and saddles. We waited our turn and then were roughly thrust towards one of the camels, it was told to sit down so that we could climb up, they are massive creatures but had lovely long eyelashes and beautifully soft faces. The camel then gradually got to it's feet, and was urged forward by its owner, he seemed to be calling it Peter which seemed an odd name for a camel and both Sue and I laughed. We were both thrust forward as it got up back end first and Sue who was sitting on the front grabbed the camel's neck to steady herself. Well Peter was not amused and swung his head round and gave Sue a filthy look, and proceeded to make a painful wailing sound and spat right at her. Sue yelped in distress but our Camel guide ignored her and headed off.

It was quite a bouncy ride and good fun, but we seemed to be going a long way, Nana was shrinking in the distance as I glanced back and I said to our Sue 'How far do you think he'll take us?' 'Dunno? Not too far I hope' she replied as she was desperately trying to wipe the camel snot from her t-shirt.

On we went, even the pyramids seemed smaller we were getting so far away. I shouted down to the camel herder. 'That's far enough mate, can you take us back?' 'You pay, you pay' he shouted up in broken English. 'Yes Yes, how much? I asked. 'Ten of your English pounds' came his reply. 'What a bloody rip off!' Sue remarked. Ten pounds back in 1984 was equal to about fifty today. It seemed very extreme for a camel ride, even though it seemed we were now half way across the flaming Sahara and Sue had no hat on. We were impatient to get back, and it appeared he had taken us away from our Nan so that we couldn't argue. Well he had two Scousers aboard his camel and he was in for a shock.

'Give him that ten thousand lira, you got back in the gift shop' Sue suggested. 'Good idea' I thought and I handed him the note 'English Pounds, English Pounds' he argued. 'They are worth more than pounds' I protested and Sue promptly started to cry. Good thinking Sue. He immediately snatched the ten thousand lira and proceeded to turn the camel back in the direction of the pyramids where we could just about see Nan frantically waving to us, as we got closer we could tell she was looking worried.

We were back on the bus in no time and heading towards the Museum of Cairo to see Tutankhamen's treasure. We couldn't wait and it was certainly impressive. The gold and jewel encrusted artefacts seemed to glow in the cool of the air-conditioned museum. Nan and Sue had to drag me back to the coach as I could have spent hours in there – I've always had an eye for gold.

(Me and Sue (front) on the back of a camel
near the Pyramids at Giza, Egypt)

# Chapter 9

## 1984 - The numbers girl

Boxing has always been a traditionally male dominated sport, not just the boxers themselves but the spectators too and at our Leisure Centre we occasionally had Sportsman's Evenings, where a boxing ring was set up with tables around it for spectators to have a meal, drink as much as they could and donate money to charity. Typically a company would hire a table or two for the male employees and a rather filthy comedian would also be part of the entertainment. The female Leisure Assistants and Lifeguards were never required to work these evenings so I had little experience or interest in what went on at these affairs. We just set up the Sports hall with the boxing ring, a temporary bar and set out all the tables and chairs during the day time ready for the evening's event.

Then it was announced that we were going to have a Sportsman's evening again but instead of boxing it was to be wrestling. Now in 1984 the wrestlers weren't the muscle bound Adonis's we see in the WWE arena, the likes of Stone Cold Steve Austin, The Undertaker and Hulk Hogan were unknown and Saturday afternoon Wrestling on ITV was a mixture of chubby, sometimes hooded individuals, who used ordinary names such as **Jackie Pallo**, **Mick McManus**, **Pat Roach** and **Kendo Nagasaki**. The two that everyone remembers had their own stage names Giant Haystacks and Big Daddy. Giant Haystacks was 6'11' and weighed in at a massive 45 stones and his nemesis Big Daddy, real name Shirley Crabtree, was famous for his top hat, union jack waistcoat and chant of 'Easy, Easy'. Grannies and kids tuned in to World of Sport on a Saturday afternoon to cheer on their favourites.

So I hear you asking 'Where is this all leading to?' Well it was all coming to our Leisure Centre in St Helens and I was quite excited, little did I know I was going to be starring in the show too. The main hall was all set up for the charity dinner and it was due to start at 9pm. The pool was closed for the evening and the staff had little to do now that the event organisers had taken over, or so I thought. Sandy one of the other lifeguards and I were sitting in reception having a coffee and chatting to Yvonne the receptionist. At about 8.45 one of the event organisers came racing through to reception to say there had been a small road accident about 10 miles away and the models due to be the numbers girls had to go to the police station to give witness statements and wouldn't be able to make it in time for the show.

Who or what are the numbers girls I wondered, well I was about to find out. The numbers girls are the models who parade around the boxing or wrestling ring at the beginning of each round holding up a card with a number on it denoting the number of the next round. Just before the announcer shouts 'Seconds out round 3' the girls slide under the ropes and exit the ring. They usually parade around in a bikini and high heels and are there to provide a touch of glamour to an otherwise male dominated event.

The event organiser was distraught. Peter our Duty Manager, piped up 'Go on you two get your cozzies on you can do it'. Sandy had done a bit of modelling in her time and was very attractive, she'd even won a small town carnival queen contest but I had never done this sort of thing. Peter was only joking of course – Oh how we laughed. But the event organiser who was sweating profusely wasn't, he seemed suddenly excited and relieved at the same time. 'Yes, Yes, girls come on, we've got the costumes you're about the right size, hurry along girls you're just what we need.' Sandy and I glared at Peter, who was still laughing, but saying 'Go on, go on, it'll be ok, it's just a laugh'

At whose expense? I thought. I didn't feel very much like being a model stuck in the same ring as Giant Haystacks. Sandy was well up for it and her previous modelling experience seemed to be fuelling her enthusiasm. So off we went to the changing rooms. It wasn't very glamorous in the stinking 5-a-side football changing rooms, but there hanging off the pegs were the skimpiest bathing suits I had ever seen. Now don't get me wrong, Sandy and I were both 18 years old and only a size 10. Although I spent most of my time in a swimming costume working as a lifeguard, this was a completely different kettle of fish; I'd never actually worn heels with a swim suit. I felt sick, but Sandy encouraged me, and we got changed and were led out to the ring.

I'd seen Giant Haystacks and Big Daddy on TV before but had no idea just how massive the pair of them were. They were absolutely enormous, and I'd never seen such a giant pair of men in lycra leotards before, the image was burned onto my eyeballs for eternity. The crowd was chanting 'Easy.. Easy.. Easy..' along with Daddy. The noise was fantastic. The next thing I knew we were being pushed up the steps and into the ring, 2 boards were flung at us, denoting round 1 and around we strode. The audience were all wolf-whistling and shouting extremely rude things, which I'm sure can't be printed here. It took less than 15 seconds and we were out of the ring and down the steps again. The crowd were all shouting, swearing and laughing. It was good fun, and we were already looking forward to round 2. I was lucky it wasn't a televised event; my Mum would have gone mad seeing me on the television wearing very little and a smile.

And that was the way it went for about 6 rounds, until; as usual Daddy did his famous splash down, and defeated the mighty Haystacks. The whole room seemed to shake, as he thundered down on the canvas of the ring and our short career as numbers girls was over. The comedian came on and we were ushered out and back to the stink of chlorine back into our tracksuits, back to reception and back to reality. All our work mates were laughing and clapping when we returned to reception, I don't think I've ever blushed quite so much as I did that day.

# Chapter 10

## 1985 – A dodgy driving test

I don't know how I found Mike Gange. He was my driving instructor; I suppose I just found his driving school telephone number in the yellow pages or Thompson local. I was eighteen, working in the swimming pool and keen to learn to drive. I'd had my provisional licence since I was seventeen but never got round to having lessons. I suppose I wasn't that eager to learn as I couldn't afford a car, so it seemed pointless. But now I was working full time and still living at home so the spare cash was useful to learn to drive.

Mike was a strange character for a driving instructor. He'd inherited the business from his father I later learned and there was some talk that his Dad had committed suicide but I didn't know that for sure. Mike had a severe stutter and smoked about 20 fags during the hour lesson. I'm not a smoker and found it very off putting, but Mike was such a laugh and very patient; he needed to be to put up with my occasional hysterics and I was keen to continue with my lessons. I drove around in his dual control white Nissan Micra like I was the queen of the road. I was actually terrible and was secretly aware that Mike was doing all the driving with his dual controls but he was in charge and I was doing as he said.

Eventually I'd had about 12 lessons and Mike said it was time to put in for my test. Back in the 80's you didn't do any theory test. It was just lessons then a 20 minute driving test with the Examiner who first asked you a few questions on the Highway Code. By the time I'd driven round all the usual test routes I'd had about seventeen lessons and Mike was sure that I'd be fine and pass my test.

In further preparation, Mum had at last given in and allowed me to drive her famous red FSO to and from work with her instructing me on what to do. An FSO is a very similar car to a Lada – it was basically a Polski Fiat and suited my Mum's socialist beliefs – it was awful, we couldn't open the sunroof when we were backing out of the drive as the water would run in on top of us, as soon as you got in Mum would shout 'don't open the sunroof!' Also if you tried to wind a window down the handle would come off in your hand, but never the less, Mum loved it.

So I was getting more and more experience, even though Mum spent most of the 5 minute drive to and from work screaming her head off at me.

The big day arrived and I was excited and nervous at the same time. The odd thing about driving a Nissan is that the indicators are on the opposite side to any other cars. It transpired that all Japanese cars are this way. Windscreen wipers and indicator levers on opposing sides. I must have had a bit too much practice with my Mum because everything I'd learned from Mike must have gone out of the window, when I drove in Mum's red FSO.

If you know St Helens driving test centre it's next door to the Area Heath Authority Office on Duke Street, and both buildings are similar modern low roofed offices with a small car park to each. Mike drove us there and we pulled into the car park and went into the waiting room. Mike gave my name to the receptionist and we sat down waiting for my name to be called.

Mike stuttered along in his usual way making wise cracks I suppose trying to relax me, but he sounded so nervous with his stammering that it was rubbing off on me.

Eventually they called my name – a booming voice shouted 'Miss Williams'. I stepped up and followed the large stern looking, blazer wearing chap out into the car park. We got into the car and the examiner proceeded to write on his clipboard and ask me a few questions relating to the Highway Code. So far so good, all seemed easy. Then he gave me the obligatory eye test where I had to read the number plate of a car that was about 30 feet away. Still all is good. My confidence was growing and we were almost ready to set off. I knew the test would only last 20 minutes and so I was confident that this time would fly by and I would be returning, joyously tearing up my 'L' plates.

How wrong could I be? Well seat belt on, mirror... signal... manoeuvre. We jolted forward and set off. Left out of the car park and we were heading towards Cowley Hill Lane. Stopped at the lights, so far so good. The lights changed and we pulled forward and went into $2^{nd}$ gear, then $3^{rd}$, then $4^{th}$. There was no $5^{th}$ gear on any car I had ever driven back then. So now we were cruising along and all seemed fine.

'Now Miss Williams, please will you take your next right hand turn?' I was now flapping as he gave me instructions on what to do next. Mirrors, check... signals, check. I slowed up changing gears and got ready to turn, and off we went. What's this, where am I? 'Miss Williams, I meant take your next right turn into a *road*, not up someone's drive way'. Oh hell, I was approaching someone's house and I would have to stop and reverse back onto the road. How could I have been so stupid? So, slowly I backed out of the driveway, and anxiously looked all around, trying to find a safe way to pull backwards into the road. 'STOP, STOP...!!!' Bellowed the instructor. 'Watch out or you'll hit that woman and her pram.' Could it get any worse? By this time, I was close to tears. But somehow I apologised profusely and I had the car facing in the correct direction and we headed off once more. We were now in the Moss Bank area of the town and it was a lovely day, I was wearing sandals and the more I start to worry about what we were doing the more my feet were hurting.

'I would now like you to pull over at the side of the road when it is safe to do so' he instructed. 'I checked my mirror and then I signalled – Oh hell the wipers, I couldn't get the damn things to stop, oh no, they were going faster and then I squirted water all over the windscreen. The examiner is huffing and puffing and eventually I stopped them and tried to compose myself once again.

'Now Miss Williams, using forward and reverse gears I would like you to turn the car in the road to face the opposite direction'. What was he talking about? My mind was blank, 'Is that a hill start?' I ask. We were not even on a hill, my feet were really hurting and the next moment I burst out crying. 'Oh please can I loosen my sandals, they're hurting my feet'. Mr Examiner raised his eyebrows and sighed. I knew by this time that I'd failed, and I was just hoping he would just cancel the whole thing and take me back. No such luck, on we continued. All of a sudden it dawned on me that he meant a three point turn was required. So I started the manoeuvre and so far I had taken at least nine turns and I had gone over every curb of the pavement, things were going from bad to worse.

At last we were on our way back. So all I needed to do was pull into the test centre, park the car and escape from the Examiner. I turned right, to pull into the car park. 'Where are you going Miss Williams, this isn't the test centre this is next door, turn around and go into the other car park. Again it took me about 11 tries to get out of the car park, I had completely lost any driving skill I had and I was a quivering wreck. I eventually got into the car park and pulled forward towards a space near the wall. We inched forward and stopped on a slight downward incline. I stopped the car and turned off the ignition key.

I was just about to turn to the Examiner to ask how I'd done. Not that I needed to ask, when he screamed at me again. 'HANDBRAKE..!! Miss Williams – for goodness sakes, get the brake on'

I'd failed I knew I had but now I had to sit through the humiliation of him telling me where I went wrong. We stepped out of the car as Mike was heading towards us all smiles as usual. The Examiner passed him and said 'Not your usual standard Mr Gange'. And that was it. I never drove again. Well not for 5 years anyway.

By this time I was married to Paul and my husband got a job which included a company car. He'd just passed his test and we had a car, he was encouraging me to take lessons again. He'd passed with the Mike Gange School of Motoring as I'd given Mike's telephone number to Paul a few months before. So I thought I'd give Mike a call. This is how the conversation went.

'Hello, I'd like to book a driving lesson'

'Ah hello, have you had any lessons before?'

'Well yes actually, you might not remember me, but I had lessons with you about 5 years ago, my name was Siân Williams then'

'Re.. re.. remember you? He started to stammer again. Perhaps it was me that caused that. 'I'll never bloody fo.. for..forget you! You were the worst test candidate I ever had' - 'Decided to have another go then have you?'

# Chapter 11

## 1986 - Who needs Pickfords?

At last I was moving out of the family home. After knowing Paul for 3 years we decided we were made for each other and it was time to live together – it was true love. That's a joke! It was more a case of the constant disapproval from my Mum that I just had to get out of the family home. We had looked at renting a house from the council but there was a waiting list and as we were both in employment, had no special needs and I wasn't pregnant, we were without the necessary points to get on the list never mind move up the queue. We looked at all the new housing estates being built and decided we had no chance at affording one of those and that Sutton Junction was the only place for us – and it was the cheapest. As first time buyers we were an Estate Agent's dream, nothing to sell and a building society keen to lend us 100% of the purchase price – ah those were the days. The sale paperwork had all been sorted and the contracts had been signed and exchanged, we were now the proud owners of our first house in Peckershill Road and we were both excited when we collected the keys and we walked around our empty house deciding where we would put all the furniture we had already collected. My Mum was not amused and she thought it was all a big mistake.  Not only was I leaving home at 18 but I was moving in with a young man. She was not impressed with Paul and took every opportunity to let everyone know. But I didn't care, I desperate to leave home. We had bought the house in joint names and we were now £6950 in debt with a 25 years mortgage. The house was small, a Victorian 2 bed-roomed terrace in Sutton Junction it needed a lot of work doing to it and was actually a dump, we had purchased a hovel but it was ours.

We had been saving our money to buy furniture for the house and as a result my bedroom looked like a warehouse with a blue-grey draylon 3-piece-suite and a double bed still wrapped in plastic. Just about everything except the kitchen sink including pots and pans, plates, ironing board, electrical items, you name it was piled high.

As well as all this I had a dog. Paul's Dad Bill worked for Manweb, the local electricity board, as a meter reader and he had visited a house were a puppy German Shepherd was being teased by 3 small kids. Well to cut a long story short, he asked the owner if she actually wanted the dog. Not surprisingly she didn't so he brought it home for me and Paul. Thanks Bill! So now there were three of us to move into the new house, me, Paul and Rocky. Mum was still sulking about my unsuitable choice of partner as she wasn't willing to hire a van and drive for us, we had to formulate a plan. We tried thinking of all our mates but none of them had transport either. Then I had a brain wave.

'Let's take the stuff on the train we'll get a Save-Away ticket and do multiple trips' I announced. A 'Save-Away' was a kind of scratch card, where you rubbed off the silver number to reveal the month and date you wanted to travel. You paid about a quid for the ticket but you could make as many journeys on the trains or buses as you liked in a day. We lived right near Rainhill station and our new house was only one stop away near St Helens Junction. They have since put a new station in between at Lea Green but that wasn't there back in 1984.

'Are you mad, we can't take a 3 piece suite on the train, they'll never let us take it on board' said Paul.

'I know that', I said, 'but we can take all the small stuff, electrical appliances, and suitcases and move as much as we can. We can then wait until we find someone with a van to move the big stuff'.

So it was agreed, 'what a plan?' I thought. I was very impressed with my fast thinking. So me, Paul, my sister Sue, Paul's brother Shaun, his girlfriend Lorraine, her brother Steve along with Ray, Carl, Geoff, Phil and various other mates and their relatives all headed off to the station with bits and pieces, this was the first run.

It was a Saturday and although the trains run every half hour it was packed and there was no room. 'Here lad, get in the Guards Van – a voice wailed in our general direction. The Guard was shouting to use to get in his compartment along with the mail. There were no seats but it was a wide open carriage with a few mail sacks and some packages. It was ideal so we all jumped in and waited for the Guard to join us as the train moved off.

The Guard was a fantastic looking Scouse chap with a big moustache; he could have played the role of a Victorian guard in an Agatha Christie play.

'Can we bring anything on the train, and put it in this carriage?' I asked the friendly guard.

'No problem girl, what do you want to bring? Some folks put their bikes in here' he laughed in his strong Scouse accent.

'I was thinking about a double bed and a 3 piece suite as we're moving house' I laughed hoping he would say yes.

'No problem girl, I'm up and down this line every hour, all day long, jump on my train, and bring whatever you like'.

'Seriously? Asked Paul

'Yeah no problem lad, just jump on. I'll let me mate know, he's on the other train so you can put anything in his van if you miss mine no danger'. He grinned, I could have kissed him but for the moustache – I'm not keen on beards or facial hair.

So we were sorted. We were moving house courtesy of Merseyrail. I stayed at the new house putting everything in its place while everyone else did the trips, after all someone had to keep an eye on Rocky.

Paul and I were in the upstairs back bedroom, just setting up the base to a single bed when I paused to look out of the window. The back bedroom overlooked Station Road and I could not believe what I saw! Shaun and Loz had the double mattress on their heads with hands clinging to the side straps as they walked along in single file. I looked further down the road and there was a line of people carrying things. Steve had a chair on his head and Carl had a wheel barrow filled with what looked like plaster or cement. Sue was dragging Granddads shopping trolley loaded with Argos boxes, she had taken the shopping bag off and found some bungee straps to hold the boxes on. Geoff had found a Morrison's shopping trolley and was pushing Phil in it.

They were the best mates in the world, what a troop! I bet not many people can say they moved house by train.

# Chapter 12

## 1989 – The elderly naturist

It was another freezing winter's morning as I sat alone on the side of an empty swimming pool. Not for the first time I was wondering why anyone would want to go swimming in the middle of winter when they have to battle through frost and snow just to get to the pool. It's a question that often came to mind but I knew the answer – pensioners! They loved it, every morning from about 8am the pool starts to fill up with pensioners, mostly gentlemen, out for their early bird swimming session. It is 7:50 and I was half asleep waiting for my geriatric patrons to hobble out of the changing rooms and plunge into the pool. They were a great bunch and I had got to know them quite well over the years. Jim and Gladys arrived together although they weren't married; Jim was over 75 and flirted outrageously with all the women he met - from eighteen to eighty. Gladys was a sweet-heart, an ex teacher who still looked like a teacher. I found myself sitting up straight when she walked towards me and I was always relieved when she smiled and chatted. She always gave me a birthday card and a little handmade present, she must have found out my birthday from the other staff.

It was amusing to watch them as they approached the pool. As people get older they lose the spring in their step so it's never a graceful dive or a jump into the water. They either just lean over until the change in their centre of gravity makes them fall into the water in a kind of belly flop (that's a dive) or they step off the edge and plummet, (and that's a jump). It's a bit like watching lemmings when it's a busy day, they just keep on coming out of the changing rooms, it's as though they feel safety in numbers.

It was the same every weekday morning; they kept away when it was the children's session on Saturday. And it was always the same people; in fact one of them was an old school teacher of mine, Mr Jones he looked like an aging Elvis when I was at school. He obviously used *Grecian 2000* or *Just for Men* as he had a shock of jet black teddy-boy hair. He now looked much older but the hair was still out of a bottle. It was lucky he was a good swimmer because if he had ever gotten into trouble I would have had to let him drown. I know that it's unprofessional but I certainly couldn't have brought myself to give him the kiss of life.

For these oldies 'early bird' sessions there was no point me going up the lifeguard ladder as you never needed to rescue them. They were all good swimmers and would swim up and down the pool, lap after lap until they had done enough.  They would then haul themselves up the steps and head for the refreshments via the changing room.  All I had to do was sit on the side of the pool near to the office where I could listen to the radio and this shift was a doddle, they didn't really need a lifeguard but you never knew if one of them could pop their clogs at any time and then it would be action stations.

The nice thing about all the OAPs is that they are so polite. Whenever they meet, even when they are swimming, they would say good morning to their colleagues and they would always meet for tea after their swim. There was obviously a social element to their visit and I sometimes wondered if they lived alone and came to the swimming to meet other folk – who knows?

So on that particularly cold morning it was very warm on the side of the pool and I was waiting for my regulars to appear from the changing rooms. I was getting ready to read a chapter or two, I always take a book to the 'early bird' sessions, when I notice a figure appear from the corridor leading to the changing rooms. I look up and have to do a double take at the figure heading towards me. My eye sight is good, but I have to blink and rub my eyes as I can't believe what I'm seeing, an 80 odd year old chap is staggering towards me and he is completely naked! I'm only 22 and although I'm married my experience of naked men is extremely limited and the image of naked, senior citizens has never entered my waking or even sleeping mind. How do I approach him? What do I say? Do I blow my whistle to alert him? None of this was in the training manual, where's my manager when I need him? Every scenario has flashed across my mind and this vision of a very old, wrinkly, naked man is now burned on my retina for eternity, even though I hardly glanced before immediately looking away. Time seemed to pass in slow motion and I'm rooted to the spot watching him without staring.

He stops half way and I think 'Oh please Lord no!' he's about to plunge in. He begins to bend over to dive in the pool when he suddenly realises that he's forgotten his trunks. He makes a speedy retreat and I am left with the image of his wrinkled rear end heading for the changing rooms. I'm speechless and am left wondering if I had imagined it.

As all the other old ladies and gents start to file out of the changing rooms and plunge into the pool, I'm still in a state of shock when I see my elderly naturist walking towards me. Oh please don't come near me, I know I'll laugh and the last thing I wanted to do was embarrass him, but how could I get away? The lovely old gentleman is upon me before I can think and is apologising profusely and I begin to realise he feels more embarrassed than I do. He explains that he'd undressed and wanted to turn left into the lavatories before putting on his trunks and coming into the swimming pool, somehow he had turned right and ended up poolside. I smile and say 'It's ok, I didn't see anything.' To spare his blushes I explain that I was distracted by the radio. He smiles, apologies again and goes off to join his comrades in the pool.

As I am sitting by the office thinking about what has just happened I look up and Ian, our cheerful maintenance man, is heading towards me with a cuppa. He looks a sight, dressed in his massive rubber gloves, rubber apron and wellies. He needs all this gear to protect himself from the concentrated chemicals used to keep the pool clean but it gives him the look of crazed scientist.

'Hi hun, what's up sweetie?' he says, 'You look like you've seen a ghost?'

'I think I have' I reply and I explain what has just happened.

'Get this tea down you then, it's good for shock'. Ian hands me the cuppa. As I sit sipping my tea I realise that I've just seen a vision I'll take to the grave. And as I write this today the memory is as fresh in my mind as it was on that day over twenty years ago.

# Chapter 13

## 1987 - Strippers and the violent Granddad

By now I'd left home and I was living in a small terraced house in St Helens Junction with my boyfriend Paul and it was a week to my 21st birthday.

'Shall we have a 'do' for your birthday?' says the said Paul.

'I dunno, seems pointless now I've left home and we've hardly any money. Your 21st is usually a thing your parents pay for when you're still at home, mine won't pay for it now I've left' I say feeling old and miserable.

'Well let's see how much it'll cost and maybe your Mum'll pay for the food if we get a disco – what do you think?' If there is one thing Paul likes it's a party..

So that's how it was organised. I was not really in the mood for a party and the thought of organising one for myself at this late stage wasn't appealing. I didn't think we'd find a venue let alone a decent disco. So without any real enthusiasm I started to ring around a few places to see what I could come up with.

As I suspected everywhere we had been before was fully booked for the following Saturday night so I dug out the Thompson Local directory and started to look further afield. It took all day but I eventually found a venue - the Sacred Heart Catholic Club on Borough Road. The nice lady assured me that they often rented the hall for private parties and yes they did have a bar and we'd be allowed to purchase alcohol and I wasn't to be put off by the venue name. The truth is that I was a little put off, Paul and I were hardly religious 'living in sin' and I imagined a priest being behind the bar and nuns looking after the cloakroom!

Next we had to find a disco and that was even harder than finding a venue. I must have rung over 50 DJs and they were all booked up but by this time I had developed some enthusiasm for the idea so I kept on trying. I was working my way through the alphabetical list and rang 'Stan Roberts, DJ and entertainer'. Stan turned out to be a seventy year old children's entertainer who had started running discos when business was bad during the 70's. Stan was free and would be pleased to provide the music. I was a little concerned about his age and then he asked, 'What type of music do you want?' I replied that we are in our twenties so we wanted modern pop and dance music. 'Oh I can't do that, it's too loud, I've got a large collection of big band and country and western, will that do?' Oh dear, back to the directory.

I was now down to V in the directory and getting desperate when the Gold Dust Disco DJ called me back - 'I've had a cancellation for Saturday so am free if you still want me – let's call it 50 quid?' – 'Great I'll have it' I replied and gratefully put the phone down before realising it was a bit expensive.

From there on things started to rock and roll and my Mum and Dad agreed to pay for the food and the disco so all we had to pay for was the hall. Barbara, who ran the cafe at the Leisure Centre said she'd give us a good deal on a buffet so it seemed that all we needed to do was organise guests.

I knew that guests would be the least of our problems… My sister and I regularly had 'parties' at our old home when Mum and Dad were away, we never invited anyone but somehow a hundred people seemed to find out and turn up with a Party 7 or a 3 litre bottle of cider, those were the days. Does anyone remember those awful sickly tasting 'Mad Dog' 20/20 fortified wines? I think they have now been discontinued due to health worries, they were dreadful but we eagerly gulped them down. Sue and I would be walking around the village and complete strangers would come up to us and say, 'Great party the other night really enjoyed it' and we didn't even know them!

So we told everyone we knew and told them to bring mates, which usually got us a good crowd. We didn't need Facebook or My Space in those days, back then everyone was always available and up for a party and there was never any trouble.  So it was all organised and we just had to turn up and enjoy ourselves.

It was the day of the party and I was working at the Leisure Centre driving the golf course tractor around the driving range collecting golf balls. It was quiet relaxing sitting in the little cage driving around as the odd golf ball rattled off the cage. As I'm chugging along in the tractor I can not only see my Mum belting along Marshalls Cross Road towards my house in her famous red FSO, but I can also hear her over the noise of my tractor, the roar of her engine, similar to that of a Chieftain Tank was deafening.

Now I was getting pretty excited as I knew she was on her way to drop of my 21st birthday present. Granddad had bought me a sapphire ring surrounded in small diamonds, which I went with him to choose and I really loved it. Mum was getting me a surprise and I couldn't wait to get home and find out what it is.

I'm sure they must have had a whip round at work for a card and present but I'm ashamed to say I can't remember what it was, I think the shock at the present from Mum has erased everything else from memory.

Andy one of our lifeguards gave me a lift home after work and I rushed in to find my Paul and Mum sitting in the lounge. She had brought a cake for this evening and on the table was a big birthday present wrapped in 21st paper, I couldn't wait to open it. Mum was beaming from ear to ear as she gave me the present and stood back to watch me open it. Now what would you get a happy, fun loving, attractive, 21 year old for her birthday – jewellery, silver, gold, clothes, shoes, maybe something to keep?   I eagerly opened the beautifully wrapped present and to my utter shock there are 3 things. A marble rolling pin, matching salt and pepper grinders and a mortar and pestle – what on earth will I use all that for – I was hardly an apothecary and I wasn't known for my cooking skills – but as usual I was very gracious and it was a nice thought, they did match my grey kitchen.

Soon it was party time and we arrived at the hall at about 7 o'clock. The DJ, Eric, and the catering woman Barbara were setting up – we went over to the DJ to tell him that my Dad was going to pay him. 'Yeah fine, whatever' he said in his fake mid-Atlantic accent 'I've got the girls with me, that ok?' I was baffled but nodded, 'Yes, fine, bring whoever you want, the more the merrier' I replied and he gave me a funny look. Off I went to check on the buffet. Barbara was up to her eyes in vol-au-vonts and sausage rolls but it all looked nice and I left her to it.

The room was a typical church hall, draughty, grim and plain, but we'd brought balloons and happy 21st banners to cheer the place up. The bar was no more than a serving hatch, just as described when I booked it but I was still surprised there was a bar at all and at such short notice I was grateful for anything.

Everything we set so I was looking forward to everyone having a good time.

Lots of people began to arrive, my other half's Mum and Dad, Joan and Bill, his sister Julie and her bloke Dave and Paul's brother Shaun along with all of their extended family of Aunts, Uncles and Cousins. They had a large family and we expected them all to come as they were always up for a booze-up – the disco was up and running and lots of people from work turned up along with our Sue's mates, their mates and the usual people we didn't even know. So the evening was underway. It was a great mixture of dancing, drinking and eating, even Granddad and Aunty Rita, Uncle Jack and a few other elderly relatives had turned up and are all tucking into the buffet.

Then suddenly the music stopped, the lights went out and we were plunged into darkness for a few seconds. Then up came the spotlight and I realised immediately what DJ Gold Dust meant when he said 'the girls' – he'd brought strippers! 'Oh hell, my Granddad's here' I thought. They proceeded to strut around the dance floor to various tunes from 'The Rocky Horror Show' wearing nothing other than some extremely revealing underwear. I didn't really mind and there was a huge cheering roar and ecstatic wolf whistles and applause as the girls came out, the lads all seem to love it, some elderly relatives seemed less than impressed but all was fine. There were a few disapproving looks from my Great Aunts Rita and Hilda but Uncle Jack and Granddad didn't seem to mind, until that is Eric, the DJ started strutting around in heels, stockings, a basque and giant black cape to *'I'm just a sweet transvestite'* doing his Freddy Mercury impression. Eric was obviously enjoying himself and was looking around the audience to find someone to join in. The next thing I saw was Eric sitting on Granddad's lap stroking his bald head. It was all getting a bit out of control and just as I got over to them Eric got up and started prancing around again, thrusting in every direction. My Granddad was virtually puce in the face and was bellowing at the top of his voice 'Keep that *homosexual* away from me! If he touches me again, I'm going to punch him!' I'd never seen Granddad so angry. I tried to explain that it was only meant to be a bit of fun but I was wasting my time as Granddad, Aunty Rita, Uncle Jack and the rest all marched out of the hall.  It was an aspect of the modern world that they wanted no part of. I remember Granddad falling out with my Mum a few years earlier, when she told him that the operatic duo 'Hinge and Bracket' were actually men dressed as women and that it was a drag act.

As you can imagine the rest of the evening was a roaring success and Paul's cousin Ian was tied to a chair and proceeded to get a lap-dance by one of the strippers – god only knows how he managed to control himself, perhaps having is his Mum and aunties watching did the trick.

It finally turned out to be a truly memorable 21st party even though I did have to go and apologize to Granddad the next day. It was certainly the strangest party that the Sacred Heart Catholic Club had ever seen although I did see the caretaker peering out of a cleaning cupboard door when the strippers cam on.

# Chapter 14

## 1987 – Promotion

I was leafing through the local paper, the St Helens Reporter one evening when I saw a job advert for the supervisor's job at the Grange Park Leisure Centre – needless to say I was a bit miffed. I was already working for the council at the pool and I felt I was an obvious candidate, but that's the council for you, they have to be seen to be acting fairly so if I wanted the job I would have to apply along with every other Tom Dick or Harry. So I swallowed my pride and applied for the job. The Grange Park Leisure Centre was part of the council's Leisure Department but located at Grange Park High School in Thatto Heath. It's a dry centre without a swimming pool but I was up for the challenge of more responsibility and I felt it was time for a change.

I really thought I'd get the job. I had a great staff record at the pool and I was good with people, I enjoyed all the sports and over the years I had done all the various jobs so I knew I would be a good supervisor. I had a great interview, with another illustrious panel, and came out feeling on top of the world, the job had to be mine and my only question was 'when do I start?'

How wrong could I have been, I was devastated to find out that I'd failed. They gave the job to a chap from my Leisure Centre who had refused to take his Bronze Pool lifesaving badge because he didn't want to work poolside. For the first time I felt cheated as I was the best candidate and I had the most qualifications but didn't get the job because they had to find a job for a useless member of staff who refused to work poolside.

I was furious and when I got home I let Paul have it with both barrels.

'It's not fair, I should have that job' I cried.

'Don't worry' said Paul, 'you'll get promotion next time, what did your supervisor say?'

'He said I should have got it, he says it's all fixed.' I was almost in tears.

'Never mind, your time will come.' Paul was trying to calm me down but it wasn't working.

'That's it,' I cried, 'I'm never applying again; I'm going to stay at home, get pregnant and become a housewife'.

Paul was stunned into silence. We'd never really discussed having children before, and although I'd just made this outrageous outburst, I didn't really mean it as I didn't actually want children at the time. Little did I know that although I hadn't been promoted at work I'd be pregnant with my first child within 28 days and shortly be promoted to the role of mother!

# Chapter 15

## 1987/8 - A New Year's Eve to forget

It was always a good night on New Year's Eve. But it wasn't going to be so much fun for me this particular year as I was five months pregnant with my first baby. I tried on everything I could find that fitted, but nothing looked particularly nice and in the end my friend Ruth from the swimming pool made me a nice silky top with lace at the front which hid my now protruding tummy. I put on a fake smiling face and we went off to a local pub the Black Horse to meet up with Paul's family as there was a bit of a party going on there. The evening was a great success, I actually enjoyed it more than I thought even though I was reduced to drinking orange juice, I felt sick and imagined that very soon I would look like an orange as I was swelling rapidly. By midnight I was very tired and fed up with orange juice everyone around me was very drunk and all having the time of their lives but I was trying my best to keep a smile on my face.

'Oh come on Paul, let's go' I moaned about thirty seconds after the obligatory 'Auld Lang Syne' I'm tired and I want to go home. 'Let's try and get a taxi and go' I continued to whine. 'But there's a party back at our Geoff's' 'Come on it'll be a laugh' 'once this baby comes we won't be able to go out so much' he continued to remind me at every opportunity. I was secretly praying that things would change once the baby came, his drinking seemed to be spiralling out of control and he spent more time drunk than sober,.

So reluctantly I agreed, and we headed off to Geoff's flat which was a ten minute walk away. Paul was completely drunk and I knew that this was a bad idea, but I agreed as I thought I could spend 10 minutes at Geoff's party and then say I was too tired to stay and escape to my Mums house just around the corner. That would force him to leave and we could call a taxi from my Mum's.

The plan was formed and off we trudged. It was a fine, dry evening and not all that cold and a few minutes later we were at Geoff's to find the party in full swing, all his family were there and a good time was being had by all. Well at first anyway. I don't recall exactly what happened but there seemed to be a bit of a kerfuffle and voices were raised and people had started to jostle. The next thing I remember was Paul's outstretched arm protecting me from falling and a crashing sound. Oh God, Geoff's front window had gone through. It was only single glazed. 'Please, Paul, take me home, I want to get out of here' I begged Paul to leave and he did, thank goodness. 'I was only trying to stop them crashing into you, and now Geoff says it's all my fault that the window has gone through.' Said an aggrieved Paul.

'Oh well let them sort it out, I just want to get home I'm really tired' I said. So we left and headed for Mums house intending to get a taxi from there.

Just as we were walking away from Geoff's I realised it was raining. 'Oh hurry up before we get soaked' I said, 'It's not raining, why do you say that?' replied Paul. 'Listen' I said, as we stopped under a street light, 'Can't you hear the rain hitting the pavement?'

 'I can hear it' said Paul 'But I can't feel it' 'Well what is it then?' I ask.

'Oh it's my arm' Paul blurted out. 'Look my hand is covered in blood'. As I looked at his hand under the street light, I see that the pitter-patter noise I heard that I thought was heavy rain hitting the pavement was actually blood pouring down Paul's arm and hitting the paving stones with a gush.

'Get your jacket off, let me look' I yelled, and then I helped Paul with his leather jacket. When we got the jacket off, I was stunned; his whole chest was covered in blood. He was wearing what was a white shirt, but under the glare of the street light, it was now completely red and my first thought was that he'd been shot! There was so much blood. I rolled up his shirt sleeve which on reflection was the worst thing I could have done. As I did so, I was splattered in the face with what was obviously arterial bloody spurting from a wound in his arm.

That was the moment, where the sight of so much blood was too much for Paul, and his legs went from under him. Oh hell! How was I going to help him? I pulled down the shirt sleeve and tried to apply pressure to the arm. Somehow my first aid training as a lifeguard kicked in. I had no fear at this point and I was sure I could manage somehow to stem the blood flow for the thirty seconds or so it would take me to drag him across the road to my Mum's house where we could call straight away for an ambulance.

'Get up, I need to you walk' I ordered, with all the authority of a paramedic. I was taking control. Paul was not completely unconscious just faint and dazed, the drink wasn't helping but we didn't have far to go. Paul staggered along, I was virtually carrying him, and at 5 months pregnant this was not easy, my face was covered in blood and we looked like a train wreck. Luckily not far to go.

At last, after what seemed like an eternity but was probably only a few minutes of half carrying half dragging a drunken, bleeding boyfriend, we were at Mum's and I was hammering on the door. There was no answer. I kept banging, 'she must wake up' I thought. 'But where is the car, oh no don't say she's gone out' I cried, Mum never went out on New Year's Eve she loved the Clive James show and was always home for it.

But that was the fact, my Mum was out, and I was alone with a now semi conscious Paul bleeding all over the front door step. So all I could do was keep him lying down with his arm elevated. I knew the blood was coming from an artery, as it was gushing with such a force. So I needed to keep pressure on the humeral artery which was just under the armpit, otherwise he was going to die. Luckily I remembered from my first aid training that I needed to keep releasing the pressure every few minutes or he'd lose his arm if he survived. I didn't know what would be worse for Paul, whether he'd rather live or die with only one arm, but all I could think about was trying to save both his life and his arm.

It seemed like an eternity, but eventually someone came along and I screamed to them for help. 'Please flag down a taxi or go to a phone for an ambulance' I yelled, the frightened passer-by fled at the sight of all the blood, which I now noticed had spurted up the glass of the front door and the lounge window. Across the road there were lights on at a neighbour's house. 'Please go over there, they will phone an ambulance' I screamed after him. All the commotion had attracted another party goer who was wandering over; he immediately leapt into action and was flagging down cars in the middle of the road. No one stopped but at last came a black cab. The driver took one look at all the blood and refused us. 'You're not bringing him in the back of my cab, look at the mess'. Off he drove, and we were both stunned. But thankfully my Mum's neighbours from over the road were coming to our help. They'd phoned an ambulance and apparently it was on its way.

New Year's Eve is the worst night of the year to request an ambulance, but about 40 minutes later, an unconscious Paul was gently lifted into the back and I got in with him. At last we were off to the hospital.

'Bloody Hell love' said the paramedic. 'He's lost a lot of blood; it's going to be touch and go'. I was in a state of shock myself 'Oh please don't let him die, we're having a baby' I was now crying hard. 'Don't you upset yourself or you'll be in need of our services to save your baby' he went on. 'We got there in a couple of minutes, Whiston Hospital was very close by, and we had full bells and flashing lights going. Paul's trolley disappeared and I was left in the waiting room with people checking me over. I was covered in blood, but none of it was mine, and I eventually found a phone, I tried my Mum first but no answer so then I called Paul's Mum and Dad Joan and Bill, thankfully they were in and were now on their way to the hospital to pick me up.

I kept asking how Paul was but no one would tell me anything, 'Are you his wife? This was the constant question, 'Well we live together, but we're not married. I'm having his baby' 'Sorry love we can only give information to his next of kin.' Next of Kin? Why did they say that I wondered? Was he dead?

Thankfully he wasn't, he went into surgery and I went off to Joan and Bill's house, there was little else I could do at the hospital, and I could hardly keep my eyes open.

The operation took a number of hours and eventually I got in touch with my Mum. She was hysterical to find the front of her house covered in blood. The only thing she could think was that I'd arrived there needing help and had lost my baby on the front door step. Poor Mum, she was distraught.

Paul was on a ward the next morning, and although I'd had little sleep, we went to see him. The surgeon came over who had done the operation to fix his torn artery and sew up the tendons in his arm it had taken a lot of work, but Paul was lying their large as life with his arm elevated in a sling suspended from a drip stand. 'You saved his life, young lady' 'He'd lost about 6 pints of blood'.

'If you hadn't known a bit of first Aid he'd have died', the surgeon went on. 'I'm a lifeguard' I feebly muttered. The shock of what could have happened was setting in. 'Well you certainly guarded his life'.

It was a many years before I ever went out on New Year's Eve again. Happily Paul was ok, our baby son Marc was born 4 months later, and we went on to have little Katie another year later, but our relationship suffered after that accident, that was the point in both our lives where we can trace back to where it all started going wrong.

# Chapter 16

## 1988 - Hard labour

I had been willing this baby to be born. I spent the whole nine months of my pregnancy with morning sickness, everything made me feel sick, particularly smells. The especially the smell of cooking bacon and my beloved morning cup coffee. I could no longer stomach it. The amazing thing was that the only thing which stopped me feeling sick was actually eating. I ate constantly, especially jelly sweets, I'd probably eaten my own weight in jelly babies and wine gums. My due date was 31st March and 3 weeks later on 20th April there still seemed to be no sign of the baby. I had gained five and a half stones and gone from a skinny eight stones to thirteen and a half. The midwife just said 'Baby will come when it's ready'. I was getting desperate. How long would they let me go over my due date? And how much weight should I be gaining?

So this particular lunchtime, I was at my future mother and father-in-law's Joan and Bill's house, Paul's parents and I were sitting in the garden I was actually sunbathing it was so hot when I suddenly realised that I was starting to have twinges, I was totally euphoric. Well that was until Bill announced that Adolph Hitler was born on 20thApril, that definitely took the shine off my excitement. Although it was only April, it was actually boiling hot, and my size was probably adding to the heat I could feel. I had no idea how long labour would be, at the ante natal classes they advised anything from around 6 to 18 hours, and I'd been getting pains for about 4 hours, so I thought it was time to head off to the hospital. Little did I know that I would have quite a while to go yet?

Paul and I were sitting in a lounge type area and although the pains were coming around every 15 minutes and were a little bit uncomfortable, they were definitely bearable and I was wandering around trying to keep moving, which seemed to be the most sensible thing to do. Sue and Mum had also arrived along with Paul's Mum and Dad and his sister, who had recently had her first baby David. The hours were ticking slowly by and not much was happening, it was getting on for 10pm now so everyone headed off home and left me and Paul to get on with things, Mum instructed Paul to call her the minute anything proper happened. I was still not progressing much and even my waters hadn't broken. As it was my first baby, the midwife decided I should stay the night, as I was definitely in labour, slow labour all the same, they thought it advisable to stay as it could speed up at any time and I'd then have to come back in the middle of the night.

So I settled down to try and sleep away some of the impending hours. I was now strapped to a monitor to check on the baby's progress. I couldn't sleep as every time I tried another pain would wake me. It was very uncomfortable but I was determined that the pain was bearable and I wouldn't need any pain relief. Well that was the plan.

I must have got some sleep eventually but I awoke to a horrendous pain. I was gasping for breath, every 5 or 6 minutes. Things were definitely hotting up but when the midwife came to examine me again, she said that I was only five centimetres dilated and still had a long way to go yet. 'Oh no!' I thought that this was it, I was hoping the baby was about to come. At least it had gone past midnight and my baby wouldn't be sharing its birthday with Hitler. Paul and I had 2 names ready for whatever we had. Amy for a girl and Marc for a boy. We both liked Marc Bolan when we met and had always said if we had a boy we'd call him Marc. I didn't even want children back then, so why we were discussing names seems really odd now.

It was now well over 24 hours since I'd started having pains and I was feeling awful, completely exhausted. I was drifting in and out of sleep for the next 5 or so hours, but still not much was happening, Paul was asleep in the chair next to my bed, snoring his head off, I was so envious. At least he was getting some sleep but I'd make sure that changed when the baby finally arrived. A young girl who seemed even younger than me came in to the room. She was a junior midwife and rather snotty looking. 'Can you help me sit up please? I'm really uncomfortable' I asked.

'Push yourself forward' she retorted rather unpleasantly.

'I can't I have no energy, I can't lean forward'

I was so large around my middle, that I couldn't sit up and with the monitors strapped across my belly, I couldn't roll onto my side to lever myself up.

'Please help me' I whimpered.

'I can't lift you, I'm pregnant myself' she blurted and stormed out of the room. I just broke down and cried. Paul heard me and woke up; he dragged me up and washed my face, then went off and got me a cup of tea. When he came back there was an older midwife there who was very caring and telling me I should now start to try the gas and air as it would help relieve the pain I was in.

The day continued much the same until about 6pm in the afternoon. I was completely exhausted and in a lot of pain now. All of a sudden there was a massive pain and I screamed out. 'Not long now' the midwife encouraged me. I was thinking back to the day before when labour had started, I thought it was pretty painful then, I had no idea what was to come!

Paul's Mum was outside; I was screaming my head off. I'd relented and had an injection of pethadine into my thigh, it didn't seem to help, and all I felt now was sick as a dog and was regularly vomiting into a kidney dish.

Although I was in a lot of pain, I could hardly believe what I was hearing. 'Can't you do something to bring that baby into the world; she's going to die if you leave her like that?' It was my mother-in-law, Joan outside in the corridor. I stared at Paul, he had the same worried look on his face that I had.

I was relieved when a doctor came in. 'Can we offer you an epidural?' Your baby is getting rather distressed and we think if you calm down it will help the baby'. My relief was short lived as I was now worrying about my baby. 'Once you've had this epidural, we'll try and break your waters for you manually this may hurry things along a bit'.

'Can't you just give me something, to make the baby come? 'What about a caesarean?' I suggested. Can't you just cut it out of me?'

'Don't be silly, you're perfectly healthy to give birth on your own, just be patient' the midwife calmly said. I didn't feel like I could be patient any longer. I was now entering the 3rd stage of labour and my temper was rising.

'Get it out of me' 'I've had enough' 'Paul, make them get it out of me.' 'I can't do it anymore'. I was getting hysterical by now.

Very soon afterwards the doctor returned and told me to bend as far forward as I could so they could inject something into my spine. This would make me lose all feeling below the waist and I wouldn't be able to feel any pain.

All I could imagine was that the stuff they were putting into me wouldn't wear off and I'd be left paralysed, but I hardly cared by then, I just needed pain relief and I didn't care what the cost was.

I needn't have worried, it was all ok. At last I had a couple of hour's relief. This wasn't going to be so bad after all.

I drifted off to a much needed sleep.

Then bang, I was back into reality with a shock. Labour was in full swing now, and people were rushing round me.

'It's time to push darling' the midwife encouraged. 'Push?' I screamed 'how am I going to push?' I hadn't an ounce of energy. But somehow, I managed it.

'Here's baby, here's the head' I glanced down, there was a baby looking right up at me with massive black eyes and a shock of black hair. I couldn't believe it.

'One more push love' 'One more big push, come on... come ooooonnnn'

A baby! My baby boy! At 19:50 on 21st April 1988 after 36 hours of hard labour, my baby Marc was born, he was perfect, I was a Mum, and he shared his birthday with the Queen.

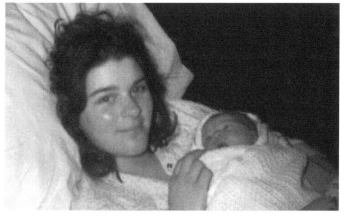

(Me and my first baby Marc)

# Chapter 17

## 1988 - A shock!

Oh no! How could I be pregnant again? Marc was only 5 months old, I'd had a hard time giving birth and I didn't want any more children. I was actually taking the contraceptive pill, but they had me on a low dosage because I was breast feeding. I went along to the family planning clinic to get it confirmed. No you're not pregnant it's negative – the stern nurse said to me. 'But I've not had any periods for the last 2 months' I told her. Well it's probably your hormones and the fact that you're breast feeding' she replied. 'Well I was having periods, can you check again please'. It's definitely negative you are NOT pregnant' she almost shouted at me. So off I went back home.

A month later and I'm actually feeling pregnant now, so I made another appointment only to be given exactly the same news. 'Madam, you are NOT pregnant, the test confirms it'. 'But I actually feel pregnant now and it's only a few months since my son was born, I know what it feels like to be pregnant. Also I'm not sure I want this baby so I need to make arrangements before it's too late'. The nurse glared at me with disapproval. Mrs... Oh I see its Miss Williams I can assure you that you are not pregnant and you really shouldn't be thinking that way'. I could see she disapproved of everything, I wasn't married, I wasn't pregnant and she now knew I was thinking of a termination. So off I went again.

Another month went by and still no period, so I had to go back to the family planning clinic again. The awful nurse was there again. 'I'm afraid I've still not had a period, so I need another pregnancy test I said. She looked down her nose at me through her half moon glasses and sneered 'Take this cup and give us another sample'. I went off to the toilet and returned a few minutes later. I was waiting in the room, wondering what I was going to do if she said negative to me again and also what I'd do if it was positive. I definitely didn't want another baby. My relationship with Paul was on the rocks, we were very short of money and the mortgage interest rate was rising rapidly with the Tory Government in power, it was already around 10% and expected to climb even higher. Paul was still out of work and there was nothing on the horizon. My job was pretty safe in local government but I was finding it hard working full time and being a Mum and supporting us financially. Paul was still drinking at every opportunity.

I snapped out of my thoughts as the nurse returned. 'Miss Williams' she called loudly and I pushed Marc in his pram into her room. 'I'm pleased to tell you that you are in fact pregnant, congratulations' she beamed.

'That's hardly the news I wanted, but I've been telling you for the past 3 months that I was pregnant, now do you believe me?' 'You'll have to tell me how to organise a termination'. 'My husband is out of work, as you can see I've got a very small baby as it is and I'm trying to support my family by working full time'- 'A new baby is too much for me'.

'When was your last period Miss Williams?' I got out my diary and gave her the date. 'Well that makes you at least 16 weeks pregnant, you've left it too late my dear, you can't have a termination now.' 'That's your entire fault, you kept telling me it was negative', I yelled. I burst into tears and stormed from her office and out into the road. I decided to push Marc in his pram all the way home from Rainhill to St Helens and do some thinking along the way. Well there was nothing I could do, I decided that I wasn't going to tell anyone I was pregnant in the hope that it would all just go away. That didn't last long and I had to tell Paul, he seemed overjoyed at the prospect of another baby and he was very good with Marc even if he was hopeless as a partner. Sue guessed straight away, but the thought of telling Mum was all too much. She didn't like Paul and didn't want me to have children; she'd go mad if I said I was having another, plus she was right, we couldn't afford children anyway. So the months ticked by and I kept away from Mum.

Well there was nothing I could do; I'd have to tell her eventually so I called her from the payphone in the reception of Sutton High Leisure Centre. 'Mum, I've got something to tell you' I stammered. 'You're pregnant again aren't you?' she immediately replied. 'Yes, I'm sorry to say I am'. Mum slammed down the phone.

# Chapter 18

## 1988 - Fiddling the lecky

One baby already, another on the way and a husband out of work meant that we were struggling to pay all the bills. But it didn't seem to matter as we were happy enough with our lot. Both our families wanted to help but we had our pride and we would stay at home in the evenings so that we could save money and pay the bills. When the mortgage interest rate increased again to almost 15% we were getting desperate but Paul had a plan. Paul's Uncle Geoff (now deceased) was a great character and could see that we were struggling to make ends meet so one evening he explained to Paul that it was easy to fiddle the electric meter with an old strip of negatives.

Apparently if you slide a strip of negatives from your photographs up the back of the electricity meter you can stop the wheel from going round thus stopping the bill from clocking up. Paul listened to this and thought it sounded an easy way to save a few bob – after all Manweb could afford it and it wasn't like stealing from a person was it? Thank goodness I was blissfully unaware of this plan and so was Bill, Paul's Dad. He was a meter reader for Manweb, the Electricity Board in the North West area and he would have gone mad if he had heard of the scheme, I think that's partly why Geoff suggested it.

It was about 3pm in the afternoon and I was heading home on the bus from the swimming pool, I was only working early shifts now as I was pregnant and I seemed to be suffering the worse of the morning sickness in the evenings, I know, I'm always different. As the bus passed our house, I noticed that the street was full of Electricity Board vans, but I thought little of it as all I wanted was a cup of tea and the chance to put my feet up. It was bitterly cold and getting dark as I got off the bus at the stop near to the back of our house and walked along the alley to our back gate. I leant my not inconsiderable bulk against the sticking gate and forced it open. As I walked up the path I was hoping Paul had some tea and toast ready for me, I was always hungry when I was pregnant. I got to the door and found it was locked – bugger! Paul always left the back door unlocked when he was at home so I started swearing under my breath as I hadn't taken any keys, Paul had assured me he would be at home all day. I decided I would visit one of the neighbours until Paul came home but as I turned away from the door I heard Rocky (our Alsatian) barking his head off. Paul would never have left Rocky in the house alone so at this point I started to get annoyed.

'Paul are you in?' I yelled. The door opened and an arm quickly appeared and I was unceremoniously yanked indoors before the door was slammed shut.

'What the hell are you up to?' I shrieked as I was dragged into the kitchen. The whole house was in complete darkness and the curtains were drawn.

'Keep your voice down' Paul whispered, 'It's the 'lecky men. They've been out there for hours banging on the doors trying to get in'.

'They probably need to read the meter' I suggested. 'Let them in you idiot' I went on.

'Shush!' whispered Paul' 'I can't let them in' Paul looked like he was sweating quite a bit and I wondered what was wrong with him.

'Why not? What's up?' I was starting to get a bit worried; this was not normal behaviour, even for Paul. My mind was racing. There I was heavily pregnant with another baby Marc upstairs and the house surrounded by the Electricity Board. I kept thinking of a small family in a wagon surrounded by Indians... and then for some strange reason I thought there must be a gas leak and the house was about to blow up. I know what you're thinking but I was pregnant!

'I've been fiddling the lecky, I'll go to bloody jail if they catch me' whispered Paul 'I've been trying to get the negative out and now I've broken the seal and the negative has slipped further in and I can't get it out'.

'What negative?' Paul explained about his money saving scheme. 'Oh God! You idiot, what were you thinking?' Then for some reason I added 'What negative did you use? It's not the ones from Marc's party is it? I need to get some reprints...'

'I don't know what bloody negative it is, what are we going to do? There's no point going mad at me now, I know it was stupid, but I'm about to get caught and Bill will go mad'

'Did he do it for you' I couldn't believe Pauls Dad would be involved in such as scheme.

'No of course not, but he works for them, he'll get to hear'

'Oh it gets better, who showed you what to do'

'Our Geoff'

'Why am I not surprised?'

'So what do we do now?' 'How long have they been outside?'

'About 2 hours'

'Shit!' 'Why didn't they see me coming in round the back?'

'I think they're having a tea-break, they had flasks out when I peeped out from upstairs'

'They must know you are in the house or they'd go'

'I heard them saying they're waiting for the Police so they can break in'

'Oh great what will we do now.' In my mind I saw pictures of me waiting outside a prison with all the other wives and girlfriends for visiting time. Paul would get out early for good behaviour but his children wouldn't recognize him and he wouldn't be able to get a job. No change there then I though as my mind snapped back to the present.

'I have a plan' said Paul

At that point I knew it was going to be something ridiculous. It always was some hair brained scheme, which was bound to fail. Everything Paul ever did failed.

'I'm going to pretend I've been asleep because I work nights'

'You're unemployed!' I helpfully pointed out.

'Shut up Siân, they don't know that'

'When they break in, I'll come charging down stairs in my boxers, and pretend that I thought they were burglars'

'What about all this barking from the dog? Wouldn't that have woken you up earlier?'

Paul thought for a minute, 'I'll say I'm a deep sleeper'

'But what about me? I'm here now'

'You stay in the baby's room, I'll say I'm alone, they won't go upstairs'.

'What if they saw me?'

'You came in the back way and they were having tea so they didn't see you!'

So that was Paul's master-plan. I shrugged my shoulders and went upstairs, thank goodness baby Marc was a deep sleeper and hadn't heard the fuss that Rocky was making every time they knocked on the door. Paul followed me up and undressed so it looked like he'd been in bed. We sat there for another half an hour, Rocky was going mad downstairs as various men were peeping and shouting through the letterbox.

All of a sudden there was an enormous crashing at the back of the house. They had used one of those rams that you see on the BBC's 'Crimewatch' TV show and the back door had splintered as a grinning Policeman started to enjoy himself for the first time that day..

Paul flew into action as the first 'lecky' man hurtled through the door. What I didn't' know was the second part of Pauls 'masterplan'. This was to pick up a vase and smash it over the head of the intruder. I was hiding in the bedroom with Marc so the rest of the story is from Paul and also what I heard at the local shop, Paul was to become a legend. The Lecky man came through the door to be confronted by a very territorial Alsatian who thought it was all good fun. Paul picked up the vase and smashed it over the intruders head but it was only a glancing blow and the victim was able to pull something out of his jacket pocket during the struggle with my lunatic husband and the dog. And that something was an electrical device called a taser – some sort of stun gun for stopping vicious dogs! There was an almighty scream and a yelp. The dog came hurtling into the bedroom yapping and barking followed by a strong smell of singed fur and dog wee. He was shaking with fear and hid under the bed. Paul was giving a good performance and was screaming 'help police' at the top of his voice to back up his claim that he had caught some burglars. The kitchen was wrecked with plates and cutlery knocked from the draining board as the broken timber door had crashed onto the floor.

There were now 5 men holding Paul down, the first was bleeding from his head where Paul had smashed my vase. The 'stunned' dog had turned to his master for safety but because Paul was only in his boxers the dog wee had managed to complete the circuit and give Paul a shock as well. Paul had also taken a blow to the head and was bleeding from his lip. In the confusion the dog had ripped his boxers from him and he was now partially naked!

Everyone calmed down and Paul launched into his story. They suggested we should fit a door bell loud enough to wake him up in future. They hurried into the cupboard under the stairs, read the meter and left, there was no mention of the seal being broken. They couldn't get out quick enough. Paul was beginning to feel very pleased with himself by now and was about to ask them to repair the door when he thought he should keep quiet.

Paul then had to pluck up courage and ask Bill to reseal the meter. Of course we had to explain what had happened and even Bill thought Paul had got what he deserved and had learnt his lesson.

# Chapter 19

## 1989 – Baby number two

So I was massively pregnant again and in a maternity frock I looked a lot like Hattie Jaques who played the Matron in a lot of the 'Carry On' films. So as Marc had weighed in at a healthy 9lbs 4oz and now I seemed to be even bigger with my second baby I assumed it must be another boy. I'd secretly been wishing for a girl. I know it doesn't matter so long as it's healthy, but as I had a boy already I really did want a girl this time.

My cravings when pregnant this time all seemed to be for minerals. And that was coal, talcum powder and chalk. Yes I was actually eating the stuff! Talc and chalk were easy to get hold of and I'd worked my way through a few containers of Johnson's baby powder, Marc had a blackboard and chalks for Christmas and I'd eaten every one of his chalks. However not many people these days had real coal fires except my Granddad, and I'd been in his coal bunker a few times lately and looked like miner about the face when I visited but Granddad didn't say anything, I don't think he was surprised to see me in his kitchen sink swilling out my black mouth after I'd finished a piece of his smokeless fuel.

Because of these strange cravings, Paul was hardly surprised when he entered the bedroom, to see me like a whale lying across the bed and the room in clouds of talcum powder.

'Have you been eating that stuff again?' I don't think it'll do the baby any good?' He said.

'No not this time, I was just drying myself off after my bath, and got this massive pain, so I must have squeezed the container too tightly and it went everywhere. This pain is killing me it won't go away. I moaned.

'Are you in labour?'

'Nah, this isn't a labour pain; it's just a long dull ache in my stomach' - 'Labour pains come and go, this is just one long pain, that's not going away'.

'Do you think we should go to my Mum's house just in case, you're about 10 days late as it is, and she's only down the road from the maternity hospital.'

'I'm not in labour!' I yelled back. Paul backed out of the room; he knew when not to argue.

I could hear him downstairs on the phone, but had no idea who he was speaking to, and about half an hour later, there was a knock at the door and his uncle John had arrived.

I was dressed by then, but still in pain with my stomach, and assumed it was trapped wind or I was about to have an upset stomach.

'Our John has come to take us to my Mum's I'm worried you might be in labour'

'Oh what ever then, we'll go, but it's a waste of time as I'm NOT in labour'

'Siân, you're actually 11 days over, you might be'

'All right, all right' 'But you'll have to get Marc ready too' I submitted in the end and let him have his way. I knew I wasn't in labour; it had only been a year since my last pregnancy so I was fully aware of what things were going to be like.

So we all piled into John's car and we went to Paul's Mum's house in Rainhill. She was only a 5 minute car drive from Whiston Hospital, and although they were at work, we could spend the day there as Paul had a key.

By now it was after 12 noon. Paul was insisting that I went to the hospital and we should get a taxi. I was pacing up and down, my back hurt and my stomach ached but there were no waves of labour pains just one long pain that wasn't subsiding, it wasn't getting worse but it was very uncomfortable.

'Ring your Mum and ask her'

'How will she know if I'm in labour, down the phone' 'She's not a midwife either, she works in an office'. 'And today she's in Liverpool Town Hall' - 'so I can't get hold of her anyway'

'Well I'll ring your Sue at work, I bet she can get hold of your Mum' Paul was being very awkward and wouldn't listen to anything I said. In the end I left him to it, and went into the lounge to watch a bit of telly.

'I've got your Mum on the phone, can you get out here?' Paul shouted from the hallway.

'Bloody hell Paul, what have you phoned her for?' I waddled to the hall

'Make me a cup of tea please' I asked him. I snatched the phone from Paul in temper and gave him a filthy look.

'Mum, I don't know why he's called you' I panted. I'm not in labour, I should bloody know. I've just got this ache, and he's doing my head in, we're at Joan and Bill's he insisted we came here.'

'You don't sound too good to me' Mum said. 'I'm fine really' I sighed. 'I know what labour feels like and this is not it' I snapped back at her.

'Phone an ambulance now!' Mum was snapping at me now.

'No way, I'll be stuck in there for hours and then they'll send me home'

'I'm telling you to phone a bloody ambulance now' 'Get Paul back on this phone to me' Mum demanded.

'She wants you, but if you phone an ambulance I'll go kill you, I'm not going to hospital' I argued back.

'She won't go Pat' - 'OK I'll try' 'you know what she's like'.

I could only hear Paul's side of the argument, and I had a good idea that my Mum was yelling orders at Paul, and by the look on his face, I don't know who scared him more, me or my Mum.

I went back to the lounge and sprawled on the sofa. It was coming up to 1pm now. I didn't feel any worse, but I certainly didn't feel any better.

Paul came back into the lounge with a worried look on his face.

'I've called an ambulance, your Mum said she'd kill me if you went into labour at home, and I ended up delivering the baby'.

90

'God she's so dramatic, I think I'd know if I was in labour'

'But you're sweating like mad' 'And you're more bad tempered that usual.'

'OK OK OK! I'll go but I'm going to kill you and Mum, when they say I'm not in labour'.

Five minutes later the ambulance arrived. I was still shouting and complaining to the ambulance staff and later the maternity ward reception staff at about five past one, when they wheeled me towards a labour ward.

'I'm not in labour but no-one will believe me'

'We'll just have a quick look, and you can go back home if you're not in labour' 'It'll only take a couple of minutes to check.' Eventually I gave up arguing and let them examine me.

Then I sat back up on the bed.

'Well dear, you're 10cm dilated your baby is about to be born' the midwife announced. I was stunned almost into silence.

'But I can't be'. My water's haven't broken. I'm not even having pains.

'I can assure you my dear, that baby is coming now'.

'Would you like some gas and air to help?'

'It doesn't work, I've just had one baby last year, and neither does that pethadine they gave me. I want an epidural'

'Oh dear, there's no time for that, the baby is coming now'.

'I waaaaaaaant my epidural' I screamed

'You have to open your legs dear, this baby needs to be born, push, push!!'

I'm not pushing, stop looking up there, I'm not having it'

'Yes you are!!'

'Stop looking'

'You don't need to be embarrassed love, I've been looking at lady bits most of my life'

'NOW OPEN YOUR LEGS!'

With that, the most massive gush of water came and without even pushing, what appeared on the bed looked like a small seal. It was my baby.

'Oh my god, it's here' I squawked.

My baby had been born all on its own, without any pushing, very little screaming nor any help from a midwife. It just shot out with the gallons of waters like a giant fish.

'You've got a little girl, well a big girl she's almost ten pounds' Yelled the midwife.

'A girl?'

'It can't be' I panted back.

'I haven't got a name and I'm so fat I thought it must be a boy' I went on.

'Well you better get thinking about a name, she's lovely'.

I'd wished and wished for a girl, so imagine my shock when that's what I'd got. I'd been stuck for a girl's name as Paul didn't like any of the name's I'd been thinking about. In the late 80s the popular names were all flowers, Rosie, Poppy or Daisy. Paul thought they were silly, so I was stuck. I'd only really thought of a boy's name and if it was a boy, we'd agreed on Gary.

I stared around the room looking for Paul; he was staggering towards me, white as a ghost with a frightful look of fear on his face.

'Her name is Katie and she's beautiful' that was all he said.

I promptly shut up for the first time that day. I had only actually been in the hospital 20 minutes before Katie came into the world. Thank goodness Paul had stood up to me and not listened to my moaning and shouting.

# Chapter 20

## 1989 - A Christening, odd shoes and no guests

We were hardly religious, but I suppose we were quite traditionalist. Like most families the only time we go to church is for weddings, funerals and christenings. As the saying goes 'Hatched matched and dispatched'. Paul was christened a Catholic and his brother was christened Church-of-England, I don't know why Paul's Mum and Dad, Joan and Bill never said. He was probably the least 'practicing' Catholic I knew but we were both in favour of having the children Christened and as far as Paul was concerned it was a good excuse for a party. In those days anything that ended up with a party and a few drinks had to be a good thing.

Once again All Saints Church in Sutton was to be the venue. All the guests were going to meet in the Prince of Wales pub before going to the church. I say 'all the guests' but what I mean is that all Paul's family and a few hangers on would be meeting there. We had arranged the Christening for noon, and as the pub opened at 11am it was an ideal place for everyone to meet.

My Mum is slightly religious, and also a bit of a snob so the idea of meeting in a pub before going to a church was completely out of the question. She disapproved of my choice of partner and that meant she disapproved of his family too. I don't think anyone would have been suitable for me, but there you go, I suppose she was right.. Baby Katie was all ready in a satin frock about 2 feet longer than her and wearing a matching bonnet. Wrapped around her was my old Christening gown, the one my Mum had me christened in. It's beautifully embroidered with a lovely fringe. We had used the same gown for Marc a year earlier so this looked like it was now going to be the tradition.

We were all set to go and Mum's new friend John was taking us to All Saint's in his car even though it was only a stone's throw away. I seemed to be living my life backwards as this was my second christening here and I wasn't even married. The vicar always smiled but I could tell he was not happy by this state of affairs. We had never thought about getting married until about six weeks earlier when Paul proposed, it was completely out of the blue. I graciously accepted his proposal and although we hadn't told the vicar yet, we know we would be back again sometime in the not too distant future.

We were all sitting in the front pew awaiting the rest of the guests. The church was an old fashioned style built out of freezing cold stone with hard pews, the back of the church had been re-modernised a bit but mostly it was the traditional type and I could actually see my breath coming out it was so cold. I was there along with the proud Dad; our Sue is God Mother again, along with Paul's sister Julie and his brother Shaun who is to be the God Father. Mum and John are here and so are Paul's parents Joan and Bill.

'Where's everyone else?' I ask Paul.

'Still in the Prince I bet' Paul laughs.

'I don't think that's very funny Paul, why didn't you get them organised?' I'm getting annoyed now. 'Shshsh' Mum hisses from behind me. 'The vicar is waiting to start' she motioned towards the very impatient looking clergyman.

'We'll.. err.. we'll have to start' I stammer to the vicar, 'The others have been... err.. delayed' I lie, and cross my fingers behind my back, how could I do that in a church, did I have no shame? I turned to see Mum with her 'I told you they were useless' look on her face.

Sue is sat to my left and Paul is on my right, next to him is Shaun, looking the worse for wear on a Sunday morning; he must have been out the night before. Sue whispers to me, 'Look at Shaun's shoes' she is always able to find something funny in everything and loves the unexpected. Oh hell (more blasphemy!) Shaun had odd shoes on. I could hardly contain myself as Sue and I start to giggle, our shoulders jumping up and down as we tried desperately to suppress our laughter. I whispered it to Paul who looked at the shoes and started to laugh out loud, he had no self control at all, until my Mum jabbed him in the back to try and restore some normality at this solemn affair.

Things moved along quite nicely and we were all round the font, Katie screamed out as expected when the water was dripped onto her head. I still kept glancing between Sue and Shaun's shoes. Shaun was oblivious, although I don't know if Paul mentioned anything as he kept standing on his own feet and shuffling quite a bit. It was fine until the candle dripped hot wax onto Shaun's hand and he yelped. Mum was almost apoplectic by this time and I think poor John wondered what kind of family he had been introduced to.

It was over at last and we headed home. As expected Paul's family and the other guests were still in the Prince of Wales and we only saw them at tea-time when they stumbled paralytic into my house asking where the food was. Mum was not amused!

# Chapter 21

## 1990 - Old ladies sauna

It was now twelve months since I had my baby girl and I decided to take nearly a whole year off work because working for local government I was entitled to full pay during maternity leave. If only I had known this when I had my son Marc, I was back to work after 9 weeks – it should have been 12 weeks off work but the little bugger was 3 weeks late and ate into my time off.

So this time I decided to take the full 40 weeks of maternity leave plus holidays, so it wass almost a year since I had worked. I was happily settling into motherhood but it was hard working full-time with two babies even though I had help from Paul, who was now working shifts, and my sister Sue. It was all going well and I was pleased that I had decided to return to work. When I returned, my pool bronze lifeguard qualification had lapsed so I wasn't allowed to work poolside – oh what a shame! In those days we had to take it every year so without it I had to do something else until I passed it again, that would make a change from being a lifeguard. I had worked in a Leisure Centre since I was 17 mainly on the side of a pool which isn't as glamorous as you might think – it's mostly spent mopping – I should have joined the navy so that at least I could have been mopping decks in more glamorous places.

When I returned to work I found out that to my horror I'd been moved from my nice modern swimming pool and leisure centre, close to where I lived, to the other side of town and to the oldest baths known to man – Queens Park! It used to be known as Boundary Road Baths when I was a kid and it was famous for being full of cockroaches, as were most old swimming pools. It was a really atmospheric place with lots of white tiles separated by bands of grey and black. It was the sort of place that was used as a film set when the director wanted the heroine to be chased through a spooky building before seeing shots of blood stained tiles and finally a shot of a partially clad body floating in the pool... I always did have an overactive imagination – back to the story.

I was welcomed by the manager who matched his surround-ings. Len Lister was in his sixties and was keeping his head down waiting for retirement. He opened my file and read a letter from the Head of Personal at the Council. He didn't read it out loud but looked at me sitting opposite.

'It says you don't have a pool bronze certificate and that I am to give you any job until you retake it. As you are female I suppose stoking the boiler is out of the question. The only vacancy I have at the moment is working in the ladies sauna and steam room – that will have to do until you re-take your pool bronze.'

Oh well it could be worse. I thanked Mr Lister; he wasn't a first name sort of chap, picked up my keys and headed to the sauna and steam room.  I had been there before so I wasn't looking forward to it. I remember it as the 'slipper baths' [I'm not that old! I never visited the slipper baths, kids couldn't go anyway, and it was only for ladies and gentlemen.] So what are the slipper baths – I hear you cry. Well years ago, before houses were fitted with bathrooms you either had a tin bath in front of the fire or you would go to the public baths. For a few pennies you could have a hot bath with soap and clean towels. The soap was awful carbolic stuff so people always took their own nice smelling stuff. Not only did you get into this massive old fashioned roll top bath full of nice hot water but you had an attendant to scrub your back – those were the days! The adjoining swimming pool was long and narrow and my Nan and Granddad could remember when the council would fit boards over the pool and hold dances on a Saturday night.

I unlocked the door marked 'Ladies Sauna and Steam Room' and entered my new domain. I was pleasantly surprised. The old cold tiles had been replaced with bright cream artex and there was a nice waiting area. At the back of the waiting area was a series of cupboards holding clean towels and to the left was a door leading to the sauna and steam room. This was beginning to look like an easy number. All I had to do was hand out the towels, tidy up the magazines in the waiting area and change the music tapes. After a few days to get settled in I would spend most of the day lying on a lounger reading celebrity magazines and listening to the music – this was better than mopping up pool side.

I had been there about three months and I was just settling down with a new magazines and a cup of coffee when I heard the door from the sauna open. It was a quiet day and there were only a couple of young Mums and one old lady using the sauna. I looked up and the old lady was walking towards to me. She was stark naked with a big grin on her face.

'I've dropped my towel and its wet, please can I have another?' She asked.

I quickly took a fresh towel from the cupboard and handed it to her, hoping that she would use to cover herself up. No luck, she started to walk back to the sauna, stopped, bent over and started to dry her feet. Now I've been around a bit and given birth so I wasn't squeamish but the sight of the rear end of the wrinkled old lady was very upsetting and the first thing that I thought of was 'am I going to look like that?' Then my mind flashed back a few years to the naked elderly gentleman that had flashed at me as he walked towards the pool and I was wondering 'why me?' what is it with these naked geriatrics? The image of that little old lady has stuck with me and it comes back to me whenever I see a little old lady on the street. Although she seemed perfectly healthy and in quite good shape for a lady in her 70s, it looked as though most of her insides were falling out - am I doomed to be plagued by the image of geriatric genitals for the rest of my life?

# Chapter 22

## 1990 - Wedding number one

We had been together since we were about 16 and knew each other from school. Shortly after the birth of our second child, our little girl Katie, Paul proposed and I was stunned, the last couple of years had been really hard and I thought we were splitting up, so marriage was the last thing on my mind. Paul had been drinking quite heavily since his accident with his arm and was still in and out of work, mostly out. So although we thought we'd wait until the following year, we began planning our wedding. I never thought we'd make it to the actual day but I was willing to give it one last go.

It was always going to be on the cheap, we had two small children, a mortgage and my other half wasn't the most reliable of people when it came to money. But that aside our families rallied around. Paul's Mum made my dress and my sister Sue's bridesmaid dress. The fact that I looked like a man in drag only added to the hilarity.

I had always imagined arriving at the church in a Rolls Royce on my wedding day but as I said earlier, funds were low and Paul's cousin Ste thought he was some sort of Arthur Daley and drove around in a very old white Jag XJ6 the Sovereign model so that was the closest we were going to get to a bridal car. Good old Andy from the swimming pool who later gave me driving lessons was a bit of an amateur photographer so had all the gear to do photos and a video. Mum was paying for the Church Choir who sounded more like auditions for the X factor (the bad ones). I did the catering, which was a glamorous thing to do on my wedding day, sarnies and sausage rolls in the local pub and it was more of the same for the evening in the Transport Social Club, however my sister and chief bridesmaid Sue, couldn't come in the evening, she had a dinner to go to with her then boyfriend Gary at Rover, as he was a salesman at Tannery Farm the local Rover dealership in Elephant Lane. I never imagined my wedding morning would be spent buttering bread, cooking vol-au-vents and sausage rolls, but there you go! Most of the rest we managed to pay for ourselves, bit by bit as we went along.

The invites had gone out and the day was upon us. My Dad and Mum divorced when I was 5 years old and although I had seen my Dad over the years we were not that close. He lives in Anglesey, North Wales so I sent him an invitation asking him to let me know if he was coming. As I didn't hear from him and I had been brought up by my Step-Dad Peter it was arranged that he would walk me down the aisle and give me away.

The time for the wedding had arrived and we were almost set to go, the church, the famous All Saints where we'd previously had the kids christened was very close to our house, so it seemed funny waiting to be collected by a car (or rather an old banger and it actually did back fire on the way) only to be dropped off again 30 seconds later, but our driver was also doing a few runs bringing all the guests. There was a knock on the door and we all expected to see our driver Ste ready to take me to the church. We were all shocked to see my Dad (the biological one) all dressed up ready to give me away, it was all very awkward. I explained that as I hadn't heard from him I had asked

Peter, my step Dad, to give me away and it wouldn't be fair to change the plan now.

Well it all came out wrong and my Dad left for the church looking rather rejected with my Mum and I was left there wondering why I was even getting married in the first place as I didn't really want to anyway. My Step Dad picked up on this and was very understanding. He said that I didn't have to go through with it if I didn't want to, but it was all too late now and everyone would be hurt so I got in the car and off we went. I know I shouldn't laugh but looking back the funniest thing was seeing my Mum sitting between my two Dads wearing an awful pink feather hat and looking like Hyacinth Bucket, she was definitely trying to keep up appearances but her face was like thunder and I knew she hated my husband-to-be with a vengeance.

It was March and there was a gale force wind and driving rain for most of the day. As I stepped out of the car the wind grabbed my dress and whipped it up around my waist, and my veil was blown horizontal across my face and was ripping my hair out at the roots, Sue, my maid of honour was desperately trying to hang on to everything and push me into the church.

As I walked slowly up the aisle I could see the afore said husband-to-be seemed a bit worse for wear he'd definitely had a shandy or two but his beaming face showed that he seemed to be pleased that I'd actually turned up.

The organist started playing – even I could tell it was off key and we were about to start singing '*oh perfect love*' or '*love divine*' I can't remember which was first but they were both as inappropriate as the other. Mum had insisted that we would have the Choir and she would pay for it. She said that the singing was always better if you had a choir leading you, and the congregation would be far more likely to join in if we did. Well she was the expert so I'd agreed. But I'd not actually seen or heard the choir before arriving on my actual wedding day. As I walked down the aisle I could see that they were there but didn't look closely as I was so distracted by a number of things, the pink chicken hat in the front row to my left, my little son Marc all lovely in his navy and white sailor suit toddling behind me trying to pick up the train on my dress and my sister almost pulling his arm out if his socket trying to drag him away from it. My daughter Katie who was only about nine months old was bawling her head off on my right along with her cousin Jamie who was only a month older than her.

So with all this going on the Choir was the last thing on my mind until they started singing. I thought it was a nice idea to have the tw hymns my Nan and Granddad had had at their wedding, after all they'd been married for 40 years until my Nan's very sad and untimely death, and I think my Mum said she'd had *'Oh Perfect Love'* at her wedding too – that's a joke in itself, but that's not part of this story. The thing I should have thought of is that not many people know Hymns these days, and apart from *'There is a green field far away'* and the *'Old Rugged Cross'* I don't know many myself. Perhaps *'Fight the Good Fight'* might have been more appropriate in retrospect? So I should have realised that picking unusual Hymns for my wedding was only going to make the congregation less likely to join in but we had a choir so all should be fine.

As I expected, the congregation were less than enthusiastic and there was only a general mumbling behind me – I never sing even if I know the words as my voice is completely flat. I'd only ever heard my new husband sound like a drunken karaoke star so

I really had to rely on my Mum, Sister, Grandad and the Choir. Grandad was in a choir himself and was in full swing with his lovely deep bass voice when I glanced at the choir. I thought the awful singing was coming from the congregation, but when I looked over I saw with my horror that it was coming from the choir and by the look of them it was no wonder. What a bizarre looking rabble? They mostly looked like they'd been dragged off the streets. At the centre was a massive man with the hair cut of Fryer Tuck and he couldn't hold a note, there was an elderly lady screeching at the top of her voice, a dwarf that you couldn't hear, a couple of teenagers who looked like punks in cassocks and a very tall thin man who was idly gazing round without singing a note at all, I'm sure I'd seen him lying on the pavement outside our local pub at least he was upright now. How I managed not to laugh out loud I'll never know but I did nudge my new husband and pointed at the choir, this was a fatal mistake as he did actually roar his head off – obviously the shandies didn't help him suppress his laughter.

We were coming to the end of the service and were about to kneel at the Alter for the blessing when my dress became tangled. As I mentioned earlier my mother-in-law had made it for me. I'd hired a hoop skirt to go underneath it, but as the dress was home-made I suppose it didn't flow quite as much as a professionally made wedding dress. Anyway we certainly hadn't designed it with kneeling on the alter in mind. It was a silky material with puff sleeves, quite tight around the bodice and then flaring from the knee and the hoop kept it all out in a circle at my feet. Suffice to say the moment I kneeled down the hoop shot up behind me and raised my skirt so that I looked like a peacock with its tail up, and now the world could see my knickers, stockings and suspenders along with the traditional garter! I was unaware at this point although there was some tittering from the pews behind me – all I could feel was my sister grabbing at the hoop and trying to force it down. Suddenly there was a cracking sound and obviously it was down, the hoop was broken but my dignity was almost saved. For the second time that day my dress was around my waist. I remember a slight groan from the male guests in the pews as Sue protected my dignity; perhaps the sight was better than I imagined! And thank goodness I'd treated myself to some quite nice undies for the special day.

We all sang *'Jerusalem'* and I was now Mrs Siân Knight!

The evening party was a disco was to be held in the Transport Club. This was a 'working-man's' type of club, actually the sports and social club for the Transport and General Workers Trade Union located at the back of the Town Hall in St Helens. We must have got some kind of discount, because I can't think of any other reason we would be there, apart from the fact that I'd been on a First Aid course there some years previously where I had to be the casualty strapped to a stretcher and lowered down the fire escape, I was one of the most frightening experiences of my life… but back to the story.

Anyway, Sue couldn't make it due to the Rover 'do', so it was up to me to make sure all the catering was laid out, and the disco chap was all set up. Paul seemed to be continually propped up at the bar, necking pints with Jack Daniels chasers as fast as he possibly could. He seemed drunk at the altar, so by now I was dreading him getting hold of that microphone from the DJ later in the evening when speeches where scheduled.

Thankfully Mum took control of the mic, and thanked everyone for coming and those who had made a special effort in providing the car, dresses, buffet (me), flowers etc.

'Oh no here he comes' I thought. Paul had got wind of the fact that my Mum had the mic and decided to try and take control. 'Shut up Pat' he yelled from the bar, and started heading our way, bashing into the back of peoples chairs and spilling his pint all over his cousin in the process. 'Please let the ground swallow me up', I was thinking to myself and hurriedly tried to get the mic back to the DJ in the hope that he'd put the next record on. No such luck, Paul beat me to it.

'I jushed like to shay a few wordsh to everybody'. Good grief, what on earth is he going to say. My mother was right; I never should have married him. But it turned out to be quite sweet; he was thanking me for marrying him. Ahhhh!

With that we proceeded to have the first dance as man and wife, where I propped up my drunken husband to Sinead O'Connor's – *Nothing Compares to You*. How very apt, as the last memory from our wedding evening was Paul's brother and a couple of his cousins coming over to tell me that Paul was asleep on the dance floor and he'd pissed himself. 'Oh no' Why had I married him?

(My first wedding, Mum, me Sue and Dad)

# Chapter 23

## 1990 - 3 wheels on my wagon

So I was having my second set of lessons with Mike again. To increase my time behind the wheel one of my co-lifeguards at Sutton High, had a bright orange Austin Alegro. Andy was a sweet lad, and had done a great job with the video at my wedding. He was a bit younger than me, and ever so keen. He had a serious girlfriend but I think he had a soft spot for me. I was married and had no intention of getting involved with anyone else but I must admit I probably took a bit of an advantage with Andy as he was only too eager to do anything for me.

Andy knew I was having proper driving lessons, and suggested that he'd pick me up for work in the mornings as we worked the same shifts and I could drive his car to and from work, as this would give me extra experience. This was all working well and my confidence was growing by the day. Mike the instructor was pleased with my progress and Andy was very patient and actually a very good teacher. He'd been driving for a couple of years and although he was a bit younger than me, I think he was feeling very proud of himself to be teaching someone else.

As time went on, I was phoning him at every opportunity to drive his car, could we go shopping could we go to my Mums, anything to get a bit more practice. I couldn't drive my husband's car as it was a company car and I wasn't insured.

On this particular day Andy and I were heading into town. I'd got Marc with me who was about two years old, he was sat in the back and although children's car seats and even the wearing of seat belts in the back were not mandatory then he had got the seat belt on around him. We were just flying along coming up to the roundabout at the top of Chalon way and there was a honking and hooting, as we careered around the roundabout, a van was behind us and was flashing his lights and signalling wildly to us. I had no idea what was wrong, until I saw Andy flinging himself into the back of the car. The car was now careering out of control. What on earth could be wrong? 'Siân, pull over' Andy was yelling from the back, just as a car wheel hurtled across my path and I swerved into Shaw Street, then there was an almighty grinding sound from the back of the car. And we stopped.

Marc had opened the back door of the car as we had gone around the corner, or at least that's what we thought, because somehow it was open and Marc was sliding out. Only the seatbelt had got hold of him by the leg. Thank goodness Andy noticed as this was the reason he'd jumped into the back. Marc thankfully was saved. My heart was in my mouth.

Andy got out and the furious van driver was shouting obscenities from his vehicle. It transpired that the rear offside wheel had come loose and we were flying along with 3 wheels on the car, and the back door open. It must have looked like a clown's car as it appeared to be falling apart.

We were all safe and Andy's Dad came and towed us home – but Andy was a bit green around the gills and I never saw that Allegro again.

Suffice to say, after another 17 lessons and wearing a short skirt and a low cut top to my examination, I passed my test with flying colours, if you can't do it on driving skill alone, then there are always other advantages to being a girl.

# Chapter 24

## 1991 - Lost babies

We had moved house, we actually had to sell, thanks to the Tories the interest rates were through the roof, Paul was out of work again, and if we didn't sell the house it would be repossessed. We had some debts but we were still left with a quite a few thousand pounds and we moved into rented property. We had moved from a two-bedroom terraced house in Sutton Junction to a three bed semi in Clock Face with a nice garden. It is so named because of the large clock face flower bed that once graced the area. The Clock Face public house now maintains the area's name.

A lot of the time I was very tired. I worked full time still and my marriage was on the rocks now after only a year. I had 2 toddlers, aged three and two which made everything very difficult. So one morning in the middle of the winter I woke to what sounded like a car door banging, I quickly opened the curtains to see a heavy fall of snow and I then glanced at the clock and it was 11am. 'Oh my god, I've slept in'. It was the weekend and it didn't really matter but Paul was snoring his head off in the bed as well. So who was looking after the children?

I dashed into Marc's room, to find there was no sign of him, then into Kate's she wasn't there either, where were they? I almost broke my neck darting down stairs.

'Paul, Paul' I screamed back up the stairs

'The kids are gone!' 'I can't find them anywhere'

'Eh? What?' he was still slurring from the night before.

'Paul help me, please, the kids are gone'

Paul was dragging on his jeans, I was still in my dressing gown and we were frantically searching everywhere. I was hoping to find them in the house hiding somewhere. I started to remember that I'd been here before. Marc had gone missing in my previous house, he was only about two then and Katie could only just walk. I could hear him somewhere but couldn't find him. And was desperately saying to Katie, 'Where's Marc, Where's Marc?' Katie could say a few words but she never did, she completely refused to speak until she was almost four. She just looked at you and you just knew she understood every word but she was very sullen. All I could hear was Marc in a muffled voice saying 'Shut the door' over and over again. I had searched upstairs, under the stairs, in the kitchen cupboards and everywhere I could think of. In the end I'd found him in the tumble dryer! He'd been trying to get Katie to shut the door, which thankfully she didn't do, as the dryer was plugged in and it would have started up and he would have been hurt or worse! I dragged him out and yelled at him 'don't you ever get in there again, you naughty boy!'

As usual he wailed his head off, Katie just stood there staring!

I was desperately pulling towels out of the dryer now to see if either of them was in there. But we'd searched everywhere and there was no sign of them.

I'd even looked in the garden and the shed. The back door was locked and the key still in it, so they couldn't have got outside anyway but I was desperate now. 'Oh Paul what's happened to them?'

Suddenly there was a knock on the front door. I flew to the door. I'd never seen such a sight in my life. Marc and Katie were stood there with a lady from down the road. I was stunned. The lady started to tell me that they were wandering down the road playing in the snow and she didn't know which house they had come from, but had followed the little Wellington boot footprints back to where they appeared to have come from.

Wellies? I looked down. Yes they had wellies on. But that was all! They were completely naked apart from their Wellington boots.

'How did you open the front door?' I was yelling by now, out of relief but also shock to find my toddlers naked in the snow.

'I climbed up Mum' then Marc started to cry.

'Don't cry baby', I grabbed them both up. Thanked the lady who raised her eyebrows and left.

They were both ok, apart from being freezing. It seemed Marc had climbed up on the ledge and opened the latch to the front door, when they had gone out the door had slammed, that must have been what woke me up.

They were safe and sound but I'd had aged about ten years!

# Chapter 25

## 1991- The honeymoon

Shortly after we moved in at Clock Face, we bought ourselves a nice car and decided that now we had the money we could have our honeymoon, although we'd been married a year, we had decided when we got married we'd wait until the children were old enough to go abroad as I wanted to go somewhere hot and I wanted the children to come too. We'd not been away together since we were 19 and we went to Majorca.

The relationship was getting more and more strained the longer Paul was out of work. I resented working every hour God sends when he was at home with my babies. I wanted to be home with them and have him go to work. I liked my job and valued my free time, but I missed my children.

We had booked to go to Tenerife in May and were due to go on the 14th. It was now the 9th a Saturday, and Paul had been missing all day. I was tired from working all week, and I'd been on my own with both children all day, been shopping and cooked the tea. The kids were bathed and almost ready for bed.

Eventually he called, announcing that he wasn't coming home for dinner, he was going out with his brother Shaun. That was the final straw. 'I've cooked your dinner, either you come home or I'm leaving you'. I stunned myself as well as him. 'I'll be back later, don't be so dramatic' he slurred. 'I mean it, come home, if you're not home in an hour, I'll be gone'. I slammed down the phone. I sat there watching the hand on the clock tick slowly round and I knew I was leaving him.

An hour later he wasn't home, so now I had to stick to my guns. I packed our things and the car and left. We were due to be going on our belated honeymoon in five days and I'd just broken up our marriage. Most marriages last at least until the honeymoon. Not this one. I'd had enough. That was ten years down the drain.

So with that I moved back home to my Mum's house and I prepared for life as a single Mum.

We still went on holiday. I was really looking forward to it. I didn't actually think he'd turn up at the airport and I was quite hoping I'd be going on my own, but he did turn up. It was the worst holiday I've ever had. Marc and Katie were too young for the heat of Tenerife. Paul and I hardly spoke. He was mostly drunk. To top it off, when we got back, we all arrived safely, but Paul's suitcase got lost and he had no clothes. I didn't care so when Mum picked us up from Manchester airport and she said that she thought we'd be back together by the time we got back, I think she was secretly pleased when I announced that we were certainly NOT back together and never would be and that she should drop Paul at his mother's house.

(Single Mum with Marc and Katie)

# Chapter 26

## 1991- Uncle Jack's camera

'Pat, move over, yes that's it, no move John over, Pat, Pat, this way Pat, look over here'.

We could hear Uncle Jack issuing instructions to the assembled family and guests.

I leaned over to Sue and said, 'My God Sue, can you see Uncle Jack over there with his camera? Now he's down on one knee Oh Lord he's coming over here, he wants to take our picture now'.

Sue was biting the back of her gloved hand trying not to laugh and I was almost choking trying to keep a straight face. We were having a great time as Mums bridesmaids and we'd decided to co-ordinate our colour scheme but thinking back navy and cream was a bit old fashioned for us as Sue was only 22 and I was only 25. Sue looked like Margaret Thatcher and I looked like a district nurse with my navy and cream dress, blazer and a small pill-box type hat. The last thing we wanted was any photographs to record our fashion disaster. 'He thinks he's David Bailey' blurted Sue. 'More like Arthur Daley' I laughed back.

Uncle Jack was a dear old soul, quite eccentric and he could have played Sherlock Holmes as he always wore a deer stalker hat. He was Granddad's youngest brother, and Sue and I nicknamed him 'the mad professor'. He was in his 70s and still rode around on a motorbike much to the disapproval of Granddad and the rest of the family.

You could always rely on Uncle Jack to make an entry. I remember I was in Granddads garden with Marc and Kate and Granddad was nodding off in the sunshine. Suddenly there was a loud roar and I looked up to the skies to see if I could see a plane. A few seconds later there is a screech of brakes as a huge motorbike skidded to a halt at the edge of the lawn. I was speechless. Who on earth was this? I looked over to Granddad completely stunned to see that Granddad hadn't batted an eyelid and seemed completely unsurprised that some maniac on a motorbike had come up his drive way. All I could imagine was that someone had turned into the wrong drive way by mistake, but Granddad didn't seem even slightly fazed.

Off came the helmet and goggles, and low and behold it was Uncle Jack. Granddad turned to look and said 'I've told you before Jack if you come of that bike in those sandals, you're going to do yourself a mischief'

I was stunned. I hadn't seen Uncle Jack for some time, and couldn't imagine he was still riding round on a motorbike. He'd had a Morris Minor Traveller when I was a child, and I always thought it was lovely to have a wooden car. It really suited him. But this brute of a motorbike? Lord only knows what Aunty Hilda thought of it. I was wondering whether she ever got on the back, fully clad in leathers, but let's not go there.

So here he was at Mum's wedding to John, with his camera, it looked like a box Brownie and he was pushing people around and getting in the way of the 'official' photographer. But he was Mum's uncle and Granddad's brother so we didn't mind; he was just so funny to watch.

Mum and John were now back from their honeymoon in Barbados and we are all around their house listening to stories of their honeymoon and looking at photographs, it looked wonderful.

Mum suddenly burst out laughing and said 'you'll never believe who's been here today? Your Uncle Jack. He wanted to put the film in for developing, you must remember him taking all those pictures at the wedding.' Sue and I were instantly laughing. 'Well you'll never believe it. He brought the camera here, as he wasn't sure how to take the film out of the camera. I was wondering 'Did he think that John had a dark room here?'

We were all laughing by now, and Mum could hardly get out what she's trying to say. 'Well we got his camera open, you won't believe it, but he had no film in it! All those pictures he was taking, all day long. And no film in the camera'

We could hardly contain our laughter, 'oh don't Mum, I'm going to wet myself' I howled.

Then Mum said 'Look at this video, we've got him on it taking pictures of everyone. John, get that video on and show the girls'

We were all hysterical, Uncle Jack had that effect on people and we all miss him.

(Mum and John on their wedding day)

# Chapter 27

## 1991- Pizza delivery

Following my divorce I had to decide what to do next and this led to many, many sleepless nights thinking about the future, was it too late to become a Dolphin Trainer? I eventually decided to give up working full time as a lifeguard at the swimming pool and go to college to study hairdressing. My Mums voice kept appearing in my head, 'You need a trade, that way you will always have a job'. College was great as it took me out of the house and I made lots of friends but I needed some money so I took on two part time jobs. The first one was working behind the bar at a friend's pub a couple of nights a week. Julia and Mel ran the Nags Head on Knowsley Road in St Helens and as we frequented the place quite often I knew some of the customers and I could choose my working hours to suit the children. The only downside was that all the regulars also knew about my divorce so after a few drinks one or two often thought I was 'available' and they would pledge their undying love for me across the bar. It was amusing the first couple of times but it got a bit nasty after that. I used to explain that I was quite happy being single with the kids but they knew best and knew that deep down I was desperate for a man – how wrong they were.

My other job was delivering pizzas and it was really good fun. Pablo's Perfect Pizzas was located on Longton Lane in the village next door to the launderette, which was quite handy if you spilled your pizza or greasy kebab down your front. Pablo was a nice guy and always gave me free garlic bread with cheese at the end of my shift. His real name was Bill and he wasn't Italian, he was from Warrington. His grandfather had arrived as a prisoner of war and his family had always been in catering – they had a chip van and drove it around Widnes. When Bill decided to open his own business he dyed his hair to look more Italian, changed his name to Pablo and invented a family history of pizza making claiming that his great-great grandfather had owned a Pizzeria in Naples. The truth was that after the war his grandfather had started a taxi service in Manchester where he made most of his money by being a bookies runner and ferrying call girls around the town – I think he was Pablo's hero. He could certainly put on the act of a typical Italian male and thought he was God's gift to women, unfortunately most women thought he was a bit odd and steered well clear of him. The shop was quite small. The drivers had to wait in the car park and we passed the time by chatting and drinking coffee as we waited for deliveries to be handed out. He used to give us discount on the coffee and I think he had a soft spot for me and as a result I was given most of the 'long distance' deliveries to increase my earnings.

We had to provide our own cars and we were then paid by the mile so on a good night you could really make a decent wage. When I couldn't find a babysitter for Marc and Kate who were 3 and 2 at the time I would wrap them up in quilts in the back of the car and they would come with me. Like all kids they enjoyed the car ride and they would soon be asleep, at the end of the night I would lift them out of the car and put them to bed. I have found it's the same with old folk. Some friends of mine took their mother to Australia because she was keen to see the country and she also wanted to visit a friend who had emigrated. Other than when they visited the friend their Mum spent most of the time asleep in the back of the car and they were convinced they could have spent a week driving around Tesco's car park – it would have been cheaper and less hassle.

Back to the Pizzas. Most Pizza drivers have small cars to reduce their fuel bill and make more money but I had a massive 2.0 litre fuel injected Ford Sierra. It was hardly fuel efficient and I am sure I would have made a lot more money with a smaller car, but it was a lovely car to drive and I could race around the area so that I could get back to the shop to take on more deliveries. The other drivers used to call me 'Speedy' because of the number of runs I could do in an evening If we were very busy we did a double run which meant taking out two orders delivering one on the way out and then delivering the second on the way back to the shop. On this particular night all was running smoothly until I dropped the first pizza off in Sutton Manor. This very strange woman shouted through the letterbox saying she couldn't open the door and that I would have to help by pushing. We eventually managed to open the door and she invited me in. Most people just want to pay and take the pizza so normally it only takes a minute but she obviously wanted to talk. She ushered me into her house which was very dark and had a gothic look about it and the more I looked at this strange lady I realised that she had a gothic look about her too. She then went into great details explaining that she'd lived on takeaway delivery food for the past 5 years as she was agoraphobic! If she lived on takeaway food why was the front door so difficult to open? I thought. This and other questions would have to be left unanswered as I had another delivery waiting in the car. I explained I had another order and my kids in the car and couldn't stop to chat but it was nice to meet her and hastily fought to re-open the front door and made my retreat as it slammed shut behind me and luckily I didn't have to make another delivery to her – I always let my colleagues have that pleasure.

When I got back to the car I realised I had been too long. Marc and Kate must have woken up and had smelled the second Pizza. One of them must have climbed in the front and they were now sitting in the back with a large slice of a 12' deep pan Hawaiian pizza with extra ham and pineapple; they were eating my next delivery with big smiles on their tomato sauce covered faces. I screamed at them and snatched back the slices of pizza, they started crying but I ignored them as I was trying to think of a solution. As I sat in the front of the car with two screaming kids and the damaged pizza on my lap an elderly lady walked past. She very kindly leant down to the window and asked if I needed any help. 'Oh bugger off' I replied and got back to my problem. Then I had an idea. I shoved the slices back into the box and carefully re-arranged some pieces of ham and pineapple to cover the little bite marks. I then closed the box and tried to make it look like new again before speeding off to Prescot to make the delivery.

I arrived in Prescot and knocked on the door hoping that I could get away with the nibbled pizza. It seemed to take an age for the door to be opened and I was just about to start my practiced explanation when I realised there was no one there. After a few seconds I heard a voice say 'keep the change' and as I looked towards the voice I see a dwarf peering around the door holding out the cash.

I struggled to keep a straight face (why do I laugh at dwarves?) I quickly started my practiced explanation. 'I realised I was running late and as I was flying around a roundabout ,the pizza heat bag slid off the passenger seat onto the floor upside down. I'm very sorry but the pizza is 'slightly' damaged. I'm happy to go back to the shop to get another if you would like.' I looked down into his eyes hoping he would be happy with the 'rebuilt' pizza.

'Oh no don't bother we'll manage with that it's not too bad' the dwarf replied as he then appeared to grow before my eyes! He wasn't a dwarf at all, he was a full size man who'd been fitting a carpet behind the front door on his hands and knees – he closed the door without knowing that my 2 little kids had already enjoyed part of his dinner.

# Chapter 28

## 1991 - The Crash

Road works again... right in the middle of the village, so heading towards Rainhill Stoops and on to Widnes was a right pain, as you were slowed by the mother and father of the slowest temporary traffic lights known to man. I was using more petrol waiting for the lights to change than I was on the whole pizza delivery. There had to be a way around it?

It was 28th December 1991 and my first day back delivering pizza's for Pablo since Christmas. As I mentioned earlier I was also at Hairdressing College and I had decided that I would have my hair dyed bright pink for Christmas! It was very festive and it made a great bold statement and the kids loved it, even if my Mum and sister gave me a few funny looks.

I didn't fancy working that night, the kids were at home with our Sue playing with their new toys and I wanted to be at home with them, but the cash came in handy so I didn't have a choice. It was a very clear night, very cold and frosty but dry so luckily it wasn't icy.

After waiting what felt like hours at the temporary lights for the 4th time that night I decided that on the way back I'd take the back road to avoid the road-works. I would go past the Manor Pub on Manor Road, all the way along to Old Lane which came out exactly opposite the pizzeria on Longton Lane. I didn't normally take this route as it was badly lit and had a few blind corners but tonight I just wanted to get home. So as the lights changed I headed off to Widnes to make my last delivery.

I was always speeding, always in a hurry and with a powerful car it was hard to notice your speed. But as I pulled off Warrington Road by the Shell Garage to my left I was forced to slow due to the awkward turning. I couldn't have been doing more than about 25mph when all of a sudden I saw an outstretched arm!

'What on earth was that' I thought as what seemed like an oil drum was launched right through my windscreen. Something heavy landed on me and I couldn't see a thing at first because of the broken windscreen and then because of the 'oil drum'. Now the windscreen was gone and I slammed on the brakes causing whatever had come through the window to get flung back out across the bonnet. I came to a stop and got out to see what had happened.

Next to my door was a man standing staring up the road. He looked like he had seen a ghost and kept staring up the road.

'He just stepped out in front of you, I tried to pull him back' he said.

We both dashed towards what I now realised was a man in the road ahead. He was a quite a large man; he must have been over 6 feet tall and looked like he weighed about 16 stones.

He was trying to sit up. My lifeguard first aid training kicked in and I said to him 'Lie back down don't move'.

I shouted to the other chap, 'you go to the pub, call for an ambulance.'

The engine was still running on my car and the headlights were lighting up the man in the road. The man, who I later learned was Colin, was groaning and from his head I thought steam was rising, perhaps it was just his breath. Colin's friend John ran to the Manor pub to phone and for a few minutes I just sat in the road with Colin in my arms. I was sitting in silence the whole the time and was wondering why he wasn't wearing any shoes or socks. The impact must have blown them off. There was a strong smell of alcohol and I just didn't know what to think. Would Colin be OK?

The next thing I remember was sirens and flashing lights and a policeman shouting 'Where's the driver?' local residents had come out of their houses and customers from the pub so there was quite a crowd' 'Where's the driver? Is this the car?' the police were asking. I snapped back to reality. 'It's me, I was driving, and I didn't see him, just his arm'.

I was lead to a police car and asked to sit inside, I watched the ambulance man shine his torch into Colin's eyes. Then they just lifted Colin by the belt on his trousers and by his clothes onto a stretcher. I couldn't help thinking that they were rough with him. The ambulance drove slowly away. I wondered why they hadn't put the lights and sirens on.

I made a short statement, and was breathalysed. I hadn't been drinking even though it was close to Christmas but I suppose it's routine. I watched everything in slow motion as my car was lifted onto the back of a tow truck. The policeman took me home and told me they'd be in touch.

When I got home to Mum I explained what had happened.

'I think he's dead Mum'

'Did they tell you that?

'No but they just went off in the ambulance and there were no sirens'

'Don't be so dramatic – they would have told you if it was serious'

'No-one told me anything' 'I need to tell Pablo – he doesn't know where I am, he'll be worried'

'I'll take you over there' she offered.

'No it's OK, I need some air, I'll walk'

So I walked slowly over to Pablo's and explained what had happened. Pablo was shocked but also thought we'd have been told if Colin was seriously hurt.

I went back home and waited.

An hour or so later, the police came to my house to tell me that Colin was dead. He'd died straight away and would have felt no pain.

I was so shocked, he'd tried to sit up when I was there, and moaned, he hadn't died straight away at all. But I was so upset it didn't occur to me to mention that to the police.

An inquest followed and I was advised by my solicitor not to attend as it would be too distressing for Colin's family. My solicitor even told me to claim from Colin's family for the damage that had been done to my car as it was found that Colin was completely to blame as he'd walked out straight into the path of my car even though the other chap had tried to stop him.

Of course I refused to make a claim – how do solicitors sleep at night? The front driver's side windscreen pillar of my 2.0 litre Ford Sierra had been totally broken in half by the force of Colin hitting my car. The grill on the car was broken and the wing mirror had sheared off. It was Colin that landed on me inside the car. I didn't have scratch and poor Colin was gone.

# Chapter 29

## 1992 – A new man

I had been back living at home for just about a year and was happily settling into life with my hairdressing course and the 2 part time jobs. Life actually couldn't be better and thinking back now, that time back at Rainhill with Sue and Terry her then boyfriend was the happiest I had ever been in my life. Sue helped out minding the kids while I worked and the rest of the time they were in play school or the college crèche. They seemed happy too. We lived in a big house and there was lots of room for them. Paul and I now had an amicable relationship and the kids saw him regularly. Life was good.

The only thing really was I didn't have any time whatsoever to go out with my friends. I didn't want to I was happy with what I was doing, but they nagged me to go out once in a while, they said it would 'do me good'.

One Thursday evening, Donna a friend of mine and Sue's called round and said there was a disco on in the Vic. The Victoria is a pub in the middle of Rainhill Village and they regularly had a disco at weekends and on a Thursday evening. As usual I declined, I always made the excuse that I had no-one to mind Marc and Kate. Until Sue piped up 'Get them in bed, me and Terry will be in all night, you go out with Donna, you never go out'. I glared at Sue; I didn't actually want to go.

'OK, just for an hour then'. I sighed. 'Great, see you later then, I'll come here for you about eight?' Donna asked.

So it was arranged, I was reluctantly going to the Vic to the disco, it would be just my luck Paul and his brother would be in there, and he'd be asking who had the kids. I wasn't at all keen. Anyway as expected Donna turned up and off we went, I'd had a few glasses of wine for Dutch courage, I was strangely nervous about going out on my own. It had been over 11 years since I'd been out alone; Paul and I always went together.

I actually started to enjoy myself, the music was good and we had a good old dance. The fellow on the door was a neighbour of ours, his nickname was Jinx and although he was a bit of a nutter he was chatty and came over for a drink. I didn't really notice the chap he'd been speaking to by the door. Donna and I were getting a bit tipsy and singing at the top of our voices. It was a good night and everyone was local, lots of our friends kept coming over saying how glad they were to see me out and I kept insisting it was a one off, and I wasn't getting into the habit of it.

While I was chatting to someone all of a sudden I felt someone grab my bottom. I swung around to find a man grinning at me with a cheeky smile. I was quite pompous and blurted out 'get your hands off me!' He just winked and said 'nice arse darlin'. I giggled and wandered off. It was nice that someone had noticed me and it had been a long time since I'd been chatted up so to speak.

The evening continued and I was a little too merry and was at the bar again and noticed the man who'd grabbed me earlier queuing for a pint. I slid up to him at the bar and said 'I'll have a vodka, if you're buying?' He grinned back at me and bought me a double. He was quite nice when we got chatting. He sort of reminded me of Patrick Swayze, but much bigger built he looked like he was a body builder, he had huge biceps in his tee-shirt. We chatted a bit about nothing really and he asked me if I lived local. He had a scouse accent and told me he was from Whiston, but he now lived in Huyton. I was looking around for Donna but couldn't see her anywhere and I made my excuses to the chap I now knew as Jimmy and wandered around looking for her. Out of no-where came Jinx. 'Keep away from him love, he's trouble'.

I was stunned. 'What? I'm not getting involved, I don't even know him, he just bought me a drink that's all, have you seen Donna?' I replied. 'I'm just letting you know Siân' said Jinx. 'Keep away from him'.

I found Donna and she said she was heading home now as it was getting to last orders. 'OK, I'll walk back with you' I said, It was only a five minute walk to where we were going. Donna was a care home assistant. The mansion next door to us had been converted into a private care home a few years earlier and Donna lived in. So we all headed off together.

Just as we got in the car park, I heard this voice again. 'Hey sexy arse, can I walk you home? It was Jimmy. 'Yeah we're all going together, you can walk with us if you like' I replied.

'He's a bit of alright' Donna grinned to me. 'Seems nice, but Jinx said he's trouble' I warned her. 'I've seen him in the Vic loads of times, he's never been in any trouble, he looks like he can handle himself though' Donna went on. 'Go on go for it, time you met someone, go with him. I'll walk back with Debs.' Donna said.

'Are you sure? It's only 5 minutes, nothing can go wrong in that time, and we're walking the same way,

I'll scream if he touches me.' I said. 'I'd be screaming too if he touched me, more like with pleasure though, ha ha' we both giggled and Jimmy walked over.

So that was the start of Siân and Jimmy, we were to be together for almost 4 years. He walked me home, and I was smitten already, I gave him the key to my car and we drove around all night long just chatting. I couldn't understand why anyone so nice would be interested in me, I was separated with 2 little kids, what did he see in me?

A month later I'd quit my 2 jobs and my hairdressing course and I'd moved with him to Blackpool. The next time my Mum saw me two months later, she was picking me up from a police station in Blackpool. She said she didn't recognise me when she walked in. I was so badly beaten my face was unrecognisable. Jimmy had done it. What she didn't know was that I was also pregnant!

# Chapter 30

## 1992 – Take me back

So after the beating of my life, I went back to my Mum and John's house very briefly in Thatto Heath. I thought I'd better go and see Paul, Marc and Kate's Dad, he hadn't seen the kids for about three months. I got the bus to his Mum's house in Rainhill. When I knocked on the door, the look on his face when he saw me all battered and bruised was shocking. Paul and I had had our ups and downs and used to fight like cat and dog sometimes but it never got violent, we just shouted. Paul never raised his hand to me, the worse he'd ever done was smash a glass at the wall. He was pleased to see the kids and I could tell he felt sorry for me.

He knew all about Jimmy and was very jealous at the time when we first got together. He wanted me back. But I told him we couldn't get back together until he found us somewhere to live. He'd had over a year to do this but had spent quite a lot of time working across Europe on building sites, just hitch hiking around. Paul eventually went working on the Olympic Village in Barcelona He was basically re-living his youth and never made any effort to do anything for his family. So when Jimmy came along and seemed to have everything, plenty of money and a keen interest in me, I jumped at it.

Paul and I talked for a long while. He said he wanted to make a new start with me. We would give it a go for the sake of Marc and Katie. I agreed and was just about to tell him I was pregnant. I hadn't decided what to do about the baby yet, but I was thinking it would be best not to have it. All of a sudden a little voice chipped in 'Mummy's having a new baby'. It was Marc.

Paul's face was like thunder. 'What you're pregnant?' he raged. I just nodded. 'Well f\*\*k off, I don't want you back' he yelled. I got the kids coats on and left for the bus home.

What was I going to do now? The first thing I needed to do was see a doctor and find out how pregnant I was. So the next day I arranged to go to the Women's Hospital up in Liverpool near the bombed out church, just off Upper Parliament Street in Toxteth. It was an all singing and dancing hospital for women and had all the latest technology. When I'd had Marc and Kate, the hospital's declined to tell you the sex of your baby as it wasn't very accurate. All you got was a grainy black and white Polaroid which barely looked like anything.  But I was stunned to see that the scan they gave me produced a near perfect image in colour of a fully formed baby. 'Don't you want to see?' The nurse said to me, I hadn't been looking at the screen I thought it was best to look away. I glanced over to see a perfect baby sucking its thumb on the screen. How beautiful I thought. At that moment I knew I was keeping my baby.

# Chapter 31

## 1992 - Refuge

I spent the next 4 months moving from refuge to refuge. Toxteth, Wigan, Warrington, Widnes. Mum had put me in touch with Women's Aid a charity who helped women suffering from domestic violence. Was I a battered woman? I didn't know anyone who was, I had no idea what defined you as that. I'd had a good kicking really when Jimmy had come back to our flat in Blackpool in some sort of rage over what I can't recall. It must have been a one off.

Jimmy followed me about. I couldn't move. If I went to my Mum's he was sat outside in a car. When I looked out of the window of wherever I was staying in refuges he was outside in the car. I couldn't escape him. He knew I was pregnant and was determined to put things right with me. My hormones were all over the place and I was struggling to look after Marc and Kate and deal with my pregnancy from these hovels they called refuges. So I was easily persuaded to take Jimmy back. I didn't tell my Mum, I just arranged with Jimmy that when the council gave me a place of my own, we would give it another go.

We were in his car one day when I asked him about the surname of our baby. 'Will it have my name or yours?' I asked. I still had my married name of Knight. He didn't say anything and I was worried what was coming next. He started the car and just drove across town. We pulled up near the benefits

138

office in St Helens on Central Street, just off College Street. 'What are we doing here?' I asked. You asked about the name of our baby' he replied and pointed across the road. 'Let's go in there' 'What do you mean, that's the Register office, and we can't register the baby until after it's born' I was confused. Not the baby's name, your name, marry me in there and we'll all have the same name'. I was stunned again. I was still married to Paul and Jimmy, although now divorced from his ex-wife Tracey, had lost his divorce papers. But within 6 weeks, I had a decree nisi, he had copies of his divorce papers and we were back at the Register office and booking our wedding. My decree absolute came through on 2nd September 1992 the Registrar raised his eyebrows when I handed over my documents and we were married on 9th October just over a month later.

# Chapter 32

## 1992 – Wedding number two

I was five months pregnant and the whole day was a disaster from start to finish. I was now living in Pennington Lodge on Sherdley Road in St Helens, this was just around the corner from Mums' house in Thatto Heath, and it meant I could now get Marc who was 4 to school in St Anne's in Rainhill. Pennington Lodge was shared accommodation for homeless people, but mainly young girls with small children. I only had to stay there a few weeks and then St Helens Council would assign me a rented house.

It was fairly nice; the only real problem was that Jimmy refused to leave me there alone. I wasn't allowed guests to stay and was worried he'd get me thrown out. I was desperate to get a house of our own and didn't' want to jeopardise that. But I was also trying to keep the peace with Jimmy and I now knew that my best way to stay in one piece was to keep my mouth shut and give him his own way.

It was the evening before we got married and I was suggesting he stay with his brother as it was bad luck to be with me. No such luck for me, he was staying and keeping a close eye on me. As if I needed any more bad luck? I felt the wedding was doomed before we got started.

I don't remember why but we were of course running late, I was extremely tired being 5 months pregnant and was getting Marc and Kate ready to take to my Mum's house, they were not coming to the wedding. In fact none of my family was coming; I couldn't blame them but still felt lonely on my own. But Jimmy's family were very nice to me, his brother Eddie was of course Jimmy's best man and Eddie's then wife Michelle was going to be my witness.

At the time we had a black XR3, my car had been sold long before in Blackpool. I was actually painting my nails as we screeched through St Helens at break neck speed that cold October morning, I didn't have any shoes on yet and was struggling to bend forward because I was pregnant to get them on with wet nails. I was almost catapulted through the windscreen as we hurtled to a stop outside the Register Office. Everyone was there already and we were late. We made a dash for it, and as I was hurried along I heard Eddie say something under his breath about Bonnie & Clyde.

We lined up and were all ready to start but the Registrar seemed hesitant. All the guests were Jimmy's family and all on his side of the room.

'Are we waiting for your family Siân?' He asked.

'I haven't got any family' I whispered. 'They can't come' I choked back the tears.

So it was all over in a matter of 10 minutes, I was now Siân Hayes. This was going to the most troubling chapter of my life and these have been the most troubling chapters of this book to write.

Off we went to the reception it was held at the Waterside Hotel, on the East Lancashire Road. It was a lovely location overlooking Carr Mill Dam and I remember looking out watching a water skier and wondering if it was cold out on the lake. All Jimmy's family were there and actually it was a nice afternoon, we had

141

a lovely meal and cut the cake. We'd not organised a party of any kind but Eddie and Michelle invited us back to their house afterwards for a little 'do'. I drove us after the wedding reception as I wasn't drinking due to being pregnant; we got into the car and headed from St Helens to Whiston, where Eddie lived. As usual there were words about my driving, there's not actually anything wrong with my driving but as Jimmy thought he was some sort of Michael Schumacher which was hysterical as he never actually took his driving test, there was always something to moan about or to criticise me for. By the time we got to Whiston, he was in an absolute rage, I was crying, 'It's supposed to be our wedding day, can't you be nice just for once?' 'This is you all over, I wish I'd never married you, if you just drove properly I wouldn't have to lose my temper' he yelled back. 'Why did you marry me? Don't say it's because you love me, because we both know you don't!' I was hysterical by now, as we pulled up by Eddies back gate, Jimmy jumped out of the car and threw his brand new wedding ring at me and slammed the door. I had never been so hurt, we'd been married less than 2 hours and already he'd thrown his wedding ring back at me. I was also furious, so I slammed the car into reverse and screeched out of the back entry and turned in the main road and spun off and away.

I didn't know at this point where I was going, I couldn't go to my Mum's; my marriage over before it had begun, she'd have a field day. I had nowhere else to go. So I just drove a couple of miles down the road to Rainhill, all of a sudden the car seemed to be spluttering, I looked at the petrol gauge 'Oh no!' It was empty.

I chugged into St Anne's church car park and stopped, I tried the engine again, nothing.

What was I going to do now? Back then there were no mobile phones, it was my wedding day and I had no money on me for a cab or even the telephone. What on earth would I do now? I sat with my head in my hands for a long time and cried.

It must have been a couple of hours when I decided I'd have to think about how I was going to get home or to Eddies. I don't know why I did but I turned the key and the car sprung back to life. I thought I'd head to Eddie's house first I knew that everyone would be looking for me, God only knows what Jimmy was going to say, he didn't expect me to drive off. The car seemed to be running OK, I would try and see how far I could get; at least if I broke down on the main Warrington Road, someone I knew may come past.

I got as far as the Green Dragon pub at the top of Dragon Lane, when the car died a death again. However I was only there for a few minutes when Eddie pulled up in his little red Nissan Cherry.

'What happened to you? Where did you go?' Eddie asked. 'It was Jimmy he threw his wedding ring at me and slammed out of the car, so I drove off, then I broke down, I think it's out of petrol' I cried. 'Our Jimmy's gone to your place; he's in a right rage because you drove off'.

'Oh no!' I was panicking now, where had he gone? I knew already. He'd be at my flat looking for me. Eddie drove me straight there, and the sight I found in the flat when I got there was shocking. It had been completely trashed and ransacked. Everything was smashed up. It looked like he'd kicked the door in; I was in tears and Eddie looked stunned.

The girl from the flat next door popped her head round the door. 'He's been arrested, the police have taken him away, he was like a crazed animal and it took four of them to hold him down and cuff him'. I apologised to her, but it was hardly my fault, or was it? I shouldn't have driven off, I shouldn't have argued back when he started shouting. I looked down and I was still clutching his wedding ring in my hand.

So that was it, he was locked up in a police cell. I called the local station, but as it was a Friday he'd be in there all weekend as they couldn't get him to court before Monday. I tried to explain it was our wedding day I pleaded and cried and explained I was pregnant but they were having none of it. I couldn't tell my Mum so I went back to my flat and cleaned and tidied everything up. So that was it, my wedding night was a disaster like the first one and I spent it alone in my little flat. I dreaded what was going to happen when Jimmy got out on the Monday.

.

# Chapter 33

## 1993 – A marriage made in hell

So that's how it continued for the next three years, fighting and arguing and the level of violence steadily got higher and higher. The council gave me a new house, a nice 3 bed-roomed semi in Grange Park in St Helens, which was close to my Mum's; I really enjoyed getting the baby's room all sorted. Marc and Kate had Bart Simpson wall paper and they loved having a garden and somewhere to play. It was close enough that they could continue to go to school in Rainhill, I took them there every day on the bus, and it was a joy to be on my own for an hour or so.

I thought once the baby came, things would settle down and we'd be happy. I was living in a dream world. I had to think everything through in my head before I spoke, to think of every single response my words could have from him before I opened my mouth. It was exhausting. Don't get me wrong it wasn't all bad, he was so funny and loving a lot of the time, I seemed to cling to the good parts. I remember thinking the minute he stopped hitting me was the best time of all, because that was the longest it would be before he hit me again next time. The most worrying thing about all of this was that there was no telling when it would happen. He wasn't the type of man who went out, got drunk and came home and hit the wife and kids. I never knew when it was going to happen or why. One day I was just driving the car along and we were getting on pretty ok, when all of a sudden he just punched me hard right in the side of the face. I never knew why, he said my driving was rubbish and I was over steering.

Baby number three came along on 17th February 1993. I was actually talking to my Mum on the phone. 'I'll have to go Mum, I'm standing here peeing myself, I need to get cleaned up'. Of course I wasn't peeing, my waters had broken and we got ready and dashed off to the hospital. We dropped Marc and Kate at their Nan's house, my Mum was going to look after them and bring them to see the baby when it was born.

Jimmy was in a bad mood the whole time his mood swings seemed to be getting worse, but he was really looking forward to the baby being born and he was desperate for a son to continue with the tradition of the name James, Jimmy's Dad was James as was his Granddad, so our baby if it was a boy was going to be James. If it was a girl it was going to be Lucy after his Nan. I had a bad feeling and was afraid. The labour was actually a blur and in fact to this day I don't remember any of it, I don't remember my baby even being born and couldn't tell you what time of day it was. I think it was late afternoon or early evening, but a boy it was, baby James. I was just so relieved when Jimmy left, I didn't want him near to my baby boy. My James was all I wanted. Jimmy kept going on that if I tried to leave the hospital with *his* baby; he'd find me and kill me.

I told the nurses not to let him back in without checking with me first. Jimmy was all sweetness and light to other people and the nurses didn't think anything was wrong. I think they just thought I had the baby blues. So later at about 1am, when he came dashing to the side of my bed asking where the baby was, I was hysterical, I almost fell out of the bed, and was screaming for the nurses. 'Who's let him in?' I shouted, 'He'll take my baby!' A nurse came up and

146

said, 'He's your husband, that's why we let him in, just calm down, he's told us he couldn't make it to the birth and wanted to see his son'. Of course it was a different shift of nurses now, and they didn't know. No-one took me seriously. 'Please don't let him take my baby' I begged them. Anyway all was fine, Jimmy was asked to leave as he was waking people and babies up and I told them not to let him back in.

The next day Mum came with Marc and Katie to see their new brother, Mum told me it was all over the news that the little boy who'd been taken from Bootle Strand Shopping Centre, James Bulger, had been found dead on the train tracks nearby. My James had been born just a few days after somebody else's James had died. Marc and Katie loved their little brother and everything seemed fine now. Jimmy was settling down, he could see I wasn't going to run away with the baby. I actually felt like everything would work out.

Later that day Sue arrived, and I was just about to go over to her with the baby, when Jimmy jumped up shouting his head off to keep her away from his baby. Sue was upset, I was upset; I put the baby back down and walked her to the door. 'I don't know why he's like this Sue, what did you say?' I didn't get a chance to say anything; I was just walking towards you'. 'Oh Sue, please will you go so there's no trouble?' I pleaded with her. 'Can't I see my new nephew first?' 'Please Sue, just go, I'm so embarrassed of him, I'll bring the baby round to see you as soon as I can'. Sue left in tears, and she didn't see her nephew for the next 3 months.

The next 9 months were awful, every time the baby cried, Jimmy would be yelling 'What are you doing to my baby?' he'd come dashing into the room and take the baby from me, he was paranoid and certain that I was pinching the baby or doing something to hurt him, just to get back at Jimmy. He seemed to be getting worse and worse, he accused Marc and Kate of hurting the baby and one day Marc had a big black eye and Jimmy told me that he and Kate had been play fighting and Kate had landed on top of him and kicked him accidentally in the face. Years later Marc told me that it was Jimmy who'd punched him in the face, Marc was five years old. Kate also told me also that he'd strangled her and held a pillow over her face, and also spit his food into her face. They were threatened that if they told me, he'd kill them. Marc and Kate have had a lot of problems over the years and I'm sure that all of this had contributed to their issues.

He made me allow James to be in the bed with us and I was terrified that either of us would roll on to him and for about nine months I hardly slept with worry.

On one occasion after a massive row about what I've no idea, Marc and Katie were upstairs, and baby James was asleep on the sofa under the window. The neighbours must have heard the screaming but no-one called the police. All of a sudden Jimmy flew towards me in the kitchen, I had my back to the kitchen door and was desperately trying for the handle, but the door was locked. The door had a large glass panel in it and I thought he was going to throw me through it, but what happened was worse, he picked up a kitchen knife! Everything happened in slow motion. He raised his hand above me and brought the knife down into my head. I don't know how but that knife was a Kitchen Devil knife, they are very strong, as he stabbed me in the top of the head, miraculously the blade snapped out of the handle. So it didn't go in very deep. However I was bleeding a lot and screaming. I turned and unlocked the door, he was grabbing at me, but somehow, I managed to lose my jacket which he was

148

holding and I ran up the back garden to the front and out of the front gate. I dashed down to the main road just as a coach of holiday makers were being dropped off. I jumped on the coach with blood streaming down my face and asked the driver to hide me. He drove off. When he stopped at the traffic lights I jumped out. My Mum's house was just across the road. But I was too afraid to go. I didn't want to upset my Mum and I didn't want her to know what was happening. I calmed down and sat on a bench by the traffic lights in Thatto Heath to think. Although I was covered in blood, it seemed to be stopping and I didn't feel too bad, so I assumed the wound wasn't very deep. I had to go back to my children, so I headed back home on foot. When I got home I crouched beneath the window ledge in the garden and listened at the front window, I could hear the baby snoring quietly on the couch just under the window where I was outside. The TV was on and I peered through the letter box. The house was silent and I just sat under the window, knowing that I'd hear James wake up if he cried and Jimmy would go to him. But there wasn't a sound. I had to get in. I went around the back. There was no sound from there either. I would just have to brave it and let myself in. When I got inside, I realised he wasn't there, he'd just gone and left the 3 children on their own, James was only a few weeks old. I locked everywhere up and sat down. I couldn't be bothered to even clean myself up.

About half an hour later there was a crashing at the front door, he was back. He'd obviously run off to find me and when he couldn't he'd returned. I refused to let him in and shouted through the letter box to him that if he didn't go I'd call the police. For a few seconds it was silent, then there was a massive crash, he'd smashed the front window, I dashed back to the lounge, the whole of the front window had been smashed through and all the glass was on the sofa – where James was asleep!

I dragged all the glass off him he was crying and had a cut on his head. Thankfully it was only a scratch. Jimmy appeared to have gone, so I called the police and Jimmy's brother Eddie.

Eddie arrived at about the same time as the police, they told me I had to go to the hospital with the baby and Eddie stayed with Marc and Katie.

As usual, I dropped the charges, the police left shaking their heads. I was stitched up and James was checked over he was fine.

And so it continued over the next few months different episodes of violence. Jimmy was always in lots of trouble with the police, for his usual driving offences. There was never anything very serious, I just wanted him locked up. I felt there was no escape unless he went to prison. Anyway eventually he had to go to court for all these small separate charges. The police knew my situation and when he eventually went to court, the judge decided that because there were so many offences that they would run consecutively and not concurrently which is usually the case. So he got 3 months for this, and 4 months for that and six months for something else and so on, but they added them all up so he now had a sentence of almost 3 years in prison. He'd only do 18 months or so but at least I was safe for the time being. I was relieved and upset at the same time. James was 9 months old, he didn't even know his Dad properly and he'd be visiting him now in Walton prison.

A couple of weeks into his sentence, I was sat at home one evening and a helicopter was circling overhead. It was noisy and obviously with the lights that were shining down it was a police helicopter. It flashed through my mind for a second, that Jimmy may have escaped from prison and they were looking for him. I laughed the thought off and went to bed.

A couple of hours later I was woken by a banging on the front door, it was Jane, Jimmy's oldest sister. 'Get the kids up, you have to come with me, it's Jimmy'. She urged me. I was shocked but did as she said.

We got into the taxi she had waiting and drove to her house.

We went into Jane's lounge, she hadn't spoken all the way to her house, I had no idea what was going on, I hardly knew Jane and was so surprised to see her. When we walked in, I couldn't believe was I was seeing. Jimmy was there. 'What are you doing?' 'Why are you here?' I asked. 'Come here baby, I've missed you so much'. He grabbed hold of me and kissed me'. I pushed him away. 'What are you doing here?' I asked him again. 'I've had an accident'. He said. He appeared to be wearing someone else's clothes. 'Who's are those clothes?', 'I've borrowed them from Ray, Jane's husband', he replied. I was so confused and had so many questions; I couldn't understand why he was there, when he was supposed to be in prison. In a high security prison!

What transpired was that Jimmy has set fire to himself. When he rolled up his trouser legs, he had horrendous burns to both his legs from the foot to the knee; you could actually see the bones. The smell was awful. I couldn't understand how he was standing let alone speaking to me as if nothing had happened. Jane had given him a couple of pain killers but by the look of his legs he must be in agonising pain. He had actually set fire to his jeans while in Prison, so that they would transfer him to Whiston hospital, which not only has the best burns unit in the North of England, but Whiston was where all his family live. When they took him there, he made his escape. He had run from the hospital in nothing but a gown and bare feet, on legs that looked like they couldn't hold the weight of a man. I was seriously shocked.

151

'I can't stay in there any longer, it's driving me mad'. 'You are mad, you need help Jimmy, no-one sets fire to themselves who is sane, you have to go back. You'll die if those legs get infected'. There was no persuading him, he wasn't going to go back, in fact his plan was even crazier than he was. He'd decided he was going back to live in Blackpool! And worse than that, we were going with him.

Oh no how could this be happening to me? Just as things were settling down, more chaos. I had to go with him. He forced me, and I suppose I was afraid to leave him, he was going to die with his legs like that. So the long and the short of it was, we were taken home to grab a few clothes and me, Jimmy, Marc, Kate and baby James were piled into Eddie's car and we went off to Blackpool again. No one ever stood up to Jimmy, not me, not his brother or any of his family; I couldn't understand why no-one just told him where to stick his mad ideas.

My memories of Blackpool were not good and I didn't want to go back. Eddie found us a holiday flat and paid in advance for a couple of weeks. The only money I had was my child benefit which was about £20 a week. I couldn't claim anything else as the police would be looking for us and could trace us through my benefits if I made a claim. I could cash my child benefit book anywhere. So that's all we had to live on. Eddie left us with a bit of extra money. We stayed there almost 3 weeks. All we had to eat was cereal and tins of beans. Thank goodness for the milk tokens with my child benefit at least the baby was eating properly. Nearly all the money went on medical supplies from a local chemist to keep Jimmy's legs clean. I had no idea what I was doing and the awful smell was making the kids sick. I begged him to hand himself in, or at least go to Blackpool hospital. They wouldn't necessarily know about him there and he could get treated. But as usual Jimmy refused. I spoke to my Mum one day, I told Jimmy I was going to a chemist and that's when I called her and told her everything. I was in for a shock. Mum had got in touch with social services and told them I was on the run with Jimmy and the kids, and she wanted my kids taking into care if I didn't leave him.

I went back to Jimmy and told him. He went mad but by this time he could hardly walk, so he wasn't in any state to do anything to me. James has just taken his first few steps. He was still only 9 months old.

I told Jimmy I had decided to go home, Jimmy wouldn't hand himself in, so when I got the chance to be away from him, I called my Mum and told her what time I'd be home, I told her to get the police so they could arrest him again and get him back in hospital I was certain he was going to die without proper treatment.

So that's what happened, we got the train from Blackpool to St Helens, and then a taxi to our house, when we got there, the police surrounded us and took him away. It was such a relief. But more bad news was yet to come. When I got into the house I found the whole place had been burgled while we were away, there was nothing left. All that was in left in that house was the beds and carpets, every single thing had gone.

In the next few days I arranged a house swap, I had to get out of that place, it was over between me and Jimmy, I had to focus on my children, Social Services were involved now and my kids were on the child protection register and if I didn't shape up I was going to have my children taken away. Within 6 weeks I was moved to a nice quiet place the other side of town called Haresfinch. I loved it there. I moved Marc and Kate to a new school and we started our new life. Jimmy's sentence was increased and he ended up

153

in prison for almost 2 years. I visited him regularly and he wrote to me a lot. About 3 letters came every day. Professing to change and telling me how much he loved me. He was in the prison hospital a lot of the time first getting treatment for his legs, he'd had skin grafts to mend the burns, but he was also having some psychiatric treatment too. When we visited the children never knew he was in prison, they thought he was in hospital. They still remember the smell from his legs to this day.

One day I got a call from the prison saying Jimmy had been attacked in there and he was in Fazakerly Hospital I knew that this particular hospital in Liverpool specialised in head injuries so I was very worried. Mum took me over there. We were shocked at what we saw. He was walking down the corridor towards us, and was in chains. He had a long chain from each wrist going to a guard on each side of him and a chain between each ankle. Because he was an escape risk, he had to be chained. He was completely unrecognisable. He'd got a broken jaw and his mouth had been wired together, but the swelling was so bad, I just couldn't recognise him.

Even my Mum looked visibly shocked to see a man looking like that in an English prison.

I felt sorry for him and assured him when this was all over, he could have one more chance and come home to us.

As I walked out of the hospital with my Mum, I knew what she was going to say. 'Are you sure you know what you're doing?' 'Don't have him back love, one day he's going to kill you'. 'I have to Mum' I said, 'He'll die without me.' 'But I promise you one thing; if he ever raises a hand to me again, just once, I'll be gone, and he'll never see me or the kids again'. 'I swear to you on my baby's life'.

# Chapter 34

## 1994 – Mum's 50th

Jimmy was still in Prison but I was back to normality now doing normal things with my family. It was fast approaching Mum's 50<sup>th</sup> birthday, I still didn't work full time and only worked part time behind a bar in Moss Bank near where I lived and was stuck for what to buy Mum for her special day. I had been agonising over what to get. Mum always wanted perfume for her birthday but I wanted to get her something special that she would remember. Then I had remembered that someone at the swimming pool had bought their Mum forty roses for her 40<sup>th</sup> birthday and I thought that was a great idea. I'd get my Mum fifty red roses. I went to the local florists and arranged it. I was going in there regularly paying ten pounds a week as it was going to cost quite a bit, they agreed I could pay it off bit by bit and then they would deliver them on the day so long as I'd paid it all off.

Sue and I had decided to surprise Mum with a massive banner on the front of the house made out of a white bed sheet we had painted with 'Happy Birthday Pat, 50 today'. It was also painted with a champagne bottle popping and a cork flying out. So we had to get the thing on the front of the house without Mum knowing. Sue's famous for her ideas and practical jokes so I left her to it. All was arranged. John was in on it too and he'd left his ladders in the alley at the side of the house so that we could climb to the top of the house and tie the banner and a host of balloons to the front.

We had filled my car with the blown up balloons in preparation, I hadn't realised how difficult it was going to be to drive to Mum's house with the car full of balloons but as it was 4am in the morning and glorious sunshine in July at least that made navigating the couple of miles from my house to Mums fairly safe.

We had to be quiet. I'm not sure if we'd had a drink the night before or not, but Sue and I found keeping quiet the most difficult thing that morning. We dragged out John's ladders and bashed them against the house.

'SShhhhh' I hissed at Sue.

'I'm trying!' she hissed back.

I held the ladder still while she climbed up. Sue had to get right up to the eaves of the house to tie the banner to the gutter on one side.

'I can hear them snoring' Sue laughed from up the ladder.

'What?'

'They're both snoring' she was laughing so hard the ladder was shaking.

Mum's bedroom was on the front of the house, right where we were and the windows were open so it was even more important that we kept quiet. But I was howling with laughter on the ground at the fact that our Sue was clinging to Mum's guttering while she and John were blissfully unaware and snoring their heads off.

Sue eventually composed herself and managed to get one end tied on and I started to climb up the ladder to pass her the first of many balloons she needed to tie on.

The ladder was shaking and we were both still trying and failing not to laugh.

'Bang, Bang!' oh hell, the balloons were bursting. As soon as we got one tied on, another burst. They were bashing against the brickwork. No sooner had Sue tied one on, than another one burst.

Sue eventually got about 5 on at one end. Now it was time for me to move the ladder to the other side and I climbed up the ladder with the other end of the banner. It was lovely and sunny but there was a slight breeze which was causing the sheet to flap and whip like a flag. This was all adding to the hilarity. I got my end tied on to what sounded like someone sawing wood in Mum's front bedroom. I couldn't tell if it was Mum or John's snoring, but at least we'd not woken them. Sue was now passing me a whole host of balloons to get tied on. The milkman then arrived and had a worried look on his face in case I plunged from the ladder and landed on top of him. But all was well and the banner was completed. The milkman was laughing too and we were all now on the ground.

Today was going to be a very good day!

It was still very early so we both headed off back to Sue's flat for some breakfast and then we had to get to St Helens Ford, which was located on the corner of City Road and Hard Lane in the town. It so happened to be also the day John was picking up their new car. A lovely shiny new white Ford Sierra, they were excited. In preparation we had been to Ford's to tell them it was our Mum's 50th birthday on the day that they were picking up their car, and we asked if we could get there beforehand to tie some balloons to the car. Ford's were more than happy for us to do that. So we filled the back seat with red balloons and also tied them to as much of the car as we possibly could. The Salesmen there thought it was hilarious.

We'd got quite a lot planned for Mum that day and we couldn't wait to find out what she thought of the banner and later the car when we got there at about ten o'clock later that morning.

'Happy birthday to you, happy birthday to you...' we both chanted the birthday song when we got there a few hours later.

'Oh thank you loves, thanks for coming round'

'What did you think of the banner?'

'What banner?'

'Haven't you seen it?' We were all inside now and Mum seemed to have no idea what we were talking about.

'Didn't you tell Mum about the banner John?' John was smirking at Mum and laughing his head off too.

'Oh I was waiting for you to get here'

'We've put a banner on the front of the house' I go on. 'Come and have a look'.

Mum went to the front door and we all trouped out into the front garden to look up.

'Oh hell, I can't believe you've done that' 'When did you put that up'

'Four o'clock this morning' Sue replied.

'I wondered why people were looking up as they passed the house; I've noticed that all morning, as people have been walking past'.

We all ended up roaring with laughter and had Mum stood on the front while we took pictures of her with the massive banner.

'You made some bloody noise doing it' John laughed. 'I was terrified you were going to wake you're mother up. I knew what you were doing'

'All that crashing and banging, were the balloons bursting?'

'haha – it must have been you snoring then Mum, we could hear it up the ladder that's why we were laughing so much, we thought it was John it was so loud'.

So that was the first of our surprises for Mum. Next to come were some lovely flowers delivered from the lady across the road. Mum loves flowers and she was really chuffed with the huge bouquet. Later we were going to Mum and John's friend's Julia and Mel's pub, the Nags Head, for a nice birthday lunch. When we got there, there was another flower arrangement, this time it was tropical flowers from John. They were absolutely fantastic. Mum loved the flowers and she was thrilled. She and John had been to Barbados for their honeymoon and Mum liked anything Caribbean or tropical that reminded her of the holiday. The flowers were like giant orchids and the colours were bright pinks and oranges and yellows, they were gorgeous.

We all settled down to a lovely lunch, me, Mum, John, Sue, Mel and Julia. We had a lovely time. Out came the next surprise, Mum's birthday cake! Sue had arranged this. It was full of candles, I don't think we quite got fifty on there but there were a lot and Mum was chuffed to bits and blew them all out.

'I'm surprised she's not yelling' I whisper to Sue.

'Yeah she usually wells up over the slightest thing' Sue replied.

'I can hear you, I'm not going to cry today, I'm really enjoying myself, you two are not going make me cry today'.

'You wait, it's not over yet' 'I bet we can get you blubbing by the end of the day'. I laugh back.

'No you won't' Mum was determined not to cry today.

I raised my eyebrows to Sue and she gave me her knowing look.

So Mum's next stop was St Helens Ford. Not only was Mum flabbergasted at the sight of their new car completely covered in red balloons. But the lovely salesmen have clubbed together and put a bouquet of flowers on the passenger seat for Mum's birthday. Mum was overcome with joy but still didn't cry.

They arrived home to us all clapping on the front door step as the balloon clad car rolled up outside.

'Did you cry when you saw the car?' Sue asked

'Nope, and I told you I won't'. Mum was having a lovely time, we were all spoiling her and we settled down for a few glasses of champagne indoors. It was late afternoon by then and another bouquet had arrived along with a few family and friends with gifts and cards. The house looked like a florist's, there were cards everywhere but I was glancing nervously at the clock, wondering where my flowers were for Mum?

Half an hour later and the door bell chimed again. 'Get the door John', shouted Mum, 'Where is he? 'In the wine cellar' yelled Sue, you'll have to go. They don't actually have a wine cellar John keeps all the cold drinks in the garden! Mum grumbled about it being her birthday and she shouldn't have to, but she got up and answered to the door. All of a sudden there was a shriek and a flood of tears. Thank goodness, at last my flowers had arrived. A glorious bouquet of fifty red roses with gypsum. And Mum was crying her eyes out. Real tears though and I wasn't sure that they were tears of joy. 'Oh Mum, what's wrong, I thought you'd love red roses and I got you fifty for your birthday'.

'Oh love, they're wonderful, you don't know what this means to me'.

And it was true I didn't. When Mum was 19 she'd had a very serious accident and had to have an operation on her back. She was the youngest person at the time to have a laminectomy which is a spine operation to remove the portion of the vertebral bone called the lamina. She had to spend many months lying flat on her back and there had been a chance that she may not walk again. Thankfully she fully recovered. Mum later told us that during her recovery as a young girl she always imagined someone coming to her with a bouquet of red roses and it had since always been a dream of hers to get some, but all her life she never had.

I didn't have any idea about all of this but it looked like I'd found the perfect present for my Mum.

'Told you we'd get you to cry'. Sue shouted. And we all burst out laughing.

# Chapter 35

## 1995 - Home again

Now it was March 1995, Jimmy was coming home at last, things seemed fine now, and he seemed so different. Mum had actually taken me to Walton to collect him, she seemed positive too, but I knew that this was just a front. The last thing my Mum wanted was for me to be back with Jimmy, but she accepted my decision for my sake. I realised now for the first time as we sat in the back of Mum's car, that I actually felt nothing for him. I was dreading having to be alone with him. I was going to try hard though to make the best of things so that I could keep my family together.

When we got home we had organised a party for Jimmy, we had a cake and his sister Maureen and her children had come around to celebrate with us. Mum was there too. It all went off really nicely.

I loved living in Haresfinch, I had made some good friends, the two Tracey's, Jackie and her husband Gary, and Brian from the next street. They all had children the same age as mine, and I regularly had all the kids round at my house for tea and they all played out in the street together. We took it in turns taking the kids to school; Brian had this massive Lada estate which he called 'bullet proof'. It actually looked like a communist leader's car so was very apt. We could pile all the kids in the back of that and Brian would just throw his keys out of the bedroom window and shout 'Take 'em in that baby, I'm off back to bed'. He was hilarious. We all got on really well. Gary, Jackie's husband had been in my class at school and both Jackie and Tracey were in the year above me at school so we all knew each other anyway, it was strange that we all now lived in the same street. I had never been happier. The only downside was I lived at number 13, perhaps that was an omen?

So we continued for the next few months, all of us were happy. Jimmy met the new friends I'd made in our little close and everyone seemed to be getting on. Then gradually, over the next few months I saw a slight change. Jimmy didn't like that I now had a part time job in the local pub. He let me go but I knew he didn't like it. He also didn't like me spending so much time with my friends. 'You don't need them now I'm back'. He would say. I stood up to him; I wasn't going to be bullied any more. 'They helped me when I didn't have you, and I'm not dumping them now you're back. If you don't like it you can leave, this is *MY* house'. I was stronger now.

Then one early evening in mid September of 1995 we were sitting watching TV. We were sharing a bottle of red wine. I stood up to go to the kitchen for something and as I stepped closer to Jimmy he stood up from the sofa he was sitting on and punched me right in the face. I hadn't actually spoken; we'd just been watching TV. I was on the floor when I felt an almighty crash into my chest, it was his boot. I tried climbing up his legs by grabbing his jeans and one of my arms wouldn't move, I couldn't see anything and the last thing I remember was clawing at his shirt and chest trying to climb up. Then it all went black.

I don't know how much later it was but I woke in the darkness I was in bed. I later found out that Jimmy had carried me up to bed. I was in that bed for almost

163

2 weeks before I could get out by myself. I didn't let the children into the bedroom for a while; I didn't want them to see me in that state, it's funny only recently I asked Marc what he remembered about when we lived with Jimmy and apart from all the horror of it, he said he remembered it being dark in my bedroom and not being allowed in.

Jimmy helped me to the bathroom. I couldn't get out of bed alone and I couldn't lift my arm up to get dressed, so he helped me with that, I had no idea what was wrong with my arm. I remember lying in that bed many nights alone, I could hear Jimmy crying downstairs, but I never asked him about it. I was trying to think how to escape and imagined somehow getting out of bed and getting a knife from the kitchen, I wanted to plunge it into his heart while he was asleep. I then imagined dragging his body out of the house and onto the railway line at the back of our garden. I had it all planned in my head. But I knew I'd get caught and then kids would have no Dad and no Mum. But I remembered the promise I'd made to my Mum six months earlier he only had one more chance with me. Well he'd had it, as soon as I could physically get out of that house with my kids I would be gone!

# Chapter 36

## 1995 – The runaway

I was back on my feet, it had been a full 3 weeks, I still couldn't lift my arm above my head and was still limping a bit I'd had a proper kicking and I still didn't know why or what had brought it on. The bruises had faded now, but it was the worst day of the week. Friday. Most people love Fridays but I hated them. During the week I could get out of the house taking the children to and from school and go for the shopping. Although I was never on my own, or had all the children with me at anytime, I felt mostly safe during the week, but as the weekend loomed so did my dread of being stuck in for 2 days and 2 nights never knowing what to expect; this was the most frightened that I ever felt.

I was more afraid of the prospect of him hitting me than when he actually did, the fear was the worst thing. It's hard to explain but that's how I felt.

I used to help out as a classroom assistant at Marc and Kate's school on a Thursday and this day I'd been called in to see the headmaster, he was worried about Marc. The headmaster told me that Marc's teacher had earlier asked Marc to get a book out of his bag in the cloakroom, but after he was gone for a while, she went to see where he was. Marc was sat in the cloakroom with his coat on and he was confused.

I broke down in tears and told the headmaster about the violence at home and said I didn't know what to do. That was the second wake-up call I needed. This wasn't just affecting me it was badly affecting my children.

Friday 6th October 1995. I didn't know it then but that was a date that was going to change my whole life. It was going to be our wedding anniversary on the following Monday, it would be 3 years. What is the symbol? Leather... hmm very appropriate, I would probably be getting a belt on my anniversary.

I was just getting the kid's coats on; it was about 8.30 on the Friday morning we would need to hurry to get to school on time. 'Mummy can I come for a ride in the car?' that was James, he was only two and he certainly didn't know and I had no idea at that moment, that this simple sentence was going to change my life. 'Can he come?' I asked Jimmy, he was still in bed and Marc and Kate were on the landing just outside the door, anxious to get out of the house as quickly as possible. 'Straight there and straight back', 'Of course, I'm only putting his coat over his jamas we'll be straight back'.

That was it, a flash of inspiration and in that second I had the four things I needed to escape. My three children and the car. It was now or never. I picked up James and went into the bathroom. Grabbed four toothbrushes and shoved them in my pocket. James' coat was over the landing banister and I grabbed that and shoved it over his pyjamas.

'Come on you two, we'll be late for school, hurry up'. Marc and Kate followed silently downstairs, I fled into the kitchen, and looked around, all that was there was a pile of ironing that I'd done the night before. I grabbed a bin bag and threw it in, handed it to Marc and said 'Take that out of the back door to the car – and be quiet'. I was still carrying James and as I ushered Kate out of the front door, I grabbed my

Freeman's catalogue from behind the sofa – we would need it to buy new clothes. What was I thinking; all I had was £30 and 20p in my purse. 'Oh who cares?' I thought 'We don't need anything, just each other'. And that was all I walked out of my home with.

We were in the car, an old Austin Maestro; Granddad had bought it for me so that I had a car. I'd done it, we were free. Now I just needed to hold my nerve and leave. But where would I go? My heart was racing and I was driving towards the school. Up the hill at Carr Mill there was a telephone box. I would stop and tell Jimmy I was leaving, that way I wouldn't be able to go back, because I knew what I'd get if I did.

I stopped at the side of the phone box. I had to think, my heart was thumping in my chest, how was I going to do this? I telephoned the house. He answered on the third ring. 'I'm leaving you and I'm never coming back', he started shouting down the phone 'you get back here with my...' I'd put the telephone down before I could hear anymore, but I knew what he was saying, he wanted his baby James.

I couldn't leave without my baby; I would never leave him behind. That was my chance to escape, I'd done it. No going back now.

But where? Where could I go now? I couldn't go to my Mum's or sister's or to any family or friends. I'd been in women's refuges before, Warrington, Wigan even Toxteth in Liverpool. They were not nice places, usually filthy and full of scruffy women, sometimes gypsies or travellers, with black eyes, dirty kids and sometimes faking their circumstances to get a council house. I wasn't like them. I came from a nice family had a lovely home and smart beautiful children. I didn't belong in the world of the battered wife. I didn't even know anyone who had been hit by a husband, boyfriend or partner. Everyone I knew was normal and ordinary.

I remembered thinking back a couple of years to the woman in Social Services who was questioning me about Jimmy's violence and my upbringing. I had told her about my grandparents and parents, how I had a happy childhood and done quite well at school. She said 'Well we've heard the 'Alice in Wonderland' version you can now tell us the truth'. I didn't know what she meant, but she went on to say that women in violent relationships had usually come from a violent childhood and gravitated towards that kind of partner. That was certainly not me, I'd had a very happy upbringing.

I was racking my brains and realised that there was only one place to go, the police station. It wasn't far away, just a three or four minute drive from Haresfinch to College Street. We pulled up in the car park outside. 'Why aren't we going to school Mummy?' Was it Katie or Marc who said that? 'We're leaving home', 'We're never going back' 'We're going to live somewhere else'. They were all silent. Then James said 'Isn't Daddy coming with us?' 'No he isn't coming; we're going on our own' I replied.

As I walked into the police station, I was so grateful to see a Policewoman on the front desk. I walked towards her; it was like being in a tunnel. Everything was faded around me; all I could see was the lady on the desk. 'Can I help?' she kindly said. 'I've left my husband, he hits me'. 'Oh love come in this room, we'll help you'. She said. And from there it was the most important turning point of my life. Another kindly older policeman was colouring in with my children, and the police desk sergeant took down all my details. 'What's his name love' 'It's James Hayes'. I didn't need to say anymore. He was well known to the police for his violence. 'We'll get you sorted; do you know where the Women's Aid office is?' 'Yes' I said, I knew it well, '42 Hardshaw Street' 'Well they want you to go over there; they'll find you somewhere safe to go'.

Five minutes later I was outside and I knocked on the door. The lady at Women's Aid who opened the door and let me in was called Ann, and the only question she asked me that I remember now was. 'Do you want to go North or South?' I looked at the children, they all looked dazed too, and they were looking at books and eating cream crackers with spread cheese on top. North or South, what did it matter, I just said I had to go far, I knew I couldn't stay local. But then I said 'South, I'd rather go south, there will be more work down there and I'll need to find a job'. So Ann got on the telephone. She was speaking to someone in Cornwall, who said they'd call her back, and then she called another refuge in London. She told me not to worry that she would definitely find me a place for tonight. 'Have you ever thought of Milton Keynes?' 'Is that far enough away for you?' I'd never heard of the place, or if I had I didn't have any idea where it was. 'Just north of London, about 50 miles north. Said Ann, she pointed to a map over her desk. 'It's about 160 miles away from here.' 'Anywhere, far enough away' I thought. 'I'll give them a call while we're waiting for someone else to come back to us.' 'Yes you do? That's fantastic' said Ann into the telephone. 'I'll give her directions and she'll meet you at the police station'.

By 1pm that same day I was heading down the M6 going south to this mysterious place called Milton Keynes, it was all a bit of a dream. I didn't have any money now; all £30 had gone into the tank of the car. But someone was going to meet me at Milton Keynes police station. All I had to do was get to junction 14 on the M1 and follow the signs for central Milton Keynes; I would see a sign for the police station.

It was belting down with rain most of the way, and the M6 and M1 on a Friday afternoon, heading south were a nightmare. A journey that should have taken about 2 and a half hours had taken us over five. The children were crying a lot of the time asking me to take them home, I was crying too but tried to reassure them. We couldn't go back now. What had I done? Where were we going to end up? Would this end up being worse that what we were putting up with? So many questions were running around in my mind.

W eventually got to Milton Keynes centre. What a place this was. It felt like I was in America. All the roads seemed to be in a grid in the shopping centre. I was going up and down these huge hills it reminded me of San Francisco. They were called Boulevards and the roads seem to have a white surface to them.

Eventually I found the police station, the children were all wide awake now, they'd been crying and sleeping off and on in the back of the car. They must be hungry by now. We all trouped in. The desk was a massive stone looking thing and I felt very small in that front desk area. I explained who I was and that someone from Women's Aid was going to meet me here. The police officer on the desk said that he would find out. He came back a few minutes later to say they were on their way; they'd be about 10 minutes and would arrive in a mini bus. I told him that I would wait outside.

It didn't seem long at all, when that blue mini bus arrived and a kind hippy type woman got out. She had sandwiches and cans of pop. And we sat in the mini bus for a little while chatting about where we had come from and where we were going to.

It was all arranged that I would follow the bus to the refuge and we'd get settled into a room. A new start. A new place. Despite everything, I knew that I was going to be happy at long last, we all were.

(Marc 7, Kate 6 in their old school uniform
from Carr Mill, and James 2 who insisted
wearing the same school jumper)

# Chapter 37

## 1995 – Where's the car?

Little did I know that when I got up the following morning, my car would have been stolen. I had moved 160 miles away from Liverpool the car-theft-capital of Europe only to wake up to find my car had been stolen in Milton Keynes. Well nothing was going to put me off this strange place, I was determined that this was going to be my home. I hadn't yet told my Mum or anyone else where I was and as the car was registered to me at my old home address, I had better get on to the police and let them know not to try and contact me at that address if they found my car. I didn't want my husband to be alerted to my whereabouts. I had been lying awake most of the night in my skanky bed in a room I was sharing with my three little kids, who were already scratching their heads, nits must be rife in this place, thinking about what I had done and was it the right decision? I had come to the conclusion that this was exactly the correct decision and there was no going back. So in half an hour I was up and dressed, sorting out breakfast for the children. The lady that had picked me up from the police station had kindly loaned me twenty pounds for the weekend so I could feed my children until I could get to the benefit's office and sort out a claim and organise my child benefit.

I made an appointment at a local doctor's surgery I had found the telephone number on a notice board; I had to find out what was wrong with my arm and shoulder. I got an appointment for the Monday morning. The doctor sent me to the hospital for an X-ray and I was informed that I'd had a broken collar bone; luckily it had set in the correct place. But that was what all the discomfort was. I couldn't lift my arm above my head for the next 5 years. Eventually it got better and now I'm fine but it was that kick to the chest from Jimmy that caused me so many problems.

About a week after I had left I thought I'd better tell my Mum where I was. She was used to not hearing from me for a few days but never more than a week or so and I didn't want her to worry. I called her up. 'Where are you?' she asked immediately. 'I'm in Milton Keynes, I've left Jimmy for good and I'm in a refuge here'. Mum wasn't surprised. 'I went around to your house the other day with your new iron and Jimmy said you'd gone, but I had no idea what he was talking about so I didn't leave the iron'. She said. I went on to explain that this time I meant it and I'd left him for good. Both Mum and I cried but with relief that day. Mum then went into action explaining that she'd be down in a couple of days and she'd take me shopping for everything I needed. I felt a huge sense of relief and was glad that Mum was coming down, the children had been very quiet and I knew they needed to see a familiar face other than mine.

Mum had never been to Milton Keynes before and I explained where it was off the M1 at Junction 14. When Mum arrived a few days later she regaled the tale to me that as she was coming down the M1 she had been looking at all the signs which said 'Milton Keynes 30 miles', 'Milton Keynes 12 miles' and so on, as she was getting closer, and when she eventually saw the sign that said 'Milton Keynes 9' she actually burst into tears while driving crying out 'Oh love I'm only 9 miles away'. Now whenever I see that sign it breaks my heart to think about how my Mum must have felt while she was driving alone all the way from St Helens to Milton Keynes to help me.

# Chapter 38

## 1995 – Another name

So following the meetings with the Police and Women's Aid, they advised me to change my surname by Statutory Declaration, and although I couldn't 'officially' change the names of my children from what appeared on their birth certificates, they could only do it themselves when they were 18, I was advised that I could actually call them anything I liked, and so long as my name was legally changed, no-one would bat an eyelid if I called the children by the same surname.

It was all arranged; I made an appointment with a solicitor and I just had to think up what surname I wanted to use. I've always had a thing about my surname. When I was at school, and my name was Williams, I hated being last on the register. It sounds silly now but I really resented that I was last to be called out and the bottom of any list. Marrying Paul, moved me up half way as my surname had been Knight, and although I wasn't ever on any register, at work I wasn't listed at the bottom whenever I saw a list of employees. Marrying Jimmy moved me up even higher as I was then Hayes. So I decided I was going to be even closer to the top if I had the opportunity to choose a name of my own.

The police had recommended that I shouldn't go back to my maiden-name or any other name I'd been known as, in case anyone (my husband) tried to track me down. It was harder than you would imagine trying to think up a new name. I obviously didn't want anything silly, it had to be something easy for the kids to spell and write down and more importantly remember and I wanted it to be short and near the beginning of the alphabet.

Well it came to me one evening when I was watching an episode of Brookside, the scouse soap opera filmed in Liverpool. One of the characters was called Rosie Banks and she'd won the lottery! Fabulous! Banks it was going to be, maybe we'd have the same luck that the character had. So now I was going to be Siân Banks.

I had made friends with a lovely young woman Amanda who was from London she had moved in to the refuge with her daughter Amy and a Glaswegian woman called Dawn who had also left her husband and was staying in the refuge with her grown up daughter Louise. Amanda and I have kept in touch all these years and we still remain good friends. Dawn insisted on calling my children by both first and surname at every opportunity. This worked well, within a few days James Banks had forgotten what his old name was. He was only 2 and a half and it was going to be easy for him to get used to his new name.

'So James, do you remember your old name?' asked Dawn one evening. 'er, yes, Jaaaames' he stretched out his first name desperately trying to think what his old surname had been. 'Bond?' he smiled 'James Bond' Dawn and I fell about laughing; 'Yes James Banks, your old name was James Bond'.

# Chapter 30

## 1995 – Flaming hell!

Eleven weeks later we were happily installed in a our new home in the new town of Milton Keynes, we'd moved out of the Women's Aid refuge and we'd been given a nice house in the North of the City on a council estate. The people at the Women's Aid Refuge were very helpful and explained how housing allocation worked for homeless people and that you were offered up to two houses in the housing system and that was it, so if you declined the first and then the second was awful, you were stuck with it. So I went with my first offer as I had no idea which was a good or bad area and the house itself was a decent sized three bedroom town house, with a lovely little back garden and luckily the area seemed pretty nice.

Mum and John had been really brilliant and virtually kitted the whole house out with carpets and furniture. I had a small grant from the Council to help and we'd got more or less everything we needed. Nagging at the back of my mind though was the thought of all my beautiful things that I left back in St Helens when I fled. Somehow I was going to get those back. More importantly every photograph I'd ever taken had been left behind, so I had no photos of the children when they were babies or pictures of me when I was small.

I was really excited as all the new furniture had been delivered and we were unwrapping sofas, the brand new carpet had been laid all through the house, so we were finally getting everything in place. After a lot of hard work we were done and with lovely new sofas and beds the house was starting to look like a home.

Six weeks after moving in Mum's John announced his plan. His friend Alf from Thatto Heath, had two burly sons with a very large van. They were going to take me back to St Helens and break the door down to my old house and help me take what I wanted whether Jimmy was there or not. I was really worried, but John said I deserved all my pictures and things. So it was arranged.

We arrived at about 10.30 one morning with Alf's sons and their giant Transit van and mum and John's Sierra. I marched up to the house with my two minders. We banged on the door. Nothing. I banged again, still silence. We looked around the back and side but there appeared to be no-one there. One of Alf's sons smashed a side window and helped me through. I was shaking but made a dash to the front door and opened it to let everyone in. Jimmy wasn't there, but I could actually smell him in that house. We had no time to lose, it appeared he had only just left and he could have returned at any minute.

Within half an hour we had stripped that house of everything I wanted. When I went into our bedroom I saw pictures of me all over the bed, he must have been looking at them. I gathered up every photograph of me and the kids and took the lot. We fled, and I never saw number 13 again. The only thing I regretted was the baby cot that my Granddad had handmade when I was having Marc was in the loft and I'd not thought to get it.

So I was now back in Milton Keynes in my new house with all my things, This particular day I was on the phone to Mum telling her just how lovely everything was and thanking her profusely and I was stretched out on the lovely carpet gabbling away on the phone, when there was a massive cracking sound coming from behind me.

In the dining room there were ceiling to floor windows looking out to the garden and when I looked out there was a huge fire outside, right next to the window. It was all the packing from the sofas and beds. The fire was so big it had cracked the glass in the windows and my full length curtains were in danger of catching fire. I screamed to my Mum 'There's a fire!' and slammed down the phone, then dashed to the windows.

'Marc, Kate, get here quick, there's a fire' I yelled. There was a thumping of feet from upstairs and down they raced. 'Hold these curtains right back, or they'll catch fire when that window breaks' I screamed to Marc. He nervously did as I said and I dashed into the kitchen and filled the washing-up bowl full of water, kicked the back door handle to open the door, and threw out the water; I was repeating this as fast as I could but with little effect and the flames were getting higher. I didn't seem to be getting anywhere, Marc looked scared and I was worried that he was too close to the fire, so I yanked the curtains off their hooks. 'Keep filling that bowl with water', I ordered Marc. 'Kate, you need to dial 999 on the phone' she was only six and looked at me with terror. I tried to comfort her. 'It's easy, Kate, just dial 999 and say there's a fire, they will then ask you some questions, you know our address'.

She nodded and for once did as she was told and I continued charging from kitchen to dining room with the filled bowls of water, throwing them desperately out of the back door, trying to quench the flames. I was exhausted and still seemed to be getting nowhere, the flames were the full height of the windows and were almost licking at the upstairs bedroom window now, the smell of burning rubber from the back of carpet and the plastic covers from the sofas was choking me and I was coughing and spluttering like a lunatic as I tried to continue. I carried on with the bowls of water, for what appeared to be ages but I suppose it was only about twenty minutes and suddenly at last firemen were charging through my house with a hose. In about thirty seconds the fire was completely gone and I collapsed in relief on the sofa. The garden was a complete mess and my downstairs windows were shattered.

The chief fire-fighter then began questioning me on how the fire started. I hadn't even thought of that. I explained that it was the packing from the newly delivered sofas and beds and the off cuts from the newly laid carpet that had been alight. But that I had no idea how it caught fire. He immediately looked at the 3 little faces all scared witless on the sofa. 'Do any of you know how it started?' he boomed at them. James immediately burst into tears. Then I was astounded as Marc confessed that he and Kate had been lighting pages from of a colouring book in their bedroom with a lighter they had found and were watching it float down into the garden. They hadn't realised that the packing would catch fire. Marc was only seven and was petrified that he would be now going to jail; he looked as white as a ghost. Kate seemed less phased and had her usual look of defiance on her face. The fireman softened but insisted to them that they could have killed us all with their silly prank which could have ultimately burned the house down. Soon the fire fighters reeled up their hose and I was left to clean up the mess with three sheepish children helping as best they could. That wasn't going to be the last time the emergency services are called to our house.

# Chapter 40

## 1996 – We've lost James

So I had settled into my new life in Milton Keynes the city of the roundabouts and after being there for about six months I'd decided that the life of a benefits-dependent-stay-at-home-Mum wasn't the life for me. So after a spell as a shop girl in the local supermarket which bored me to the core, I had found a local hotel in the historic town of Stony Stratford which was looking for part-time bar staff. I'd worked behind a bar before and I thought that this would be ideal. It would be far easier to find a babysitter for the evenings than it would be during the day, plus bar work is like as a social life but you don't spend any money you earn it. It would be perfect!

I got the job and the work was easy, Stony Stratford is only a short five minute drive from where I live. The Cock Hotel is a 16th Century Coaching House steeped in history and apparently haunted, not that I ever saw a ghost. It was owned by a local business man who was well known in the town and was a family run business and not part of a chain.

This was one of the best summers I can remember since moving to Milton Keynes and I was really relishing the fact that I was only working evenings at the local hotel. I could spend every day in the garden or take the children to the great outdoor swimming pool just half a mile away in Wolverton. As a committed sun worshipper I was in heaven. We were thoroughly enjoying our new life in Milton Keynes, there is so much for a young family to explore and do, with beautiful parks and countryside and it's a far cry from the industrial Merseyside we had come from.

I stayed good friends with Dawn from the refuge and her daughter Louise moved in with me. A friend of Dawn's, Martin, had a dog called Monty and as the kids loved it when they could play with Monty I volunteered to look after him while Martin was a work. Monty was a Border collie with a gentle nature and he was great with the kids. They would keep him on the go all day, so much so that he would sleep all weekend when Martin took him home. Being a sheep dog he would always try to 'round up' the kids and bring them towards me. It would have been great if it had worked but they were more trouble than sheep and Monty soon realised he was fighting a losing battle. My children and I love dogs and although I didn't want to commit to having a dog of our own, looking after Monty from Monday to Friday was a good substitute.

On one particularly sunny day the kids were in the garden playing with Monty and I was sunbathing with my Dawn. It was getting too hot, even for me, so Dawn and I retreated to the kitchen to get a drink when Marc came racing in from the garden.

'Monty has gone out the back gate' he yelled.

 I dashed out of the kitchen and flew down the alley at the side of house. I was terrified of losing Monty as he was not our dog, I'd have a lot of explaining to do to Martin. He had been lost once before and Martin had to pay £90 to the dog warden to get him back. Luckily Monty had been electronically tagged so they quickly found Martin's details and returned him. With this in mind I was particularly careful about not letting Monty out of the garden so I was panicking as

I ran out into the street. I rushed around the corner and there was Monty sniffing another dog, 'Phew' I thought, that was lucky. I dragged him back into the garden as I was telling him what a naughty dog he was, I don't think he was listening. I closed the gate securely and with the panic over Marc returned to the garden with Monty and Dawn and I went back into the kitchen to fix our drinks. It was getting near lunch time so I decided to take some sandwiches out into the garden for the kids. I shouted out to them to come for lunch and Marc and Kate came running straight away but there was no sign of James. 'Where is James?' I asked. 'He was with Monty' replied Kate. Well Monty was now playing alone with his ball in the garden so I went back into the house and called James, no answer. I ran upstairs to find him but there was no sign of him, he had vanished.

I then headed back down to the garden, shouting for James all the while. There was still no sign of him.

'Did he go out with Monty earlier' I ask Marc. 'Yes, I think he took him out' Marc replied.

Dawn shrieked in her Glaswegian accent 'That James Banks, you know it would be him'. I think she was more worried than I was.

So we secured Monty in the house and the three of us, Dawn, myself and Marc headed out to the street to look for James. But there was no sign of James anywhere, so we all spread out and took different routes to the usual places he may be. There's a small park at the back of our house with swings and a slide, I headed there. Dawn went up to the centre green where there is a larger park with swings and Marc headed towards the back field. There is a small stream there and the kids often play around it. After about twenty minutes or so we were all back at the house and no-one has found James. Kate had scoured the house and he wasn't back there either. I was panicking by then, he was only three and although he played out close to the house with his brother and sister he was not allowed to stray from our front garden on his own. James was always a bit of a dare-devil he thought he could do exactly the same kinds of things that his older brother did but didn't realise that Marc was five years older. He could ride a two wheeled bike at two and a half years of age, and was regularly falling out of trees from about three years old. He'd already broken his arm from climbing on top of his toy car to see over the garden fence to look at our neighbour's racing dogs. What kind of scrape was he going to be in now?

My panic was now starting to rise. 'I'll have to call the police' I said. Dawn agreed and I dialled 999. I explained that I'd lost my three year old son and the officer on the phone took all the details. He was very calm and did his best to calm me down – he failed!! I had hardly put down the telephone and there was a siren and a screeching of brakes at the front of the house, there were police cars filling the street. The house was soon equally filled with Police officers, I had never thought there would be so much help so quickly, I had imagined them saying call back when he's been missing 24 hours or something, but I soon realised that if a child goes missing its panic stations and they mobilise everything.

James was convinced he was 'grown up' and had taken to exploring on his own. The last time he did it was a few weeks earlier during a trip to the shopping centre. We were with Marc and Kate's Dad Paul, and his then new girlfriend Sarah, when James decided to 'go walkabout' he was only gone five minutes and we found him hiding in between clothing racks in Dorothy Perkins. I was frantic with, images of James Bulger flashing through my mind. (The little boy who'd been kidnapped and murdered 3 years earlier from a shopping centre in Liverpool, at almost exactly the same time as my James had been born.)

After a thorough search of the house, including the loft and the garden shed, the police instructed us to stay at home while they took control of searching the estate. This went on for over an hour and my heart was in my mouth, how could I lose my baby son when he'd been safe at home with me? Dawn was being strong and completely confident that he'd turn up but it didn't help. 'That James Banks won't go off with anyone, he's clever' she assured me. One of the policemen returned to the house to ask for addresses of all the kid's local friends so they could start checking out other addresses. I was now hysterical. I told the police that he'd if gone to a friend's house; their parents would have brought him back or telephoned to say he was there. But never the less the police wanted addresses and Marc and Kate helped me sort them out, at least it was a distraction and gave us something to do. Where could he be? All the officers had radios and between the crackles and pops I heard voices talking about the ETA for the search helicopter. This made me even more hysterical but the police woman waiting with me was fantastic and explained that it was normal procedure – oh that's OK then!!

So there we were. Marc and Kate balling their eyes out and Dawn doing a poor impression of being calm and me hysterical. Poor old Monty sat in a corner looking confused by all the fuss. We had five police cars, more than twenty officers and now a helicopter searching Stacey Bushes looking for my son. Obviously I was glad of the help and desperate for them to find him but at the same time I was mortified with embarrassment and terrified of the trouble I was going to get into for losing him, or so I thought. Half an hour later the helicopter was noisily hovering overhead. I was still wandering from room to room in the house hoping to God that he'd turn up somewhere, when for some unknown reason I bent down to look under the bunk beds in Marc and James's room. I couldn't believe it he was there! Asleep!

I was so relieved that I was crying with tears streaming down my face as I dragged him from under the bed and hugged him, almost squeezing the breath from his body. Now I had to go down and tell the police. 'Oh hell!' I thought what on earth were the police going to make of it? Then I remembered that they had searched the house already so they must have missed him too. I carried him down stairs. 'He's here' I yelled between my sobs of relief and fear. A very stern looking police officer asked me where he was. 'Under the bunk-beds upstairs' I replied. So much for their detective work!

What transpired was that he'd actually been walking along the street when he saw all the police cars so he ran home down the alley, climbed over the fence into the garden and dashed up the stairs to hide under the bed because he was frightened. Somehow he'd managed to escape detection by all of us and the police.

I was so happy and relieved that I didn't care what they said and to be honest I don't remember much about it. Afterwards Dawn told me that the police were as relieved as I was and they all left with smiles on their faces. I spent the next few days wondering if there would be a bill in the post for wasting police time and for the cost of the helicopter search but luckily nothing arrived.

# Chapter 41

## 1996 – Danger on the ice

As I have said before I like Milton Keynes and it's a great place to bring up children. However it is a city based on some odd regulations and one is that there should be not be any television aerials on the outside of the houses. It was one of the planning principles along with 'no building shall be higher than the tallest tree' and that one didn't last long either. Milton Keynes is provided with its own cable TV system originally operated by Cable and Wireless, then NTL and now Virgin Media. It's an old analogue system so goodness knows what you are able to receive these days. Most people now have Sky dishes and lots of people have added external television aerials to receive Freeview, what will the planners say? One of the additional channels we used to receive via the cable is MKTV and I was quite fond of having MKTV playing in the background as I did the housework – there were no presenters it was just music with a picture show telling you about what's going on in and around Milton Keynes. To keep every ones attention they sometimes had quizzes and competitions and general advertising features, it was a bit like an up market ceefax, just what you would expect in Milton Keynes.

I had the TV on with MKTV providing some background music as I was doing the ironing when I saw a competition to win four family tickets to see local hockey team, the MK Lightening, at the local ice rink, Planet Ice. Whenever I see competitions I am always tempted to enter, not that I ever win anything and this one just needed you to phone in and leave your answer. So I dialled the number on the screen and left my answer with my name and address, I can't even remember what the simple question was. I put the phone down and got back to my ironing thinking nothing more about it. About twenty minutes later there was my name on the screen – 'Our winner today is Sian Banks and she will be receiving her prize tickets in the post'. I couldn't believe it – it just goes to show you always have a chance.  I know what you are thinking, that's not much of a prize, but I felt like I'd won the lottery and picked up the phone to tell my friends Julie and Dawn. They were equally impressed and we decided to buy some additional tickets and make a night of it.  By the time we had included the kids, the kid's friends and other hangers on there were over fifteen of us going.

'Planet Ice' is a massive ice rink near Central Milton Keynes. The outside looks a bit dated and wouldn't win any architecture awards but it's a great night out. We arrived in good time to watch the hockey match I can't remember who the Lightening were playing, you'll see why later. I do remember it was an exciting game to watch, I have always loved the speed and the spectacle of Ice Hockey with the players padded up like Michelin men hurtling around the rink, crashing into each other and being sent off to cool down. After the match they removed the goals and repaired the ice before opening up the rink for the spectators to have a skate. You can hire skates and access to the ice is free as the lights are turned down and the music starts for an evening of 'ice disco'. The kids loved it as its pretty dark with flashing disco lights and very loud dance music. We were all having a really good time on the ice. Marc (8) and Kate (7) were pretty good skaters and had been skating many times before so they were off on their own speeding around the rink trying not to knock anyone over. James was only three and couldn't skate at all, so I was slowly skating round holding him up between my legs. From his shrieks of laughter I could tell that James was enjoying it just as much as the others, and although I didn't get much of an opportunity to skate, I could see all of our party whizzing round having a great time. Every so often we would sit at the side to have a drink and a chat before going back onto the ice for another go.

So James and I were in the middle of the ice rink, he was all kitted out with a bobble hat, thick coat, mittens and scarf and his little red face was beaming, he loved it. Most Mums and Dads with little ones were in the middle while all the main action and speed skating was taking place around the sides. It was quite a challenge to get on and off the ice though the constant stream of more accomplished skaters, especially when you have a three year old who is either desperate to get on the ice to have a go or desperate to get off for a rest.

As James and I were taking some tentative steps to start him gliding we somehow knocked into each other and our blades got tangled. I was worried about falling on top of James but somehow I managed to manoeuvre away from him and land very, very hard on my bottom. Oh what pain! How I stopped myself from screaming I'll never know. I was sitting on the ice with a pain I could hardly bear at the top of my thigh but I was more worried that I might have hurt James or upset him. I somehow managed not to faint or cry although I knew I was close to doing both. 'Now what?' I thought. The pain was awful and I didn't seem to be able to move my legs. I could feel my jeans getting wet from the ice so I knew that when I did stand up it would look as though I'd wet myself – the thought of being so embarrassed was adding to my pain. James had managed to stand up by himself next to me and was wondering what was going on and why hadn't Mummy got up to play like she normally did.

I was trying to look for the others but it was dark, the disco lights were flashing and the music seemed louder than ever. I kept feeling as though I was about to pass out as I sat there shouting for Marc and Kate at the top of my voice, James was crying by now he knew something was wrong. I saw Marc and Kate whizz by and then Julie and Dawn flew by next, how on earth was I going to attract anyone's attention as everyone must have thought that I'd just fallen over like everyone else, after all every few seconds there was someone's bottom hitting the ice and no-one ever took any notice.

I filled my lungs for one last shout as Kate skated past and she came over to us, by now James was balling his eyes out and I was getting close to doing the same thing.

'I can't get up Kate, I've hurt my leg' I whimpered, 'can you get James to the side?' Kate now also looked upset, and I tried to keep calm so as not to worry her too much, 'and get Dawn, I'll need her to help me get up'. Kate wanted to stay with me but eventually she took James to the side, he must have sensed that I was hurt and I didn't want him watching as Dawn and Julie lifted me up off the ice, it wouldn't be a pretty sight. Kate had found one of our group to look after James and had gone looking Dawn. With James being looked after I had time to assess the damage and I couldn't feel my legs apart from an enormous pain in my thigh. I could feel myself drifting off when a loud Glaswegian voice shouted. 'There's always one, Siân, and it's always you' I few people have said that over the years! Dawn laughed as she made a grab for my arm to lift me up. 'STOP STOP' I yelled, in agony, 'my leg, oh God Dawn what have I done'. I was now crying in agony and Dawn realised that I was really hurt. I still thought that I was just badly bruised with having landed awkwardly so I had no idea what I had actually done.

'I'll go and get help' Dawn said but I was begging, 'please don't leave me'. People were starting to look, and I'd got this awful feeling that the warmth I could feel underneath me meant that I had actually wet myself – I didn't know what was worse the embarrassment or the pain. It was still almost pitch black with the disco lights and I could feel myself feeling faint again as I watched skates whizzing past and people's concerned faces looking at me – it all seemed surreal.

I was suddenly snapped back to reality as the lights came up and a voice came over the sound system saying that there had been an accident and they would have to clear the ice for a few minutes. I remembered him apologising and saying it would only be for a few minutes. I was now sitting alone on the ice with everyone looking and coming towards me was Dawn with three burly looking St John's ambulance first aiders and they were dragging a stretcher with them. 'Please no, how bad can this be?' I thought. I hung my head in shame and embarrassment and then to my horror I realised that the warm, sticky feeling underneath me was being caused by blood, my blood, and lots of it. With the full glare of the bright lights on I could see a pool of dark red slowly creeping across the ice from beneath me. It seemed worse with the lights on; I began to worry about what had happened. Before they moved me they carried out all the checks to make sure they wouldn't be making things worse and they eventually lifted me from the ice and onto the stretcher, it then became obvious what had happened, my jeans were sliced open and so was my leg. It looked like James's ice skate must have gashed my leg open when we both fell; no wonder I was in pain.

I still think the embarrassment of everybody watching was worse than the actual injury and I just wanted to pull my knitted hat down over my face. As I was carried off the ice I could see the ice cleaner dragging out a hose to wash away the blood, my blood. Many of the skaters had taken the opportunity to have a drink or something to eat but there seemed to be hundreds lining the route to the first aid room. They were all staring at me with miserable faces, I felt like their night was ruined just because I slipped over.

The First Aid room was more like a store room with a first aid box and a bottle of Aspirin and it was freezing. I'm sure they kept it cold to help stop the blood flowing. Now don't get me wrong I am a great supporter of the St John's and they do a fantastic job with little support and few resources but the young lad who appeared to be in charge didn't inspire confidence. He was no more than about seventeen and wore a uniform about two sizes too big for him and his bedside manner left a lot to be desired.

I was lying face down on some kind of therapy bed and it smelled of big muscley ice hockey players. He began to prod around at the top of my leg and said, 'It'll need stitches and lots of them, it's completely gashed open and it's not a clean cut'. By then everyone was in the room, Dawn, Julie, all their kids and friends all staring at me. The very clinical and very loud description of my injury didn't help matters and most of the kids all started crying again, James hadn't stopped, and poor Marc and Kate look like they'd seen a ghost. I did my best to put on a brave face but I think the loss of blood was beginning to have an effect and all I wanted to do was sleep.

It didn't take long for the ambulance to arrive and we were soon at Milton Keynes General Hospital. I was cleaned and stitched up and the Doctor told

191

me to go and see my own doctor to have the stitches removed about 10 days later. For some reason they were reluctant to give me any pain relief, I think it was because of the blood loss, so they had to suffer me screaming and moaning as they sorted me out, I tried to be a good patient, honestly. Dawn had taken the children home and was waiting at my house. My problem was that I couldn't bend or sit down so I had to lay on my side in the back of the taxi that was taking me home. I spent the next few days either standing up or lying on my side but I was lucky and it wasn't too bad.

A couple of days later, there was a lot pain from the cut and it felt very hot to the touch. Dawn was around quite a lot to help me with the kids and after she looked at the wound she insisted on me calling the doctor as she thought it didn't look too good. I rang the doctor's surgery and they said they would send my doctor around later that day. Dawn had cooked tea and we were watching TV when the door bell rang followed by a hammering on the door.

'I'll go' said Dawn, 'Whoever it is needs a lesson in patience.' Dawn went to the door and came back with an odd expression on her face 'There's a wee bag lady at the door. Says her name is King'. I was confused for a few minutes then realised it was my Doctor, Barbara King, she was a funny old lady, and you'd never think she was a doctor if you saw her as she always went round in a dirty old rain coat. But, give her credit, it was late in the evening and she was there to take a look at my leg. She was never a sympathetic Doctor, always very matter of fact, but her heart was in the right place. She gave me a prescription for some anti-biotics and told us where the late night chemist was open.

I don't think I've been skating since and although I used to love it, I don't think I'll ever go again.

# Chapter 41

## 1996 – The Millionaire

I had been working at the Cock Hotel in Stony Sratford for quite a few months I guess when this old chap in his 70s checked in. He seemed to be a permanent guest and was known as Mr Ball. He always seemed to pay me special attention and was a decent tipper. I was always kind to him even though he did seem a bit creepy in that he would always request that I serve him, in fact he would wait until I was free, even though Josie my colleague would be standing around waiting to serve someone. He always held my hand for that extra few seconds when I gave him his change. His favourite tipple was a single malt and he always smoked those terrible Cuban cigars – in the days before the smoking ban. Well he had been resident in the hotel for about 3 months and there was a private party he had organised in the function room in the Marquee suite at the back and Mr Ball had specifically asked for me to work on that bar. This was all leaving me feeling rather uncomfortable as he seemed to be behind me every time I turned round, grinning like a maniac. Half way through the evening, Chris the owner came through to see all was ok, and asked how I was getting on. 'Oh fine except for the host' I said, 'He's all over me like a rash, as usual Chris' 'Ha ha' boomed Chris, 'Play your cards right and you'll be the 4th Mrs Marshall'. 'What do you mean?' I asked, completely puzzled. 'I thought his name was Jim Ball?'

'Don't you know who he is?' Chris replied. 'I've no idea; I thought his name was Ball?' 'No, he's Jim Marshall, owns Marshall Amplification' – 'You must have known?' 'He's left his wife and is staying here until his new house is ready'. 'Oh!' I replied, still completely unaware of whom this geriatric groper was.

I thought no more about it and as it was time for my break, I got myself a coke and went for a sit down in the front bar. My Mum had insisted on my having a mobile phone as I was alone in Milton Keynes, and they were quite new back in the mid 90s and weighed a ton. All of a sudden my mobile rang and it was my sister Sue asking how I was and we had the general chit-chat, I was just about to say goodbye when it occurred to me to ask Sue. 'Hey, have you ever heard of Marshall Amplification?' 'Yeah why?' replied Sue, 'Well that OAP I told you about that's always asking me out for dinner and trying to grope my arse at every opportunity, do you remember?' Ha ha, yes I remember why' 'Well apparently he's Jim Marshall who owns it' 'What is it?' I asked her. 'Oh my God Siân, he's a multi-millionaire, you know Marshall Amps, those massive speakers all the rock bands have on Top of the Pops?'

'No!' I reply; stunned. I'd still not got a clue. 'How do you know it's him?' asked Sue. 'Well Chris the owner here told me, apparently he's staying here under a fake name, Mr Ball' I said. 'He's an old friend of Chris's' 'Chris is probably winding me up'.

'Well if I was you Siân, I'd get in there' laughed Sue. 'You must be joking he's in his 70s by the look of him even his son is about 20 years older than me' I laughed back.

So that was the start of it. The very next time I worked I noticed out of the window a limousine pulling up and the so called millionaire leaving the bar to get in it. I'd never heard of Marshall Amps, or the famous Jim Marshall so it was all still a mystery to me. But something had sparked my interest (I know what you are thinking reader, the money! Well you could be right) so I started to ask other people if they'd ever heard of Jim Marshall and his speaker business. I was astounded to find that everyone did. My sister's boyfriend Neil at the time was a rock guitarist and actually owned a Marshall Amp, I saw the famous amps on Top of the Pops and every music channel on TV, they seemed to be everywhere and following a trip to B&Q in Bletchley, across the road I noticed the famous Marshall factory, with the name emblazoned across the front. It all seemed true. Jim was and still is a well loved local hero who regularly raised money for the Variety Club and gave very generous charitable donations to the local hospital. He was on the front of the Milton Keynes citizen, our local newspaper regularly.

And that's how it continued for about another 3 months, Jim asking me out for dinner, me declining and eventually trying to change my shifts so that I wasn't in the bar when I knew Jim was going to be. I felt like a laughing stock, this randy old goat at least 40 years my senior constantly asking me out for dinner.

Christmas had come and at last Jim had moved out of the Cock Hotel. He popped in for the occasional late night snifter after attending some charity event, and his driver John would pop in and say hello. On this particular occasion, Jim shuffled up and handed me a Christmas card. 'Oh thanks Jim, you didn't need to' I haven't got a card for you. 'No need my dear' 'just a little something to show my appreciation of how kind you have been while I was staying here'. I opened the card to find two £50 notes inside. The card was a Marshall company card emblazoned with Marshall across the front in a snow scene. I was stunned. 'I

195

don't want this money Jim, the card is enough that's very kind, please take the money back' 'Now my girl, most people I meet are only nice to me because they know who I am, you never knew and you were always polite and kind' he said 'I'm polite to everyone who comes in Jim' 'It's my job'

'All the same it's unusual for me to find that' 'please let me take you somewhere nice for dinner to say thank you properly' 'you can bring your boyfriend or someone with you if you prefer'. I kind of felt sorry for him at that moment, and was very sorry for thinking he was a dirty old man. 'No thank you Jim, I really don't think it's appropriate' 'What about if I cook dinner for you then?' he asked 'At my house?'

Well as you can imagine this really sparked my curiosity, I'd never been inside a multi-millionaire's house before and was interested to see what it would be like. 'OK then Jim' - 'I'll come' I replied.

So it was arranged, he gave me his address and was about to see the inside of the newly purchased Marshall mansion. Jim took my address and said that his driver would pick me up at the arranged time. How exciting.

I went for dinner just thinking that this was a one off, Jim's opportunity to thank me, and my opportunity to have a nose round the millionaire's house. What a perfectly wonderful time was had by all. Jim was a good cook and prepared chicken with asparagus and lyonnais potatoes. We had champagne and a lovely dessert. It was all very proper and Jim was the perfect gentleman. He even put the cork back into the unfinished champagne and told me to take the rest and have it for breakfast. At the end of the evening, John, Jim's driver arrived, I thanked Jim for a perfect evening and John drove me home. I never expected to hear from Jim again unless he happened to pop into the Cock Hotel when I was working.

So few weeks later, when my phone rang and it was Jim asking if I could accompany him to a charity event I was astonished. The event would be in London and as he was now divorced from the 3rd Mrs Marshall he didn't have a companion who could come to these types of events with him so he was asking if I would I like to. I explained I hadn't really got the wardrobe for this type of thing, but he told me not to worry, but to buy myself a nice evening dress and he would give the money back for it and any other accessories I might need. I was stunned but gratefully accepted and after the phone call I immediately telephoned my Mum. 'Oh my God, Mum you won't believe what's just happened' 'Jim Marshall, has asked me to accompany him to some charity event in London and has said that if I get an evening dress and all the gear, he'll give me the money back.' 'What will I get?' I shrieked. 'I'll send you some money', said Mum 'Make sure you get a good dress, go to House of Fraser or somewhere like that it'll be a posh do, if he's told you to get a nice evening dress'. So Mum sent me some money and I went shopping and got all organised for this 'do'. I got a midnight blue full length evening dress, with a split right up the side to the thigh, I've still got it now, it was absolutely gorgeous and more money than I'd ever spent on a dress before, I got matching shoes and a little purse, I was really excited.

A few days later I got all ready for the event. Jim arrived at my front door and said I looked lovely, he immediately handed me an envelope to reimburse my expenses, which I placed in my new evening clutch bag, he took my arm and led me to his limousine. I felt like a movie star, and I'll never forget the lovely time I had. Jim's friends were all from the entertainment business and this particular event was raising money for Jim's favourite charity the Variety Club and had lots of his 'star' friends attending. The now late Ernie Wise and his wife Silvia... Frankie Lane... Gloria Hunniford and her partner and also Jim's closest friends the wonderful Burt Weedon and his wife Maggie I seemed to remember Burt Weedon from the Basil Brush show, he played a guitar. Everyone was so kind to me. Even though at the back of my mind, I thought they must think I was some kind of gold digger. I was only 30... Jim was 42 years my senior and although the perfect gentleman, I wondered what everyone else thought I was doing. Little did I know that those thoughts would play on my mind an awful lot over the next few months?

# Chapter 42

## 1997 – The Frankfurt cuckoo clock

My next expedition with Jim was to a music show. This was very much like the Ideal Home Exhibition or the Motor Show at Earls Court. A massive exhibition of musical instruments and sound technology. It was in Frankfurt and I was absolutely thrilled to be invited.

After the excitement of being invited I realised I had better get a passport. With all the fuss of moving house I'd lost mine plus I had now changed my name, so I would need all my papers to show my new details.

I'd already got a copy of my birth certificate, but I needed a copy of my first marriage certificate when I married Paul. I also then needed the decree absolute from when we divorced and my subsequent marriage certificate for when I married Jimmy! I had my divorce papers so it was just the 2 marriage certificates I needed. I was still legally married to Jimmy so didn't have any divorce papers but I had my Statutory Declaration of name change. What a palaver? Life does get complicated.

Jim told me I could get the marriage certificates at Somerset House so that was our first stop. Jim's driver was going to take us to London in his limousine. James was now four and not in school yet so we took him along for the ride and John, Jim's driver took care of him in the car. Somerset House was a fantastic place; I could have stayed there all day looking up birth, marriage and death certificates of old relatives, but time was ticking on. I now had my documentation and we needed to head off.

Jim had arranged it all, I had an appointment at the old London passport office in Petite France just around the corner from Buckingham Palace and we arrived there in time for my appointment. It's a lot easier having a chauffeur driven limo than having to rely on buses and the tube.

I was so embarrassed having to use all of these documents just to get a passport. As a company director Jim had signed my photograph but it was the other paperwork. I had divorce papers dated 2nd September 1992 and a marriage certificate dated 9th October 1992 – what on earth did it look like?

Anyway after many raised eyebrows, the passport was issued and it would be ready in about 2 hours. In order to obtain a quick passport I had to state why I needed it so quickly and I am sure the passport staff thought I was going with Jim to do more than look just at the exhibition. After lunch we collected the passport. Frankfurt here we come!

I'd never flown with British Airways before and my experience in flying had always been budget airlines with package deals on holiday. As you can imagine Jim had booked us in Business class and we had the executive lounge to ourselves at Heathrow, free food, drinks, newspapers and magazines, I could get used to this.

It was only a short flight to Frankfurt, just about an hour and a half, but it was wonderful, we had lovely food and plenty to drink. Jim even bought me a lovely gold watch from the Stewardess. I am normally keen to get off the plane but this time I wanted the flight to take longer, the service was fantastic. When we arrived at our hotel in Frankfurt I was amazed. Jim had booked me a suite of my own. Not only did I have a triple-sized king-size bed, but a lounge area as well. The walls of the room weren't wallpapered. They had silk material on them and we were on the Penthouse level of the massive Marriott hotel, we had a fantastic view. Not that Frankfurt is a very nice to look at but all the same I was in awe of everything.

The three days we spent in Frankfurt whizzed by in a flash and I realised just how famous Jim was. At the music exhibition there were hundreds of people all queuing up getting Jim's autograph. Jim just smiled and was so gracious and he had time for everyone even though he must have been getting very tired signing autographs all day long. His signature is exactly the same as how it's written on his amps and I'd never realised that until that day. Later we had dinner with an old friend of Jim's who owned Zildjian the company that makes the cymbals for drum kits. Jim was a drummer himself and had a full kit of drums in his office in Bletchley. Jim's friend was charming and would steer the conversation away from the music industry whenever I started to look bored. He explained that the name 'Zildjian' literally means 'son of the cymbal-maker'.

'Zil' is the Turkish for 'cymbal'.

'-dji' is the Turkish suffix for 'maker'

'-ian' is the Armenian surname-forming suffix for 'son of'. He was a lovely fascinating man and I'll remember that dinner for ever.

My Great-Aunty Rita, my Nana's sister, had a cuckoo clock when I was little and I had been fascinated by it. Her son-in-Law Geoff was in the army and had brought it back from Germany many years ago where he had been stationed with her daughter Sue. They had also brought Cow bells and lots of other interesting German souvenirs but it was the cuckoo clock that always drew my attention when I visited her. I would always say to Aunty Rita 'please can we have the bird come out, and she would gently move the hands to the half-past or o'clock position to make the bird 'cuckoo'. I loved it.

I knew that cuckoo clocks were more usually from Switzerland but I was certain that I'd be able to buy one in Frankfurt so before we went home I was determined to find one. One afternoon when Jim was having his nap, I headed off out of the hotel. I had armed myself with a map from the concierge just in case I got lost.

A few minutes later I was entering a road called 'Kaiser Strasse' literally translated as King Street. I was amazed to find little old ladies who looked like they'd come from Eastern Europe and dressed like the Matryoshka Russian dolls, all sitting with babies in their arms on the pavement begging for money. It wasn't like this in Milton Keynes so I hurried on. Further along there were 'ladies' sitting in dimly lit shop windows wearing lots of make-up and very sexy underwear. As I walked on the pavements seemed to be full of men talking to more 'ladies' standing outside the shops. Now you may not believe this but I have led a very sheltered life and it took a long time for the penny to drop and for me to realise what was going on. I was almost running when at last I found a clock shop so I rushed through the door away from the unsavoury goings on in the street. The shop was amazing; it was full of cuckoo clocks. Some of them were immense, over four feet high with not only a bird popping out, but ladies, men and animals all dancing and spinning around when they chimed. They were fantastic but all I wanted was a cute little traditional one and I couldn't make them understand so I headed back to the hotel, past the 'ladies in the windows' and the begging Russian dolls.

Jim was wondering where I'd been and I told him. 'Dear child', he exclaimed 'The Kaiser Strasse is the 'red light district' you mustn't go there alone!'

'But I really want a cuckoo clock I've wanted one since I was a child' I said.

'OK, but I'll come with you, let's go and have a look' he replied.

So off we went back to the clock shop. As you can imagine Jim tried to persuade me to have the all-singing all-dancing, monstrosity, but I stuck to my original dream and we purchased a lovely little traditional clock. After all how on earth would I get one of the large ones home? I still have the little clock and it's a lovely reminder of my fantastic time with Jim in Frankfurt. All the local kids now say 'can we have the bird out Siân?' and I'm just like my Great Aunty Rita rotating the hands to make the bird come out of the clock for them.

# Chapter 43

## 1997 – The back seat of a limo

The charity events became a regular occurrence and it was really good fun, I now owned lots of beautiful evening dresses that Maggie Weedon had picked out for me and I was really getting into the swing of things. Jim's friends were all nice and although I still felt a bit awkward around them I was certainly enjoying the experience.

I was also getting used to being chauffeured around in the back of a limo – it was certainly the best mode of transport I'd ever had. Jim's limo was a huge stretch Volvo, with beautiful upholstered leather inside, very tasteful not like these huge white monstrosities you see for hen nights. I even got taken home from the hotel after work one evening; Lord only knows what my neighbours thought. I lived on a council estate and not many limousines pull up in our street. The children have even been taken to school on a couple of occasions in the limo, and what a sight that was pulling up outside Greenleys first school and a driver letting out my nine year old son Marc and eight year old daughter Kate. We definitely got some funny looks. But what a thrill it was to go shopping for new dresses in Oxford Street and Bond Street in London's West End, and not to have to drag the bags back home on the train, but to have a car and driver outside waiting to pick you up and help you with your things.

There was really only one downside to the limo, and that was John our driver insisted on travelling everywhere 'cross country'. I never really found out whether it was Jim or the driver who didn't like motorways, but cross country in a limo is a very strange experience for a couple of reasons.

The first is that if you have ever travelled in the back of a limousine you will realise that they are rather bouncy cars, they can travel fast but due to the size and shape I wouldn't have thought it should be recommended. You get thrown all over the place and a rather strange sensation of sea sickness prevails. The second maybe something to do with the amount of space you have and you're not as tightly packed into the back as you would be in an ordinary sized car, or whether the long wheel base of the vehicle creates this sensation I don't know, but all the same I've never been travel sick in a car before but I certainly felt a bit queasy in the back of that car.

Also due to the fact that we always travelled 'cross country' to our destinations and 'sat nav' wasn't about back then, we were invariably running late so John the driver always had his foot down. This made for an uncomfortable journey. As I mentioned earlier, I was usually nervous before these functions and often had a couple of glasses of wine or a shot or two of vodka before I left the house – just to steady my nerves of course. Maybe that's why I was queasy? Anyway we'd be in the back of the limo, careering at break-neck speed down a country road being thrown all over the place. Jim was very excitable at times and regularly got thrown across the seat and landed in my lap – grabbing any spare piece of my anatomy he could lay his hands on. The drink I has necked only added to the hilarity so by the time we reached our destinations, along with feeling slightly queasy I sometimes looked a tad dishevelled. Jim's antics were leaving me feeling a little more than uncomfortable.

The rest of the evening was a lovely affair the champagne flowed and I was a little too eager for a regular refill. The impending return journey playing slightly on my mind, only added to my willingness for another drink.

On another occasion we'd been to the Variety Club Ball at the Grosvenor Hotel in London's smart Mayfair. It was a wonderful event organised by the Lady Water-Rats. The aim was to raise money for 'Sunshine buses' for disabled children so that they could get out and about, and it was a charity that was dear to Jim. Just going through the entrance I saw a sight I'd never experienced before. There were gold statues of Greek style Gods all along the wall, it was only later I realised that these were real people spray painted gold and who were standing completely motionless. There were also real parrots everywhere it was completely amazing, a world away from the council estate I lived on in Milton Keynes. Velvet curtains parted, fire eaters blew flames from their mouths and trumpets sounded and we were ushered along to our table. The room was immense; there must have been a hundred round tables each sitting about a dozen guests. Each guest had a gift on their plate, the ladies had perfume and the gentlemen had cufflinks. Amazing waiting staff appeared and refilled glasses and brought out course after course of wonderful dishes.

My head was swimming. There was an auction of items, Jim bidded for a solid silver dressing-table set of mirror, comb and hair brushes for me and I've still got them now. There was a musical show with dancers, tumblers, acrobats and ballerinas, and various different celebrities said a few words. The whole show was lovely. I was absolutely stuffed with food and drink and getting more and more tired. How on earth did these people all seem so awake, had they been in bed all day long? They were all getting on, in their sixties and seventies but they could easily all out last me, I was flagging.

Then all of a sudden, the relentless waiting staff appeared with a cooked breakfast, it was 3 o'clock in the morning, and the whole evening was still in full swing and now breakfast was appearing, I'd drunk and eaten all I could manage and was praying for an end to the night. And thankfully at last it came. Off we all trouped to the car; air kisses all around us with the theatrical 'lovies' all wishing us a good night. I'll never know to this day how I made it to the car I was so drunk.

As we stepped out of the Grosvenor there was a sudden flashing of light bulbs, what was going on I thought. It seemed to be cameras flashing and voices shouting and I realised I had forgotten that all these people I was with were celebrities and entering and leaving events was all part of what they were used to. I was on the pavement side of the car and thank goodness the door was being opened. Everything was whizzing round but somehow I was inside the car. 'Oh no' I thought, ' I have to be sick'. A massive wave of nausea overcame me. I grabbed for the door handle and leaned out. All I remember is the flashing of cameras and me vomiting into the gutter.

Whether that photograph ever appeared in any magazines or newspapers I'm blissfully unaware, but I've always worried that those pictures one day might come to light. Let's hope this story doesn't become a best seller.

(Jim Marshall, me (centre) and friends)

# Chapter 44

## 1997 - A New Man

My Granddad died while I was at the London Variety Club Ball in March of that year and it hit me hard, it brought home to me just how old Jim was, he was a similar age to my Granddad, in fact they shared the same birthday - 29th July.

One day Marc who was nine years old by then came home and asked me an odd question. 'What's a prostitute Mum?' I was shocked he'd ask such a thing and I said 'Why are you asking Marc?' 'Well my friend's Mum said you must be a prostitute because you keep getting picked up in a limo'. I was astounded. Was that what my friends and neighbours thought? I was helping Jim with his charity work and although he bought me some lovely dresses and paid for everything, he was getting nothing in return other than my companionship.

I decided there and then that I wanted Jim's and my relationship to end and happily Jim found friendship a few months later with Silvia and I understand that they are now happily married.

I was still working in the Cock Hotel, after things had fizzled out with Jim and I was very relieved in some ways although I'd had a fabulous time with him.

One evening this gorgeous young man came into the hotel reception, I happened to be there waiting for the receptionist to return with cellar keys so I could change a barrel for the bar.

'Have you got any rooms available' the dark handsome man asked.

'I'm sure we have, but I'm from the bar, you'll need to wait for the receptionist she'll be back in a few seconds' I smiled back.

'Do you work in the bar then?'

'Yes' I replied.

'I'll be back later then, hope to see you' he gave me the most dazzling smile, his teeth were perfect, and he had a look of a young Tom Cruise.

Wow that blew me off my feet I thought as I headed back to the bar. I turned around to see him still smiling at me.

I'd almost forgotten about him but a couple of hours later, in he walked. He sat at the bar all evening, chatting to me as I served the customers. He was really nice and very good looking. I knew he was a bit younger than me, I was 31 and he looked about 25 to me. But we never mentioned our age.

A local was sat at the bar near to him. 'No point chatting her up' he said. 'Why's that?' the handsome stranger asked him. 'Everyone chat's her up, but she won't go out with anyone' he said and I laughed. 'Is that right then? You never go out with anyone who asks you?' 'Ha ha, no I don't' I laughed, 'most men who come in here are married, sometimes I see them take their rings off as they come in to the bar'. 'But it's not just that, you get a reputation if you're a barmaid who goes out with customers, so I've never bothered.'

'Won't you make an exception for me?' he asked suddenly, I was shocked. The local piped up 'You're wasting your time mate'. 'No he's not; I'm going to make an exception seeing as he's so cheeky'. I stunned myself with that response.

We both laughed out loud and later made arrangements to meet the next evening. I was off work the next night so I'd get Louise my lodger to babysit. I now knew the dark-haired stranger as Mark and I gave him my telephone number and soon after that he left. I had no idea if he was going to actually call me or not, or whether he was just flirting. Maybe he was just seeing if he could get me to say yes. I didn't know if he had a girlfriend or anything much about him apart from the fact he was from Brighton and he was working in the area for a few weeks.

I had been dating a man called Alan for a while, Dawn had introduced us, it was nothing serious and we just used to meet up now and again for a drink, he had a little boy called Daniel who was the same age as my Kate and all the kids used to play together, in fact I was more of a babysitter for Daniel when Alan had him for the weekends as he was separated from his wife. But we were good friends all the same.

Alan came around after work on his way home sometimes, he was bricklayer and he'd come for a cuppa. This particular day, he came round and I was all excited. 'I've got a date, I've got a date' I was shrieking. This chap Mark, asked me out last night and he's just called me to meet me tonight. Alan was pleased for me. I knew it wasn't going anywhere with Alan, and this confirmed it, as he was pleased I'd met someone else.

So I got ready and met Mark. We had a great night, we never stopped talking and laughing, it never occurred to ask Mark how old he was as we got on so perfectly

211

well. Later that very night he came back to my house with all his stuff, and moved straight in with me and my children and my lodger Louise. We were mad about each other; I can probably say that Mark was the love of my life. We had our ups and downs, and I never really felt that his Mum thought I was what she had hoped for him. Well that's not entirely true, she liked me and was extremely kind to me, and we are still friends today but I was 31, twice divorced with 3 children from 2 different marriages, and I wasn't having any more children either. Whereas her son was only 21, which I only found out a few weeks later after meeting his family who were Italian Catholics. I wasn't exactly what she had hoped for her only son.

# Chapter 45

## 1997 - The 3 Amigos

I was really excited! My first foreign holiday since my honeymoon with my first husband six years earlier, we'd even had to take the children to that, Marc was two and Kate was only a year old, and as we'd already split up in the time between the wedding and honeymoon, we only went together because the holiday was paid for, so not a good time was had by all. But this was going to be different, it was the first 'girls-only' holiday I had ever had.

Louise and Julie, my friends and I had booked a fortnight in Ibiza. It was going to be fantastic, I'd paid the deposit, and we had about £500 each to pay 6 weeks before we travelled.

I shouldn't have been surprised but a mere seven weeks before we were due to go, Louise and Julie backed out, and I was left to pay the full balance and go on my own, which was one and a half grand – I could have gone to Barbados for that and seen my Mum's honeymoon photos for real. So I needed some stand-ins to take the girls' places or lose my deposit.

Who could I ask? Well it was simple really, the only two people you can depend on who have some disposable income – your parents! So John and Mum it was!

'Mum have you booked your holidays yet?' I tentatively asked over the telephone.

'Not yet why?' Came her reply.

'Well Julie and Louise have backed out of our holiday to Ibiza and I wondered if you and John fancied coming instead so I don't lose my deposit?' I laughed thinking of Mum and John in San Antonio.

'Ibiza?' 'Oh love me and John are too old for all that raving and gawd knows what that goes on there'

'Oh come on Mum, it's just a Spanish holiday island, we don't have to go clubbing' 'The place was there long before 'Pacha', 'Amnesia' and 'Es Paradis'

'Eh?'

'That's just the names of the clubs' 'Will you just think it over with John and see what he says' It's all booked and I've paid the deposit, you'll just need five hundred quid each, it's half board so the food is sorted, then your spend'

'OK I'll see what John thinks and we'll let you know'.

So that's how it went. Strangely enough John was up for it. As an Engineer in the Merchant Navy, John had been around the world at least five times, and there were very few places on planet earth he'd never visited, or in fact been thrown out of. But Ibiza was one of the places he'd never seen.

It was all arranged Marc and Kate were going to their Dad's place in the Isle of Man. Mark my now live in boyfriend and Louise were staying at home and were going to look after James. Mum and John came to stay with me the night before and we left for Gatwick the following morning. Mark drove us. On the plane I decided to buy a few drinks to get the holiday off to a good start and tucked my purse into the seat pocket in front of me just for safe keeping. It was quite a raucous flight with lots of party go-ers all getting ready for the fortnight of their lives.

We eventually arrived at our hotel and it was lovely, right on the beach with a beautiful pool it was just like the brochure which was surprising, we did get a few funny looks checking in where the average age in the lobby was seventeen. But we didn't care we were on holiday and the sun was shining.

I'd forgotten that Julie, Louise and I were going on the cheap and had a room between us, three single beds in one room. Mum and John must have wondered what they were coming to, but we all mucked in. John by the wall, Mum in the middle and me by the window. After all we wouldn't be spending the holiday in the room. We had an en-suit bathroom so Mum was happy.

So next we went out to the pool Mum and John intended to spend a lot of time relaxing, I fancied a boat trip as per usual and there seemed to be lots of entertainment on at the hotel so Mum was happy too. I just needed to find my purse so I could get some more to drink by the pool, where on earth had I put it?

'Muuuuuuuuum!!!!!!!' I screeched.

'She's probably seen a cockroach, John' 'She hates the things from when she was at the swimming baths' Mum said to John.

'It's in the seat pocket' I yelled, on the plane' 'All my traveller's cheques' 'what will I do'

'What's she on about?' John muttered

'Oh you daft idiot, I told you to slow down on the drink when we were on the plane' Mum yelled back at me.

'Don't worry Pat, if it's Travellers Cheques, she can get them replaced', John assured us. We'll give you some money now, and you can pay us back. We'll never get them now, it's a Saturday, but we'll go and find an American Express shop in the main town, they have them everywhere and they'll replace your Travellers Cheques straight away.

'Oh John, thank goodness you were with us, I'd never know what to do' I said as my panic subsided.

'Well he's been round the world five times, Siân, of course he knows what to do' Mum retorted.

So panic over, we could relax, John was taking charge of the situation. We headed off to the pool and I clutched the 500 pesetas that John had loaned me, Lord I needed a drink.

So about eight vodka and cokes and a large jug of sangria later I was quite, well actually very squiffy and so was Mum, John had knocked back a few San Miguels and we were enjoying the sun.

I was desperate for a good tan and intended to spend as much time by the pool as I could. Mum had bought us these new fangled swimming costumes that were a kind of mesh, you couldn't see through them but apparently you could tan through them, so we were giving them a try. So far so good. We had the camera out, and Mum and I were taking very amusing pictures of each other diving onto lilos in the pool.

John spent most of his time wandering around finding the local paper shop and getting to know the locals.

It was about 7pm when we eventually left the pool to head back to change for dinner.

I was certainly feeling a lot worse for wear, but was deter-mined to have a nice evening.

The restaurant, or rather canteen, was a decorated in a 70s style, there was masses of salad, risotto, fish, pasta, paella and cold meats, it was self-service but you could help yourself to as much as you liked. There was hot food too, mostly curry, chips or rice. But it was good food and we enjoyed it. I helped myself to more sangria.

'Slow down on that stuff, it's cheap and you'll have a terrible head' Mum warned.

'We're on our holidays Mum' 'Let's have a good time' I took no notice of her advice.

That evening we decided not to stay in for the entertainment but go out to a local bar, where there was an act on.

So we sat through a comedian, then a banjo player and a couple of games of bingo, and I knocked back a few Bacardi's along with Mum.

The next morning a expected, I was feeling pretty rough and decided to have no more to drink but I was going to spend the whole day by the pool, I was running out of peseta's anyway so needed to hang on to what I'd got. The sun beat down all day, but I was pretty quiet and mostly fell asleep by the pool, Mum and John went out for lunch and left me to it.

By the evening, I resembled a lobster, and the tan through costume had been lashed it definitely didn't work, but I was covered in tiny red spots where the sun had gone through and burned me, I was just hoping they'd all spread out and cover me completely in a few days. We had a quiet night in after dinner listening to a Frank Sinatra tribute, which was quite good.

The next day was Monday and we had to head off to the old town to find the American Express office where I could get my money back for my Traveller's Cheques. Luckily I'd listened to John and got them in the first place and safely put the counterfoils with the numbers on them into my case before leaving for our holiday. So I had the proof and my passport. John had found out where the place was and we headed off on the bus just before lunch. It was absolutely roasting inland, the temperature was up into the high 30s and it was sweltering. I was feeling worse and worse as we got there. To make matters even worse when we eventually found the place it was closed. It seemed to be siesta and they wouldn't be open until 4pm. So we wandered around the shops that were open then found some shade to sit in.

'She doesn't look very good John' Mum said.

'No bloody wonder the way she was putting it away over the last few days'

'Oh don't row, please, I can't stand it' I moaned

'Well it's your own fault, you always have to go mad, John's right' Mum snapped back.

'Yes you're right, I'll not bother with any more drink and we'll have a nice time, once we sort my cheques out'

Eventually it was time to go back to the shop and we got the replacement Travellers Cheques, and headed back on the bus to our hotel.

Spanish buses are not the most conducive mode of transport to aid in the recovery of a hangover, and by the time I got back to the hotel, I was rather green around the gills.

'Go and lie by the pool and rest' Mum advised.

'I think she's got sunstroke, by the look of her' John said

'All that bloody drink and laying in the heat all day long, she never wears a hat and the sun on the back of her neck in that heat today has only added to it'

John of course knew exactly what he was talking about; I did in fact have sunstroke and spent the rest of the next few days swaying in and out of consciousness either by the pool under an umbrella or in doors.

But luckily by the beginning of the second week I was all better and was excited by the prospect of this boat trip we had booked.

The trip was to take us around the island on a pleasure cruise, there was sangria to be had, and then we stopped in a small beautiful cove where the water was crystal clear. We would then set off and disembark from the boat and have a barbeque by a swimming pool with lots of games. This was all hosted by the reps and looked like jolly good fun.

When we arrived in the beautiful cove the reps threw bottles of champagne into the water and everyone was invited to dive off the boat and down to recover a bottle which you could keep if you got it. This should be easy for an ex lifeguard I thought. I'd get down there for the lot! Hmmm not as easy as I thought, I just couldn't get down that far, both Mum and I had done quite a bit of scuba diving and I was an excellent swimmer but could we get those bottles? Could we hell!

John advised us that it was a scam and that they dropped them off in a location where they knew no-one would be able to get them; he swore he saw a frog-man in scuba gear later retrieving them all.

Soon we were disembarking from the boat and enjoying a lovely lunch of huge sardines and beef tomatoes. All cooked fresh by chefs at the side of the pool. Now it was time for fun and games. As usual I had put away quite a lot of sangria, but luckily so had Mum and John so they weren't complaining about me. Mum and John just relaxed and watched everyone else. They were mostly teenagers and singles in their early twenties and they were having competitions which mostly involved throwing each other into the pool. There was a Spanish compare chap who seemed to be organising all of this.

There were a few young families also with children and watching them all diving and jumping into the pool made me miss my own children and I wished they'd been there with me. As we were sitting by the pool 3 young kids about 10 years old or so, were trying to tempt each other to back dive and somersault into the pool, they were just in front of where we were sitting.

'Go and show 'em how it's done' Mum yelled to me. The children all looked around in our direction. I was blood red in the face.

'Go on Siân, she used to be a lifeguard', Mum hollered 'she'll show you how to back dive and somersault' Mum laughed to the kids.

'Will you?' one asked?

'Oh go on then' I smiled back to them. And I spent the afternoon back diving and somersaulting to much applause from the kid's parents and most of the kids around us joined in. Everyone was very surprised to see how well I did it. Mum and John roared with laughter.

220

Later it was time for beach volley ball and Mum had drunk quite a few sangria's now and was eager to join in too. We were divided into teams, boys versus girls and there were about forty aside. It was just for fun and we hardly got to touch the ball there were so many people playing. The whole day was great fun and at the end of the game of volley ball, they were taking photos of everyone. All the girls lined up and I was really giddy after all the drink and diving in the pool and as they took the pictures all the girls, me included lifted their bikini tops and screamed 'TITS' out loud. It was all in good fun.

Now it was time to get back on the boat and head back to San Antonio. As we disembarked we could buy photographs of everyone that the photographer had taken during the day. On sale also was a video. I hadn't noticed anyone with a camcorder but Mum decided she wanted to buy this, to see if we were on it at all. 'You might be on it doing back dives into the pool with those kids' Mum said. So she got a copy.

The last few days were lovely and we spent the days by the pool, and the evenings either watching the hotel entertainment or going out to see Mum's favourites which were drag acts in various local bars.

Soon it was time to leave the clubbing capital of Europe. After our plane landed and I was sure I had all my belongings, Mark and little James picked us up from Gatwick airport I was so excited to see them both, and Mark thought I looked lovely with my tan. Mum and John had left their car at our house and were staying overnight and then driving back to St Helens the next day. Paul had arrived at my house with Marc and Kate to bring them home and Louise my lodger was there as well.

So we all settled down for a nice take away in the evening. 'Let's watch that video' Mum shrieked. 'You

221

know the one from the boat trip, I'll get it out of my case' she said. So we all sat in front of the telly and watched. Every so often there was a little flash of green bikini, that was me, then you saw me diving full pelt off the boat to try and get a bottle of champagne, oh there was Mum, waving from the water as I came up again empty handed. Then a full shot of Mum's bottom as she turned to try with vain to dive down. 'Oh get it off, look at the size of me', Mum wailed. We were all shrieking laughing. The camera moved around and all of a sudden there was me back diving into the pool. 'Look at your Mum James' John said. Then we were at the volley ball. 'Oh no' I screamed. 'Get it off, turn it off' I pleaded. I hadn't seen the camera man whilst we were playing volley ball, but I knew what was coming next. 'No leave it on, I want to watch' Mark replied. There it was for all to see. My huge boobs right in the middle of the shot as I lifted my bikini top with all the other girls, the cheeky cameraman had zoomed in on me. How embarrassing in front of my current boyfriend, my ex husband and my children. On this particular occasion, what goes on in Ibiza didn't stay in Ibiza, now everyone saw me making a fool of myself. But they all laughed, I was completely mortified and I think the kids were slightly stunned.

# Chapter 46

## 1998 – A proper job!

Well my prospects of getting a job as a dolphin trainer now seemed pretty remote, my career to date had started in a swimming pool which was about as close as I was going to get to dolphins and for the last seven years had been very varied from working in pubs and hotels to delivering pizzas and working in a local shop, but as I had 3 young children and my youngest James was still under 5 and not at school full time I was limited in what I could do. Mostly I could only work in the evenings as it was easier then to find a babysitter. My latest job was to be working as a PA to a Managing Director for a local technology company. It sounded grander than it was and I had sort of fallen into it. I was working behind the bar in the Cock Hotel when one of the regulars, Ian, mentioned that he was looking for a part-time secretary. 'I can type' I announced. 'And I'm looking for a job during office hours once James goes to school full time next month' I went on.

'Really? You know how to operate a computer and you can type properly?' Ian asked. 'Yeah of course' I lied. 'What's involved what do you need someone to do?'

Ian started to go on about schematic diagrams using AutoCAD and working with 'Office' whatever that was. Also involved would be answering the phone, making sales calls and managing his diary. I had actually never even switched on a computer, but I had played solitaire in my Mum's office on her computer once so I continued to nod in all the right places when he talked about the various duties. I told him about going to secretarial college when I left school which was true and he seemed pleased when I mentioned my typing speed. When Granddad had died he left me a bit of money and I had been thinking of buying a computer. I told Ian this and it was arranged that as part of what his company offered was building computers he'd let me have one at cost price.

So it was all arranged, the following month I'd be starting a new job as Ian's PA. All very grand and I was looking forward to it.

I dropped James off at school on his first day and arrived at Ian's offices and workshop at the back of Stony Stratford High Street at around 9.30am. After the obligatory introductions to everyone else who worked there and we had cups of coffee, Ian sat me down in front of his very high tech looking PC. He showed me some examples of schematic diagrams he had created in AutoCAD. They were basically maps or diagrams of offices showing where all the windows, doors, desks and PCs were located and where all the network points would be installed when he did the work for his customers. This was the type of thing he wanted me to create. I sheepishly explained that I had never used such sophisticated software as AutoCAD and he said that, this was OK he hadn't expected that I had, and I could create them in PowerPoint and eventually he'd train me how to use the other software.

PowerPoint? I wonder what that is, I thought. But Ian opened the application and told me to copy what was on the paper in front of me using the drawing tools in PowerPoint. I picked up the mouse and looked at it. Ian looked stunned. I put it back down and tried to make it land on things, I was right clicking and left clicking but the mouse wouldn't land on anything. I couldn't drag or drop I didn't have a clue.

'You've never used a computer before have you Siân?' Ian gently asked. 'No not really' I said. But quickly replied 'I can really type quickly though Ian'. He opened up another application called Word and said 'Ok show me'. 'Dictate to me then Ian, say anything and I'll type' I was more confident now. Ian looked doubtful, but I was raring to go. As Ian started speaking... 'Dear Mr Jones... I am writing to complain...' My fingers moved quickly over the keys, I could keep up with him no matter how quickly he spoke, and I could see he was impressed.

'OK then, you can have a month's trial. I'll show you the whole Microsoft Office Suite' he went on 'If you can pick it up in a month, the job is yours. It was daunting but I was determined. Ian built me a computer and I was absolutely thrilled with it. It cost eight hundred pounds was fully loaded with Windows 95 and Microsoft Office. The hard drive had a capacity of 250 megabytes which was huge at the time, but is absolutely laughable now as my mobile phone has a capacity of 16 gigabytes. I practiced the skills Ian was teaching me during the day every evening when I got home.

I got the job permanently with Ian and worked there part time between 9.30 and 12.30 for about 6 months, fitting it in with James, Kate and Marc going to school. I was still working at the Cock Hotel part-time a few evenings a week, but what I really wanted was something more permanent where I could progress. Ian's place really was just a temporary thing to help him get his business organised and he didn't have the capacity for anything full time. So I started looking around. I noticed an advertisement for a receptionist

225

in Wolverton Mill, which was really close by to where I lived and in fact walking distance. It was almost full-time the hours were 9am to 3pm and that was perfect with the kids being in school.

The company was called Sanders & Sidney which sounded like a firm of solicitors to me, but the advert said they were an Outplacement organisation, whatever outplacement was, I'd never heard the term before. I needed to send off my CV to someone called Celia and provide a covering letter. These were things I'd never had to do before so I did some research on my new computer.

I was connected to the Internet but this was a dial-up connection back then, and the Internet was still in its relative infancy as far as mainstream users were concerned. I found a website which talked about the perfect CV and found a template in my Microsoft Office programme called a resumé which seemed to be the same thing as a CV. I've always been quite fussy about how things are laid out, even back in the days of my secretarial college, I always made sure bullet points were perfectly aligned and margins even, and the spacing in my letters was accurate. So with all this in mind I decided to create my perfect CV. Little did I know that Sanders & Sidney were in the CV production business themselves and my CV would be critically scrutinised. I got a bit carried away and although the layout was very good and nicely lined up, I put my name in a blaze of colours across the top in a fancy font. I cringe now at the thought of the thing.

Well a couple of weeks later, I was at home one evening in my nightdress watching TV when the telephone rang, it was a chap announcing himself as Roy Eaton and he was Client Services Manager at Sanders & Sidney, and would I have time for a short telephone interview for the role I had applied for? Oh hell, I wasn't prepared for this, I'd never had a telephone interview in my life and never been scrutinised in my nightdress either, not that Roy knew at the time but I certainly felt vulnerable in my attire. It was a bit like a surreal dream where you wake up naked in a crowded shopping centre and everyone is looking.

Anyway Roy asked me questions about my skills and experience also he told me a bit about the role, by the end of the call I felt like I'd stumbled through and sounded as I was, completely unprepared. So imagine my surprise a few days later when I get a letter inviting me to a formal interview. I met Roy in the flesh so to speak and also the Managing Consultant Celia, who was very nice as well. I must have had a good interview, because a day or so later Celia invited me back to offer me the job, I've never forgotten her words. 'Siân you had the least qualifications and experience of everyone we invited to interview, but after seeing such a colourful CV like yours I just had to meet you'. She went on to say that I'd had a very nice interview and they were going to take a chance on me as they felt that I fitted in with the culture of the organisation. I was thrilled and immediately accepted.

I've now been with the organisation for 12 years it has changed its name to Penna and I have had about four different roles but it's the best place I have ever worked! And my colleagues are the best I've ever had!

# Chapter 47

## 1998/9 – A New Year's Eve to remember

It had been ten years since the horror of my first husband Paul's accident on that fateful New Year's Eve when I was pregnant having my first son Marc, and I was still not really one for celebrating New Years Eve. Mark and I were settling in for a quiet night when suddenly our Sue called on the phone – 'Happy New Year' she shrieked. 'I thought I'd call you now before the telephone lines all get jammed at midnight' she went on, sounding slightly worse for wear already, and it was only 9.30.

'Where are you?' I asked.

'Allan and Nigel's, they're having a house party you should have come, Mum and John are here too'. 'Yeah I wish we had come, we're stuck in with the kids watching telly' I replied 'We couldn't get a babysitter'. There was another shriek and Sue screamed her goodbyes with Mum in the background yelling 'we love you'.

I put the phone down and realised how much I was missing my family.

'We should have gone up to Mum's for New Years' I moaned to Mark, 'They're all at a party round Allan and Nigel's, it'll be a right scream, you know what those two are like.'

Allan and Nigel are my Mum's two gay friends, who live round the corner in Birchfield Street. My Mum's street is on a 1970's housing estate where the houses are all terraced or semi-detatched and mostly small 3 bedroom town houses with little back gardens or yards. It's not the type of street where anyone could fit a swimming pool in the back garden let alone afford one. But Allan and Nigel are the campest pair you could ever meet and they have made their house very special. They decided they wanted a huge jacuzzi bath-come-shower with built in sounds system, and had to have the staircase removed and the upstairs window taken out just to get it in. But the best thing about their house is the swimming pool in the back garden. Now this pool isn't your average blow up kids affair, oh no. This is the real deal, with a filter system, a pump and a heater all installed in the garden shed. It's huge and almost fills the whole back garden; I bet you can see the damn thing on Google Earth.

'Well let's go up there then' Mark piped up.

'It's nearly 9.30 now, we'll never get there in time for midnight' I said but in my mind I was working out if we could actually make it.

Mark could see I was thinking about it 'I bet we could make it if you put *your* foot down on the motorway' he went on 'It's only 160 miles away and the motorway will be empty.' '*My* foot down?' I queried with him. 'Well I've had a couple of cans now so it'll have to be you', he replied.

I was still unsure, 'But the kids aren't ready, and what will we do with the dogs we can't leave them over night'.

'Come on Siân live a little, it'll be a laugh, Allan and Nigel are a scream, and your Mum and Sue will be made up if we surprise them'. Mark was now keen for us to go and said 'What's the alternative, sit here all night watching Clive James on our own?'

It was sounding all the more appealing, so in less than 5 minutes, the kids were dressed and in the back of a convertible Ford Escort, which I had actually bought from Nigel a few months earlier. Now we had to get the dogs in on top of the kids and this wasn't going to be easy as we had two very large and heavy Great Danes that were all legs and Max just wanted to play. Well we eventually did it but it was all a bit of a squash. 'Ah my leg, get off me Max' screamed Marc, 'She's got her nose in my face Mum' moaned Kate about Silk our other dog, 'Well' Marc went on, 'Her bum is in my face' 'He's farting on me Mum' complained James. That was the general conversation for the next 160 miles. In the end Mark had to get James on his knee in the front, just to make more room. I was fine as I was driving.

So off we went, only six miles to junction fourteen of the M1 motorway. Then it was motorway all the way to St Helens. The M1 and M6 can be daunting they are always full of traffic. But I couldn't believe it. Nothing on the M1, and I'd only seen three lorries and no cars at all on the M6, we were over half way there and we hadn't been going an hour yet. We'd averaged 110 mph all the way so far, god only knows how the car managed it with three kids, two adults and two Great Danes, but we were flying along, ignoring the yells from the back as dogs shifted position and Kate constantly asking to stop at services for the loo.

We were now on the M62 and only fifteen miles away, we had half an hour to spare we were going to make it before midnight. The party was only a short five minute drive from junction seven of the M62 so we would definitely make it.

'Hurry up Mum' moaned Marc, 'I think Max needs a wee, he won't sit still' 'Nearly there' I prayed that we wouldn't arrive with my kids soaked in dog pee.

And we didn't. We screeched to a halt outside Allan and Nigel's to find the party was in full swing, the house was jumping. We dashed across the road and into the house, kids, dogs and all. Allan and Nigel had about five Yorkshire Terriers along with a Poodle called Blackie, and it could have got messy, but thank goodness their dogs along with their cats were safely locked in an upstairs bedroom.

Mum and Sue nearly fainted as we waltzed into the front room. 'I wash jusht shpeaking to you on the phone where were you, I thought you were at home?' a drunken puzzled Sue asked. 'We were, we just drove here, an hour and three-quarters and we've made it in time for midnight, just to see you lot'. So all the hellos and hugs and kisses from Mum were over and we just had drinks thrust into our hands in time for midnight, when the next sight I saw was one of the most comical moments I can remember.

Goodness knows what Glen was doing on the sofa with Allan, Glen is another neighbour of Mum's and friends with Allan and Nigel. Glen and his wife are a bit strange and affectionately known as the 'fatties', they remind us of the 'Go-Lightley's' the hugely overweight family that advertised Benson's beds in the early 80s. Anyway whatever was going on with Allan on the sofa Nigel certainly didn't like it and he came screaming out of the kitchen in his mincing way armed with a very large chocolate gateaux. It was going to be handbags at dawn. Well gateaux at midnight at the very least.

Nigel hurtled towards Glen with the gateaux and it was flung like a comedy custard pie, right into the face of the unsuspecting Glen

Everyone was hysterical; we'd never seen anything so funny in our lives. Sue snorted her Bacardi and coke out of her nose she was laughing so hard. The dogs were bounding in all directions and trying to scoff the gateaux. It was certainly worth that 110 mile per hour drive of 160 miles in less than an hour and forty-five minutes just to see Nigel armed with his gateaux. . We never found out what had upset Nigel so much, just as well I suppose.

# Chapter 48

## 2000 – Great Danes

The sun was beating down and I decided I needed to be out-doors soaking up the rays. 'Let's take the kids and the dogs to Caldecotte Lake' I suggested to Mark my soon to be husband. So we loaded our kids and two Great Danes into the back of our BMW estate and headed off to the lake.

Now for a local history lesson. Caldecotte Lake was a small farm pond that has been expanded to be part of the series of flood control lakes in Milton Keynes. These 'balancing lakes' have become wildlife havens in the city and are now used for water sports and leisure activities. The name 'Caldecotte' is thought to come from the term 'Cold Cottage', a basic travellers shelter often found in remote and lonely places. When the lake was excavated in 1982 they found the remains of a roman village and bits of a dinosaur skeleton. The skeleton is from a 165 million year old sea creature called an Ichthyosaur and it is now on display at Milton Keynes Library.

We had been to the lake many times before and as it is away from the road, the dogs are fine to be let off their leads. If you've ever met a Great Dane you will know that they are the gentle giants of the dog world, really good with children and no problem with other dogs. The biggest problem is how people react to them because they can look a bit scary due to their size and the fact that they can look menacing when they come bounding towards you to make friends.

As I said earlier we had two Great Danes. Silk was a brute of a dog thirteen and a half stone in weight and at about ten years old then, she was a quite old for a Great Dane. She was black in colour and was previously Mark's dog when he lived in Brighton, Mark announced shortly after we decided to move in together that the dog at his Mum's house was actually his and she'd be coming too, that was quite a shock at the time! Silk was very gentle and we loved her to bits. We actually thought she was on her way out a couple of years earlier, so we decided to get a puppy so that when she did die, it wouldn't be so bad for the children. But when we bought Max, at 12 weeks old, Silk seemed to get a new lease of life and perked up and had carried on for a couple more years. We thought Silk was big but Max was huge. If Max stood on his hind legs and puts his front paws on your shoulders he was over 7 feet in height, no wonder some people are afraid of them.

So picture the scene. It was a boiling hot summer day – hundreds of kids and families all playing on the grass at the side of the lake. There is a new pub, built like a windmill, so people had spread out on the grass having a drink and playing with their kids, it's a really nice place for families.

We arrived at the car park next to the pub and opened the back of the car. Two hot and thirsty Great Danes dashed out and headed to the lake, they had been before so knew that it was play time. Max was splashing in the shallows, when all of a sudden there was an almighty scream; we turned to see mild mannered, gentle Silk dragging a swan out of the bull rushes at the side of the lake. The swan was beating its wings trying to escape but Silk had got it by the throat and wasn't letting go.

Children were crying, Mums and Dads were hysterical. Max was oblivious to all this and realised that as no one was taking any notice of him he would proceed to take the biggest dump I had ever seen in the middle of all this mayhem. Everyone was shouting, my children were crying and Mark was up to his knees in water at the edge of the lake trying to separate Silk and the swan. To add to the confusion I was up to my elbows in Max's dog poo, trying to get this smelly steaming mountain into a very large carrier bag without the aid of a shovel or gloves.

Mark eventually managed to free the swan from Silk's jaws but it's didn't look in good shape, so I suggested putting it out of its misery. Other Dads were phoning the police and the calm of the sunny afternoon had completely evaporated. Reluctantly Mark held the swan's head under water for what seemed to be an eternity, and eventually the noise and the thrashing stopped. Then we heard the distant wail of a siren, here we go again, why is it always us in trouble? I thought to myself.

The crowds were keen to point the finger and the police soon had enough evidence to arrest the 'murderers' so we were carted off to the local police station for our own safety as the crowd was starting to get nasty. The kids were crying and I think they thought that they are going to be beheaded because all swans belong to the Queen and she always has people beheaded when she isn't happy.

When the police listened to the story they realised it was a tragic accident so apart from a ticking off and a 'keep those damn things on a lead' warning we were allowed to go home. We all piled back in to the car to be greeted by the smell from the carrier bag full of Max poo, the hot weather hadn't helped. We never went back to Caldecotte Lake ever again.

# Chapter 49

## 2000 – 3$^{rd}$ Time Lucky

Mark and I had quite a stormy relationship at first, what he had failed to tell me for some weeks was his age, I just assumed he was about 25 a few years younger than me, what transpired was that he was in fact 21! A full ten years younger than me. But all in all we got on quite well, he was quite fiery as was his Italian nature, but he was a kind and decent young man, and worked hard which was important to me. I used to tell my friends I wasn't looking for a father for my children I was looking for a playmate! He was always on the Playstation with them and for someone so young he really was a good Dad to them all.

Mark and I actually split up for about 3 months in 1999 but when we got back together Mark proposed on one knee in a restaurant in front of his Mum, Dad and sisters, I was gobsmacked. Although I declined his proposal at the time, and I'm sure his Mum breathed a sigh of relief, one day when we were drunk in the famous Cock Hotel, he asked me again and I said 'Yes, so long as we can get married on 29$^{th}$ July, on my Granddad's birthday, here at the Cock'. I hoped they wouldn't have a vacancy, but they did so it was all arranged.

It was the morning of my now third marriage and we were getting ready, Sue was my maid of honour once again, and at every opportunity she was spouting the famous saying 'three times the bridesmaid never the bride' but she was in a right flap, we were supposed to be all organised and we'd arranged to put the dogs into kennels so that we could all get ready in peace. However when Mark returned home the day before with the dogs still in tow, it transpired that they wouldn't take the dogs as we didn't' have their latest injection certificates to prove they were fully vaccinated. It was too late now to get them from the vet's. So we now had to cope with getting ready with two giant great Danes bouncing around. Neil, Sue's boyfriend was driving along with Allan and Nigel who were coming down from St Helens, everyone else had arrived the day before and had booked into hotels in Stony Stratford, and Sue kept looking at the clock wondering where Neil was, this was all adding to her tension. She'd got Kate, Marc and James ready and they all looked beautiful, despite the fact that James had decided to cut his fringe off the night before, so I had to spike up his hair with masses of hair gel so that it wouldn't show in the photographs.

Just as we are about to leave for the register office, we realised that the dogs were missing! I was in my wedding gown, Sue in her cream bridesmaid dress along with the other bridesmaids we were running around the estate trying to herd the dogs back. Silk was actually bounding full speed along the H2 main road causing cars to swerve in all directions, but eventually we got them back. Sue looked slightly bedraggled and hadn't managed to get her own make-up on and she looked close to tears.

The bridesmaids, Sue, Kate and Demi, who was Mark's youngest sister all piled in the Rolls, Harry my next door neighbour insisted on travelling in the front with the chauffeur leaving his poor wife Carole to jump in to someone else's car and off they went. I now had a few moments on my own with John before the Rolls Royce came back for me. John was really pleased for me that at last things were finally working out and I was so glad that he was going to give me away.

We eventually had a beautiful wedding at the register office and later in Stony Stratford for the reception and evening party. John paid for the reception and all the champagne which was wonderful. I had a proper wedding dress, the first one I'd had even though this was my third time. I even got to travel there in a Rolls Royce, which had been my dream, I still had nightmares about my other journeys the first wedding in Arthur Daley's Jag, and the second in Jimmy's XR3i where he drove like Sterling Moss. My neighbours Carole and Harry had paid for the Rolls as a wedding present and it was fabulous. Neil arrived just in the nick of time with Allan and Nigel who liked to make an entrance at the last minute, Sue breathed a sigh of relief.

Mark and his best man Andy looked stunning and Mark cried when we said our vows and both our mothers did too. At last this was the perfect wedding and I was sure it was going to be third time lucky for me. I was now Siân Allen. I had successfully worked my way up the alphabet from Williams to Knight to Hayes to Banks and then to Allen. This was my fifth surname and I had no intention of changing it again. This was to be happy ever after

Carole and Harry lived in the bungalow next door to me. Harry was a funny one sometimes – he spent a lot of his time speaking in tongues, he called it his Israeli language, which was interspersed with Portuguese. I think he liked to say things to Carole that no-one else understood. Harry insisted that he was Israeli he wore a star of David around his neck and he told everyone who would listen that he'd been a mercenary in the Israeli Army, chopping people's heads off and the like but I don't think anyone believed him. His name was Harry Felton and he'd grown up in London, so I don't know where this strange story came from. He and Carole had run a bar in Portugal for a while so that's where the Portuguese came from. Anyway no-one took much notice as he was a kind chap too. But when the speeches where going on Carole kept raising her hand and getting out of her seat until she couldn't contain herself any longer and she insisted to Mark that Harry be thanked for providing the Rolls Royce. Everyone was stunned. Harry and Carole where getting a mention just the same as everyone else in our thanks but nobody had jumped up requesting this. He also insisted that he wanted a steak for his meal and not chicken like everyone else and had been up to the restaurant to change his order. Nobody was too bothered, except that my Dad was paying and he hadn't asked.

Apart from that the whole day went off without a hitch. The evening party was to be held in the marquee suite at the Cock Hotel, 'Cueball' and Jim from the black thunder at the local Horizon radio station were the DJs. Jim now runs a local disco company bookmeadisco.com and is very successful. Jim's Dad Chris used to own the Cock Hotel and Jim was also a resident DJ there and a good friend of ours. Everyone had gone back to their rooms to change for the evening, and Sue was blowing up balloons she'd got a tank of helium from somewhere, these were for the function room and she was also making table decorations. When everyone came down to the party we were surprised to see that Mum wasn't with us yet, and neither was John. I asked Sue and a few others but no-one had seen them. I guessed they were tired as we'd swilled a good few bottles of champagne in the afternoon perhaps they were having a snooze.

Eventually Mum and John turned up. But Mum had a big cut across her nose. 'What on earth happened to you' I asked. 'Everyone has been worried where you were'. 'Oh don't ask' came John's reply, 'She's bent over washing her hands, god only knows how but she's head-butted the sink and nearly knocked herself out' I was shrieking laughing, but Mum was not finding it funny. The rest of the evening went off without any mishaps and everyone had a thoroughly fabulous time.

(My 3rd time)

# Chapter 50

## 2000 – Wee willy winky

My family loved Mark and we all got on like a house on fire, we spent a lot of time on motorways, his family was in Brighton and mine in Liverpool and it was almost equidistant between the two so we visited them every other month or so. On one occasion we were staying at my sister's flat in St Helens Junction. Mark was a bit worse for wear having been on the 'pop' all afternoon. We were sharing Sue's sofa and the kids were at my Mum's house when all of a sudden Mark was wandering round in Sue's lounge. I asked him what he's looking for and I was trying to keep my voice down, but he was like a complete zombie. Then I realised he was looking for the loo. Oh hell, he was peeing against Sue's lounge door. I desperately tried to get him to stop and ushered him into the bathroom but by the time he got there he was all done, I quickly found Sue's mop and bucket and cleaned up the mess, of course our poor dog Silk got the blame. She'd never peed anywhere in all the time we'd had her, it felt awful blaming her, but Sue was fine. At least now Sue, you know the truth!

Mark's toilet antics happened quite frequently, after a few shandies he seemed to forget where he was and never made it to the toilet, on another occasion we were staying in the Cock Hotel in Stony Stratford.

Mark made his way to the wardrobe and promptly peed in there. He even did it at home. He'd gone to bed early after a few drinks watching the football, and I was sitting at the dining table when all of a sudden I could hear water running, I dashed out into the hall to find Mark peeing over the banister on the landing and down on the to the stairs, he only just missed from peeing on my head. That was the final straw. So I found his trainers and I peed in them and left them to dry. I never confessed but he complained for weeks that his trainers were stinking of cats, before he bought a new pair.

# Chapter 51

## 2002 – Gone

So the next year and a half passed fairly non-eventfully, Mark and I were very happy, well I certainly was and felt that he was too. We had a few ups and downs like any marriage, I'm a bit bossy and after my bad marriage with Jimmy I wanted everything my way and Mark was a bit stubborn but generally we got on really well, the spark was definitely still there. Mark now worked in Curry's the electrical store which is only about five minutes in the car from where we lived. I had just got a promotion and my job although for the same company had moved to London, I was very excited to be working in the West End and didn't mind commuting every day it was quite a novelty. I was just starting my second week in my new job and Mark and I had had a bit of a row over the kids and a stupid game of Monopoly. Mark and his sister Michele were playing the game with Marc, Kate and James and as time went on the kids were getting bored and were messing around. Michele quite rightly tried to chastise them and actually said she'd smack them if they didn't behave. I was quite tired when I came home from work, so when the kids told me the whole story, I lost my temper and shouted at Michele, telling her she had no right to threaten to 'smack' my children, as she was only 21 and they were my children. I suppose I was a bit over the top, and I over re-acted. Anyway, Mark took his sister's side and we ended up both sulking a bit. A couple of days later and things were still a bit strained but I was fine with things and had put it behind me. Mark still wasn't speaking to me much and as soon as he got in from work he was on the computer upstairs, so I just thought I'd leave him alone to simmer down. Eventually we were speaking again but it seemed to be just one word answers and in the end I sat down and told Mark that we needed to sort things out. Mark wasn't very forthcoming but we ended up coming to an agreement that if I wasn't there, and he or his sister needed to chastise the children, then it was his job and not hers. I was happy with that after all he was helping to bring them up.

So on the next Saturday, I dropped Mark at work and thought everything was now ok again. When I picked him up again, he didn't speak in the car and I asked him what was wrong. He didn't really give me any explanation, just shot up the stairs to the computer so although I felt hurt I left him alone. Eventually I went upstairs and tried to speak to him again, he was having none of it, he immediately shut down the PC and stormed downstairs, I begged him to talk to me, but he flatly refused and said he was going out. 'Out where?' I asked. 'Just out!' He shouted.

That was that. Later I went to bed there was no sign of him and I fell asleep. When I woke up he was back home and I tried to move over to his side of the bed but he just shrugged me off and got up. He got ready for work and I dropped him off. I was heartbroken that he wouldn't even talk to me and explain what was wrong. We seemed to have worked out our disagreement so I had no idea what was wrong now.

On the Sunday evening much the same happened again, he came straight back from work and then announced he was going out. This time I wasn't so agreeable and demanded to know where he was going and that he explain to me what was wrong. He just stormed out of the front door, slamming it behind him. Later that evening I was helping Marc with some homework on the PC and I don't know why but I looked through the recent history of Mark's internet browsing, something just didn't feel right. What I found shocked me, Mark had been texting someone from the computer. And he hadn't wiped the history. From what I was reading it was obviously a woman and the texts were of a sexual nature, and the texts he'd got back were the same. I was stunned. I had no idea that he'd met or was seeing anyone else, we had been sleeping together up until a few days before, and this small row was the only problem we'd ever had. Or so I thought.

I called him on his mobile. He didn't answer but I continued to try and was bombarding him with texts. Eventually I called the mobile number of the person he'd been texting from my PC. Mark answered it. He was with her. He was very cross and told me never to call this number again, and to not bother his friends. I asked who he was with but he slammed the phone down.

I didn't see Mark again that evening, and I went to bed crying my eyes out. When I woke up the following morning he was back, but he wouldn't even speak to me, I begged him for an explanation, pleaded that he sorted things out with me for the children's sakes. But all he said to me was that he couldn't bear to be near me and the children weren't his and that I shouldn't try to use them against him. He flatly refused to give me an explanation for the texts. I couldn't believe it.

But I still didn't think our marriage was over. I thought he'd just been flirting with someone, while we were arguing to take his mind off things. I had to leave for work so I needed to get ready, I begged him to talk to me that evening so we could work things out. All day at work I was worrying.

When I got home from work that evening, Marc, Kate and James were all sitting there watching TV. 'Where's Mark' I asked them. 'Don't know, he wasn't here when we got back from after school club'. Replied Kate. When I turned I saw his wedding ring and mobile phone and keys on the ironing board. There was no note but I knew at that moment he'd gone, he'd left us for good.

# Chapter 52

## 2002 – The road to recovery

That hit me hard. I had no way of getting in touch with Mark, he'd left his phone and his parents had moved to France that week. I also found that he'd removed his name from our joint bank account and he appeared to have disappeared into thin air. I went to Curry's where he worked but they told me he'd handed his notice in at work on the Monday he'd left me and never returned. I was stunned. So I just had to get on with things. I continued to go to work and manage with the kids and their after school club. I left work early so that I could collect them most evenings. My work colleagues and boss were very supportive. I don't know how I got through those early weeks. Every time I got home to the train station in Milton Keynes I expected to see Mark standing there saying it had all been a big mistake and he was back. But he was never there.

I stopped eating, and in the next few weeks I actually lost three stones. I felt awful but looked amazing and all my friends were commenting on how great I looked. Only a few knew just how I really felt. I moved back to work at the Milton Keynes office in Wolverton Mill, I was still doing my new job but I was now working in my old office which was more convenient and allowed me more time to be with the children.

I was shocked to see Mark walk in to my office one day, I don't know how he knew I was there. He immediately told me he wanted a divorce. I hadn't actually seen or spoken to him in over 3 months and here he was large as life asking me for a divorce. I suddenly decided that I wasn't going to make it easy for him. I told him yes he could have a divorce, but I was divorcing him on the grounds of adultery. And that if he didn't agree to that then I would make him wait 5 years. I was already an expert in divorce law, having done it twice before. Of course he agreed. So my petition was granted that our marriage was to be dissolved due to irretrievable breakdown on the grounds of adultery between Mr Mark John Robert Allen and Miss Unknown.

So that was it, I changed my name again; I was now back to Siân Banks and single.

I didn't find out who Miss Unknown was until very recently. She was a girl he worked with at Curry's. They are now married and have two little girls and I'm happy for him. We would never have had a family together and the age difference must have played a part in it for him although it never did for me. I just resented the cruel way in which he left me and the children and I'll never forget the day Kate was hysterically crying in the garden just begging me to get him back. I had no idea where he was or how to find him and Kate never recovered from that and the counselling she's had in recent years has revealed that it was his leaving, when she was only 13 at such a vulnerable age, that has caused her so much of the anguish and rage she has felt. Mark left me up to my eyes in debt and it took me 7 years to pay everything off. We'd bought a lot of things including an expensive car on credit and it was all in my name. That didn't matter too much when we had two salaries coming in, but now there was only mine, I don't know how I would have coped without my parents help. Mark even left his Great Dane Silk with me. I had to pay for her upkeep and all her vet bills. I hope he never does that again to anyone else again.

# Chapter 53

## 2003 – The best ever chat up line

I had been invited to my friend Josie's wedding. Josie's first partner Andy was my ex husband Mark's best man and although both relationships had crashed and burned, Josie and I stayed friends. So much so, that Josie had asked my daughter Kate, who was then 14, to be her bridesmaid. I was really touched by this, as Josie has lots of half sisters and cousins and a very large family, and we only worked together for a short time, I was really surprised that she'd asked my Kate.

It was Josie's hen night and we'd all been to Central Milton Keynes and the night had been really great. We always ended up back in Stony Stratford where we have all worked together from time to time. It's a small market town just outside Milton Keynes and has one main high street. But the great thing about Stony Stratford is that there are about a dozen pubs along this high street all within a very short walking distance so you can fall out of the Cock and into the Bull (this is where the cock and bull story originated) very easily.

I'd decided to leave the George pub and find a taxi on the High Street, so I was tottering along slightly worse for wear heading in the wrong direction when a voice called to me. It was Roy. Roy is my best friend Andrea's husband; they frequent the Vaults bar in Stony next to the famous Bull Hotel. 'Siân, come and have a drink, Andrea is here' Roy called from the cobbled entry between the Bull Hotel and the Vaults bar. I wobbled over and into the Vaults where Andrea was sitting at the bar. We chatted for a while and I got another drink, completely forgetting that I was on my way home. The Vaults is probably one of the smallest pubs I've ever been in, it's certainly one of the thinnest as the distance from the side wall to the bar is only an arm's length and you can actually stand with your back to the wall and reach the bar to get your drink, This makes getting past people to go from one end of the pub the other very difficult and sometimes embarrassing as you squeeze past.

It was as I was inching past some people to go to the ladies that I got squashed up against this hunk of a chap, with arms like Schwarzenegger sporting a number of tattoos, he gave me a cheeky smile and a cockeyed wink and I smiled back. When I returned to the bar, there was no sign of Roy and Andrea but the burly chap with tattoos was still smiling and he asked if I wanted another drink. 'I'm with my friends but they must have gone to the Bull next door' I replied. But this chap seemed quite nice so I accepted the drink and we got talking. By this time I was very worse for wear but this chap seemed quite attractive and I was happy to be chatting. I remembered the various questions, 'where do you live' and 'what do you do', but couldn't remember many of the answers apart from the fact he had been telling me that his Granddad had been a crocodile hunter! I also remembered something about Belize. Anyway after a couple more drinks I could hardly stand and explained I needed to get a taxi home. We both staggered out onto the High Street as a taxi was dropping some people off and I asked the driver to take me to my address.

We set off and I realised that the chap I've been speaking to in the Vaults is now sitting in the back explaining that he's going to an address on the same estate so we may as well share. The taxi driver was gabbing into his radio in some foreign language and Indian music was blaring from the radio as we swept along I could hardly make myself heard to give the driver my address, but eventually we rolled up at my house and I paid the driver.

My mysterious companion staggered off up my road to his destination on foot and I called out 'byeeeee' as I tottered off down the steps to my house in my very dangerous heels.

The next afternoon, I was nursing the hangover from hell on the sofa watching an old movie on TV. I couldn't have felt worse, but kindly my son Marc was bringing me regular cups of coffee and the odd round of toast as I asked for it. I was just thinking 'Never again...' when there was a knock at the front door. Marc went off to answer it. When he returned with a shocked look on his face, I asked him who was there. His reply was very odd. 'There's a man there'. 'Who is it, what does he want?' I asked. 'Dunno who he is, but he's asking for you'. 'Me?' 'What does he look like?' I was stunned as to who could be calling at the house on a Sunday afternoon asking for me, no-one ever knocks at the door asking for me, it's always for one of the kids. 'He's a great big skin head, with a scar down his face and a gozzy eye and he's carrying 3 cans of Tennent's'. I was amazed at Marc's powers of observation and his apparent total recall and laughed out loud. I had no idea who this person was who had asked for me, even with a very accurate but odd description that Marc was giving me.

I got up from the sofa and gingerly made it to the front door. When I opened it I was gob smacked. It was the burly chap from the Vaults the night before. I vaguely remembered thinking that he seemed quite nice looking. Just goes to show what beer goggles can do. He was very odd looking with his wonky eye and a huge scar which ran the full length of his cheek from his eye to his jaw line, he appeared very drunk still. From what I could remember he was still wearing the same clothes. 'Oh it's Crocodile Dundee' I laughed as I glanced down to see him clutching a few cans of Tennent's Super strength lager. 'What are you doing here?' I asked puzzled I was wondering how he knew where I lived. I vaguely remembered him in the taxi but he certainly didn't come back to my house. 'Thought you might like a drink sometime' he slurred. 'I'm not keen on Tennent's' I laughed. 'No not that, let's go out sometime' he went on. I was keen to get rid of him and I was beginning to wonder how I even looked at him the previous evening. So in my haste to be shot of him I agreed to meet him the next evening at a local pub. I had no intention of turning up and that was the last time I would see him as he staggered off again.

Later that evening I decided to have an early night after the heavy Friday and I hoped that by Sunday I'd feel a lot better and not waste the whole day laying around on the sofa.

I woke early on Sunday feeling much better and I spent most of the day doing a few jobs around the house and preparing the kids uniforms for school. I had forgotten all about the crocodile hunter from the previous day when at about seven in the evening, there was a knock at the door again.

'Oh No!' I thought as I answered it this time, 'it's him again'. How on earth was I going to get rid of him? He was standing there again looking sheepish. 'Still coming for that drink?' He asked. I sighed deeply and reluctantly agreed; I thought that if I went for one drink I could then let him down and make up some excuse for not seeing him again. So I asked him in while I quickly changed and then we got in my car and I drove us over to Halle's Comet which is a local pub near to where he lived.

It actually turned out to be quite a nice evening and Stuart, I now knew his name, was quite a laugh, although he did get extremely drunk. Anyway I made my excuses after a couple of drinks and headed off home.

As it happened Stuart regularly kept turning up and my youngest son James took quite a shine to him. I was never over keen on him but after a few weeks we ended up going out together regularly and about six months later we ended up moving in together. Looking back now I still don't know why that happened, perhaps I was vulnerable after Mark left. I was never that keen on Stuart and I certainly didn't love him. He turned out to be a raging alcoholic and he was also 10 years younger than me, but we ended up living together for 2 years! What was I thinking?

# Chapter 54

## 2005 – The Train

It is great working in London I only go there once a week now as I'm permanently back in the Milton Keynes office. But whenever there's a birthday, leaving party or any kind of celebration everyone goes and you don't have to worry about driving home or finding taxi's as we all travel home by train. I have a slightly further journey than my colleagues who mostly live in London, but it's only 5 stops on the Northern line from our new offices in Moorgate to Euston and then a 40 minute journey to my home in Milton Keynes and I live 5 minutes from Wolverton Station – so generally I was home in just over an hour – usually!

Well this occasion was a developer's leaving party, I don't remember exactly which month it was but it was definitely winter as I had a full length red woollen coat on and it was snowing so it was very cold. We were in a very smart bar in Soho and a good time was had by all – I'm careful (usually) not to drink too much as I have to find my way to the station and onto the train home while lugging my heavy laptop bag and all my paraphernalia. After about four glasses of wine (my usual limit) I decided to say my goodbyes and head off from Soho to Oxford Circus tube which is only a short five minute walk. Outside I stepped into the freezing cold and within about ten seconds I went from slightly merry to completely legless, tripping down the steps and falling full length across the road with my laptop, bags and everything shooting off in all directions, 'how on earth did this happen?' I thought. I got up and grabbed my stuff hoping that no one had noticed. I was covered in dirt off the road but thankfully still in one piece so I staggered off to the tube station, and to be honest the next half an hour is a bit hazy.

The next thing I remember was being on a train going North so somehow I must have managed to get to Oxford Circus, then to Euston, find my train and platform and board the correct train with my ticket and belongings, so far so good. Now I just had to keep awake so that I got off at the right stop, the train was packed and it was standing room only so I was clinging to a support rail for dear life and trying not to make eye contact with anyone. I remembered hearing the doors close and the noise of the train as we pulled out of the station; thank God I'd soon be home.

Well the movement of the train had a disastrous effect on my internal organs and I began to feel quite queasy but still in control – just. Well perhaps not – I held my hand in front of my face, 'oh hell I'm going to be sick' I realised. There was no room for me to rush to the toilet, even if I knew which direction to go for the toilet so all I could do was keep swallowing hoping to god I could manage to keep it down.

No such luck! Projectile vomit left my body faster than that train was heading north and splattered everyone within about 3 feet. I remember that people were shouting, screaming, swearing – calling me all kinds of names as people were pushing and shoving eventually I got to a toilet and remained there for the rest of the journey too embarrassed to come out. I was covered in vomit with no way of cleaning myself up but somehow, thank God, I still had hold of all my bags.

The next thing I knew I was slumped on the floor of the toilet (this wasn't to be the only occasion this evening), with someone banging on the door saying we're at the final destination. 'Oh no where's that?' I wondered. I staggered out of the toilet to be greeted by train cleaners who said that it's Birmingham New Street. It couldn't have been any worse, or so I thought. I headed off to the main departure hall to find out what time the next train would be leaving back to Milton Keynes to find the place was like a morgue. Not a soul in sight, what time was it? I wondered. It was 1am? I'd been on the train for about 3 hours before anyone found me! Eventually I found a man working there who informed me that the next train south was at 5am – what was I going to do? I had no money for a hotel, but how could I turn up at one anyway covered in mud and vomit – it was in my hair and all down my coat, I couldn't find my mobile phone, it was absolutely freezing and when I looked outside it was actually snowing. I finally decided to go to the waiting room there was nothing else I could do but wait.

The waiting room was on one of the outdoor platforms and was all glass and unheated it must have been the coldest place in Birmingham or even the world. I dragged my belongings in and sat and waited trying to get comfortable on the steel chairs. I actually felt fully sober by then, but needed my bed desperately and couldn't get comfortable no matter what I tried, the minutes ticked by so slowly and I couldn't even doze off. So I started to wander around just to warm up and to see if I could find somewhere else to sit and wait and I ended up in the second toilet of the evening.

I couldn't believe it as I walked in I was hit with the most heat I've ever felt, it was like an oven in the ladies loo in Birmingham New Street – whoopee! I would sit on the loo for the next few hours at least I'd be warm, so I dragged all my things into a cubicle and sat down on the lid of the toilet in the warmth. You've guessed it; I leaned against the wall and eventually nodded off.

The next thing I knew there was crashing and banging and people shouting 'get her out' 'she must be a junky' and I was being dragged from the cubicle by cleaners and the British Transport Police. How could this evening get any worse? I asked myself. And quite indignantly I started to explain that I was actually an Applications Manager with a very responsible job in IT in London who'd missed her stop and could not get home until the next train at 5am – of course because of the state I was in no-one believed me so I was lucky not to be arrested. I was ushered out into the cold again and I heard people telling me to keep out of the toilets. I looked at the time and little more than an hour had passed. How on earth would I make it through this night?

Well of course I did and I was in the freezing waiting room and eventually it was 5am and my train arrived. I got on and found a seat, home and my bed were calling. Thank goodness it was now Saturday and I'd be in bed within the hour – or so I thought!

Fifteen minutes into the journey and an announcement came over the train tannoy. 'Due to signal failures this train cannot go south and is now being redirected to Manchester anyone wishing to get to London needs to change at Stoke on Trent and continue with their journey'. I was virtually at breaking point, I was now on a Virgin train heading north instead of south, covered in vomit looking like death with a whole load of angry commuters who all appeared to be looking at me because of my appearance and the awful smell.

Well we got to Stoke on Trent, changed and eventually got to London by 9am where I found another train to take me to Wolverton in Milton Keynes which is my stop, my eyes were like organ stops and I was fighting sleep but there was no way I was missing this stop again and going back to the hell hole that is Birmingham New Street in winter.

257

# Chapter 55

## 2005 – Milton Keynes A&E

We had moved offices again at work and now had a nice office on the ground floor of Mansell Street, which is close to the 'gherkin' in London's city area near Aldgate Tube Station. Next door was a pub called 'The First and Last'. I think they must have known our Development team when they named that pub, because we were first in there after work and last to leave in the evening. I didn't go out with my colleagues very often as the horror of falling asleep on the train after a few drinks was still very fresh in my mind. One lovely summer evening the whole team had planned to have a few drinks after work and it was nice sitting outside in the sunshine. We'd been there about an hour or so, when my mobile rang. It was Marc. 'We're at the hospital Mum, you'll have to come, James has had an accident and they can't operate on him till you come.' I was almost hysterical and didn't even bother to find out what had happened, I grabbed my bags and screamed goodbye to my friends and flew to the tube station.

I didn't have long to wait before the tube arrived and it was only about 6 stops to Euston Square. I got out at the other end and ran up the steps then all the way along Euston Road to the mainline station at Euston. When I got there puffing and panting and feeling the panic rising in my chest, wondering what on earth was wrong with James to my horror I saw that every train from Euston going north up the West Coast

Mainline was cancelled. Every board had the word cancelled in bright orange letters scrolling across it. It was about 7.45 in the evening, how on earth was I going to get home? I headed to the Silverlink customer service desk. Silverlink were the train operators that ran the trains between Birmingham and London on my line.

It turned out that there was an overhead power line down and nothing could get along the line for the next few hours. No Virgin trains and no Silverlink trains. They said they were going to get a single train stopping at all stations that was due to leave at around 10.30pm. Oh no! There was nothing I could do but wait. How could this happen on a day when I needed to get home so urgently? So there I sat on the main concourse at Euston watching the clock tick round and hoping against hope that one of the cancelled signs would miraculously change showing a train leaving for Milton Keynes. Well as expected nothing unexpected happened and no miracle train turned up to take me home any earlier. So I was there until 10.30.

Eventually after what seemed to be a lifetime of worry, wondering what had happened to James I boarded the only train that was leaving London and heading in my direction. What turned to be relief was quickly replaced by frustration as the train called at every station between London and Milton Keynes, this took over two hours so it was now 12:30 when I stepped off the train at Milton Keynes and flew to my car in the multi-story car park. Less than ten minutes later I was parked at Milton Keynes General Hospital and was charging across the car park to accident and emergency. I dashed towards the counter and gave both mine and James's name and was ushered through to cubicles at close to 1am. James was hysterical as was Kate but they were being calmed by a very nice nurse with an American accent and between Marc and Kate they explained to me that they had all been playing out in the street when James had fallen off his bike and gone straight over the handle bars. He'd skidded across the floor and as I could tell by looking at him he'd ripped open his chin and a large flap of skin was hanging down.

He had refused to allow anyone to touch him until I got there and he'd been there since just after 6pm that evening. The kind nurse explained that they had to stitch him up shortly or the skin wouldn't be suitable to stitch at all and he'd need surgery to repair his face. Once I had got there James started to quieten down. His experience of hospitals made him really frightened as had lots of accidents resulting in visits to A&E over the years.

It all started with a freak accident in the frozen foods store Iceland. Marc and Kate had been swinging on the front of the trolley I was pushing, but the weight of them on it tipped it forward and James who was only about a year old had been catapulted out of the trolley seat and head first into an open freezer resulting in a gash in his head. We'd gone to A&E in Whiston on Merseyside, back then and I was appalled as a nurse approached James with what looked like a staple gun and although I was yelling at the top of my voice 'NOOOOOOOOOOO' they just went ahead and stapled his head without any anaesthetic, which frightened the life out of both him and me. It took me 3 years after that to be able to cut James's hair. I had to wait for him to fall asleep before I could trim it as he wouldn't allow anyone with scissors anywhere near him.

After that James had had many more accidents, the first few being 3 broken arms. He'd broken his left twice and his right once before he was five, and on two occasions it had been so bad that it meant general anaesthetic and an operation to have them manipulated back into the correct position. He'd gone to school on his first day with his arm in plaster and it was a regular occurrence for him. James then had more stitches in his head when he'd run into a tree in Willan Lake, he had stitches in his wrist when he'd been swinging from his wardrobe and caught it on a sharp screw. Then he was scraping glue off a picture rail with a sharp chisel and put it through his hand, which meant another trip to A&E for even more stitches. He'd even run into the handle of a door and had the most massive shiner you've ever seen.

Kate had been just as bad. We'd not lived in Milton Keynes for very long when she'd climbed up onto the kitchen sides to get jam out of the cupboard, dropped the jar and then stepped on it and sliced open her foot. After that she'd had a couple of freak accidents, the first when she was running down stairs with a fishing net on a bamboo rod, and somehow she'd fallen on it and it had gone down her throat! The next was even more bizarre! She was running up the steps from the outside of our house to the road with a pencil in her hand and she'd tripped and put the pencil right through the side of her face, this resulted in a small stitch to her cheek. Then one summer when she was staying with her grandparents in St Helens she had fallen from a 10 foot wall where she'd been climbing and broken off her two front teeth. But Kate's worse accident was a broken leg, where she'd been climbing on the roof of a school, again in the summer holidays and had slipped, she had tried to save herself from falling into a skip and ended up falling completely off the roof and breaking the leg, cutting open her head and hurting her hands too. That was the day before we were due to go on holiday to Blackpool for a long weekend and we had to hire a wheel chair for her.

Marc had suffered a number of injuries too. His ranged from kicking a ball through a glass window in someone's conservatory and slicing the muscle in his calf, this required surgery to repair his muscle and he now has a 10 inch scar down the back of his leg. He was 'jumped' outside our local shop one Christmas Eve and had his head smashed against some iron railings, the lump on his forehead was so big it deformed the whole of his face so that he was barely recognisable, he looked like a Klingon out of Star Trek and Kate and I were virtually incapacitated in laughter just looking at him but we took him to hospital anyway. In another fight he was kicked so hard in the head that he ended up on a ventilator in intensive care and he's also recently been stabbed! You'd think we lived in Beirut rather than Buckinghamshire. So along with my 'Dancing on Ice' accident the Banks' are regulars in Milton Keynes A&E.

So back to James' story.... After James had been injected with some local anaesthetic and Kate had stopped screaming 'don't let them hurt him' at the top of her voice I calmed James down and we were all ready to go home. James looked like he had blue whiskers coming from his chin and now has a very nice scar the full length of it

# Chapter 56

## 2005 – A Family Reunited

I used to love watching Surprise Surprise with Cilla Black and more recently Heir Hunters, where long lost relatives are found and reunited. But I always thought it was a bit of a fix. How could you possibly have family that you didn't know about? We had always been a small family as my Mum was an only child and I had only one sister so perhaps this was influencing my view of the stories on the TV.

We'd not been in touch with our Dad that much over the years since we'd become adults. Our parents had been divorced since I was five and Sue was only eighteen months old although as children we saw him regularly – Christmas and birthdays and we used to stay in Wales with him and our other Nana during the summer holidays. Dad had a sister and a brother but we'd not seen them or our three cousins since we were in our teens. So that was the extent of our family and all of the grand-parents were sadly now gone so we definitely knew our whole family. Dad had remarried a couple of times since his divorce from our Mum, but hadn't had any more children. Angela his second wife sadly died young and Liz, his third wife, already had a grown up son when they married a few years earlier. So that was it, just me and Sue – two girls, with no-one to carry on the Williams name. Without any brothers the Williams name in our family would die with Sue.

I'd left James's dad 9 years earlier when James was only 2 years old so he didn't know his Dad or his Dad's side of the family. It had always played on my mind that I was the only parent James had. If anything happened to me, who would look after James and how would he ever find out that he had a very large extended family on his Dad's side. Jimmy, his dad, had three sisters Jane, Maureen and Irene and a brother Edward and they all had large families so by my reckoning, James probably had about fifteen cousins. There could be even more by now, I had no idea. So over the last few years I thought about putting markers on the Internet on the family tree websites, so that if ever in the future James wanted to trace his dad or his family he'd be able to do some research.

I had no intention of introducing him to them or ever going back home. It was too late and there were too many unhappy memories.

I'm on Facebook, Twitter, Linked-In – lots of social and professional networking sites, but before that, the big site for finding people was Friends Reunited. It was great and I'd even met up with an old school friend who now worked in London after getting in touch. Friends Reunited have a sister site called Genes Reunited which allows you to search for your ancestors in over 600 million family trees including census, birth, marriages, death and military records. It's the quickest way to discover your family history! There are now lots of other sites like this where you can register your details. I'd even found an ex-pats site for people who used to live in Holyhead in Anglesey and registered there. So there were markers all over the Internet on family tree sites showing who my family was and links to in-laws and ex-husbands families, then if James or the others ever wanted to find out more, they could.

So on 16th June 2005, which was the day after my daughter Kate's 16th birthday, I wasn't that surprised to get an email from someone called Donna asking me if my father was Stewart Williams. It was twenty past six in the evening. I was sitting on the sofa with my laptop on my knee watching TV and catching up with a bit of work. Mainly I was deleting spam and junk mail from my hotmail account. But this particular email caught my eye. As I said I wasn't surprised as I'd previously had an email from a lady in Wales asking if I used to live in Ael-y-Môr in Holyhead. That was the name of our family home until I was five; it meant House by the Sea in Welsh. My Mum and Dad, Sue and I had lived there. It had originally been a barn and our Grandparents Elizabeth and Llewlyn had owned the original house Lewascote and the surrounding land. Lewascote was an acronym for the family names. L was Llewelyn our Granddad, E was Elizabeth our Nan, W was for Wynn their eldest son, A for Ann their daughter and S was for Stewart our dad. COTE stood for Corner Of The Earth and I loved it when my Nan told me this. The house was originally a stately home owned by Lady Kathleen Stanley and our Nan and Grandad rented some of the 39 rooms out. Later the house was demolished and our Nan and Granddad designed their dream bungalow to be built on the grounds they called it Bethlyn after their own names, but our Granddad died before he ever got to move in.

Our Dad had since sold the converted barn house and the lady living there now was interested in the history, so I told her all about it. This seemed like a similar type of email. This is an exact copy of the email exchange; I've kept the emails as they are very special to me. The conversation went like this.

> *Donna: Is your father called Stewart Williams and previously lived in Ael y Môr and now lives at Bethlyn Holyhead?*

*Me: Hello Donna. Yes that's my Dad, I lived in Ael y Môr as a child until I was 5 years old and my Nana and Granddad, Elizabeth and Llewelyn built Bethlyn. Nice to meet you, how do you know my family?*

*Donna: This might come as shock to you but Stewart Williams is my father too I've known about you for years but was too scared to get in touch but I'm glad I've traced you through friends reunited I also know that you have a sister called Susan I'm sorry but I thought Dad would have told you by now.*

That was the most jaw-dropping moment in my entire life; I dropped the laptop onto the floor! I was completely stunned, this couldn't be right, how could Dad have another daughter? I'd been to his house every year; there were never any other children there. I would have known if Angie had a baby, we were quite close. This must be a mistake. All kinds of things were flashing through my mind. And the thing I kept thinking the whole time was that it was some kind of scam. Dad had been ill for many years with asbestosis, which is a form of lung cancer. He'd had a decent compensation payout and wasn't short of a bob or two. He had sold his own house and after our Nana died he'd bought out his sister and brother and now lived in our grandparent's house. Perhaps someone knew he was ill, and was after his money? But I needed to find out more… I had to play it cool.

The email exchange continued like this.

*Me: oh my God. He never told us anything, I wonder why not, I've got to call my sister and tell her, what a shock but great news too call me if you want to. How old are you?*

266

> *Donna: I'm sorry if I've shocked you but I would really really like to hear from you again please reply.*

So I had to call Sue. I rang her mobile but she was driving, so I blurted out 'Call me as soon as you get home, I've got news to tell you and you're not going to believe it, call me straight away'

Sue must have been worried sick, but eventually she called me back, I was almost hysterical by this time, pacing up and down willing the phone to ring.

'What's up mate?'

'Oh God Sue you're never going to believe this'

'What?'

'Someone called Donna has been emailing me, are you sitting down?'

'Yeah what's up? Who's Donna?'

'She says she's our sister!'

'What?'

'That's what I thought, how can we have a sister, but she says Stewart is her Dad too, and she's known about us for years'

'She must be mistaken, there's probably loads of Stewart Williams in Anglesey, and everyone there is called Williams'

'Well she knows all about Ael-y- Môr and Bethlyn'

'Are you sure?'

267

'Yes I didn't tell her anything, her email was asking me was my father Stewart Williams and he used to live in Ael-y- Môr and now lives in Bethlyn'

'Well email her back and find out more, I'm in all night now, so keep me informed, and find out how old she is, he couldn't have had her before you, he was only 18 when he married Mum'

'I will, I will, I'll find out everything, I bet it's some kind of hoax and she's after his money'

'You might be right, do some digging'

So I continued to email Donna and this is how it went.

*Me: I've spoken to Sue and she's so excited too. Please get back to us soon love Siân x*

*Donna: Hi again hope you are well I'm so made up that your happy to find out about me I'm 30 years old live in RAF Valley Anglesey and have 3 children... Sorry for the shocking news but I have more news I also have a brother called Nigel who is also Stewarts son. love Donna xxx*

*Me: Do you know why Dad never told us anything in 30 years? My Mum is in Spain I just rang her to tell her, she said that Dad was with someone after they split up in 1971 and before he married Angie, but she never knew he had children. I have 3 children also 17, 16 and 12. Marc, Kate and James. I'm so shocked that Aunty Ann or Nana Beth never mentioned you. I was with my cousins Michael and Peter in Cyprus at RAF Akrotiri when I was 18 and they never said a word - no-one did, I don't understand why not? We really must keep in touch I've so much to tell you about me and Sue and my family. I live in Buckinghamshire - Milton*

*Keynes and work in London. I'm 39 Sue is 35 how old is Nigel? love Sian x*

*Donna: Nigel is 32 and he's in the army he's married an Irish girl so he's based there now and has been there for the last 5 years. Dad has never had much to do with me or Nigel so maybe that's why we were never brought up but I'm so made up that we are talking it's something I've wanted to do for so long I don't think Dad knows I know you are even born it's my Mum that's told me everything about you and Sue I phoned Nigel and told him that I'd traced you and he is so exited we've wanted to see you for so long. Love Donna xxxxxxxxxxxxxxxxxxxxxxxxxx*

And that's how it all got started. We exchanged telephone numbers and we continued to have telephone calls and send pictures to each other via email, and Sue did the same. It was all like a dream. Speaking to Donna I felt so close to her, I really felt like I had known her all my life, what a waste of 30 years, not knowing about them. They were so lovely and just like us.

The next day I was working in London on the 17th floor of our London offices with my good friend Lynne from Edinburgh, we had just launched invoicing via our Consultancy Tracking System and Lynne and I were training everyone in the business on how to use it. Lynne asked me what was wrong as she'd noticed I was quiet that morning. 'Oh Lynne you won't believe this' I said. I've just found out that my Dad had two more children after he and my Mum were divorced, they've tracked me down, and it's been *30* years! Why didn't he tell us, why did he lie to me for all those years?' I broke down crying. Lynne cried along with me but was so supportive I don't know how I'd have got through that day without her. The next few days were hard, but gradually we got used to the fact that we had a new

269

family and I was keen to keep in touch with Donna and find out more.

The most poignant thing that Donna said to me on one of our telephone calls was this. 'Siân, I've known about you and Sue for about 15 years, I think my Mum told us when I was 15' she went on 'And for the past 10 years I've wanted to find you and when I tried it took me 10 seconds to find you.

Donna went on to say, 'I don't know why I did it, but I put your name into Genes Reunited and a rough guess for the year you were born. You were the only Siân Williams registered on the site born around that time. It said your middle name was Patricia and you had a sister called Susan. I phoned my Mum and said could this be her? And my Mum said 'Well their mother was called Pat, and the baby was called Susan so it must be them.'

We all arranged to meet up and it was one of the happiest days of my life, Me, Sue Nigel and Donna, all together at last. Our Dad made a huge mistake not telling us about each other, and we have never found out why he didn't but this really has been a happy ending, we're all still in touch. We love each other to bits and our little family has now grown to include a brother and sister and lots of nephews, nieces and cousins.

(Nigel, me Donna and Sue – reunited at last)

# Chapter 56

## 2005 – The office Christmas party

The company I work for is very traditional and always arranges a Christmas party for its staff. These are very well organised and civilised. There's no photocopying of bottoms, or getting in the stationary cupboard with the boss. Or at least if there is, I'm either never invited or oblivious to what's going on around me. My colleagues are professionals who are very dignified at all times. So the Christmas party is usually a quiet affair, a few drinks, nibbles and the obligatory quiz. Being based in Milton Keynes I'd never been to the main London office parties and as the average age of the Milton Keynes consultants was probably about fifty-five only myself and the other office girls Andrea and Caroline were younger, so the local office parties were very quiet. Most people had to drive so it was a nice dinner at the local pizza restaurant and then home, all tucked up in bed before 10pm.

Following the closure of the Milton Keynes office I had been moved to London and this was to be my first experience of a London party and I had assumed it would be much the same as our MK ones but a lot bigger. I commuted for the first four months every day into London and it was easy enough. After that I was all set up to work from home and just went into the office one or two days per week, it suited me well.

What I didn't realise was that because everyone working in London mostly lived in London; they were all able to take partying very seriously and took any opportunity to enjoy themselves. Christmas, birthday's, leaving parties, the birth of a new child, someone only needed a new hair cut and they were all down the pub to celebrate. In fact when we worked in the Mansell Street office it seemed that everyone was out every Friday, whether there was a celebration or not. One of our developers was a crazy South African who seemed to be able to consume huge amounts of alcohol most evenings after work. Tequila shots were Terry's speciality and no expense was spared. I don't know how the London development team managed to keep it up and come into work and do such a good job, but they did and a very good time was had by all. I expect it was because they did it so often that it became second nature to them. I was keen to join in even if I had to travel home on the train after the party. Christmas was upon us and I was looking forward to my first London office party.

I decided to take this seriously, it would be a chance to meet all the staff at head office I sorted out my party outfit. It wasn't new but I hadn't worn it to any work parties so it would be new to my colleagues. I'd had my hair done and headed for the office.

Everyone was to bring some drink and nibbles so I was laden with lots bags on my journey into London. A few bottles in a cardboard Tesco bottle carrier, a few packs of nibbles, my party outfit and my makeup! The company had provided some party games to keep everyone amused. These included giant Jenga and Twister. These were great fun as it is always amusing to see the senior staff, who are normally out of breath after walking to the coffee machine, bent double trying to place a foot on a coloured circle. As the bottles emptied and everyone began to relax it was time to have the quiz. This was a company institution and everyone would form very competitive teams. It was

273

all good fun and Terry was in charge of the drinks and he appeared to know his stuff. I think it was his way of not having to take part in the games. Lord only knows what he was giving me, but it was very strong and I remember being 'merry' to say the least.

My team was doing very well in the quiz and I remember thinking that it was a fun party without any excessive drinking and silliness. The next round was 'Guess the Santa' a company favourite. The week before the party lots of photographs were taken of colleagues wearing a Santa hat and beard and you have to guess who they are. So everyone is handing round the photographs and looking into the eyes of colleagues as we move around the room trying to make out who was who. I get to one of my colleagues who I'm pretty sure is in one of the pictures, and I'm looking into his eyes.

'Oh you have dark eyes, I've never noticed before, are you Santa number five in the picture?'

'Yes very, very dark eyes' he leers back to me.

I'm quite taken aback, is he coming on to me? Or is it my imagination, he's not like that at all normally, and I was very surprised to see him wearing a pink tutu and a ski mask to the party, but I take no notice and have a harmless flirt back. 'Oh yes... very dark, sexy eyes. You're quite the dark horse aren't you?' I joked along with him.

The night was in full swing, and I was getting drunker and drunker. The dark eyed chap was fuelling my stupor by continually bringing me a variety of cocktails, which appeared to get stronger and stronger all the time. The next thing I knew I was bottom up on the floor in a game of Twister. It was all hilarious good fun as we collapsed laughing on the floor.

Our office was in the City of London near Moorgate in the heart of the square mile. St Alphage House was an old building, not very posh, but we were on the seventeenth floor, and had a fantastic view. The city looks lovely at night. We work in the IT department and in the support area was the secure communications room. This was where the servers were stored, and there was a security lock on the door, to protect them. The office had windows from ceiling to floor so we had a great view out, but no-one could see in as we are so high up.

I was helping myself to another drink; I needed orange juice, as I was feeling a bit worse for wear. All of a sudden someone grabed my hand and we were heading towards the secure communications room. My God was anyone looking? Everyone else seems occupied with dancing, jenga, twister and drinks – no one was looking. A stranger was pulling me along.

The next think I knew we were in the communications room, 'how on earth did he get it open?' I wondered. The next moment I was making a pathetic attempt to fight off the stranger basically I wasn't fighting him off at all! I was then squashed against the full length glass and the stranger has metamorphed into an octopus with hands and arms everywhere. The cold glass against my skin quickly sobered me up.

'Stop Stop, I need the loo' I gasp, he was kissing me and it was all very nice but I had to get away, I don't do this kind of thing for God's sake! All of a sudden I came to my senses thank goodness. 'OK hurry back' he slurs. 'I'll wait for you here'.

I quickly made my escape. I grabbed my bag and coat from my desk and hurried off to the lift in reception. Luckily the party was in full swing and no one noticed my swift exit.

That was the longest ride down in an elevator I've ever had, my heart was beating like a drum as I went down all seventeen floors but I had thankfully escaped with almost all of my dignity intact, before things got completely out of control.

I'm sure some of you reading this book will wonder just who the stranger was and how he got into the Penna party and into the 'comms' room. But a message to him if he's reading... Your secret is safe with me!

# Chapter 57

## Benidorm 2006 – My 40th Birthday

Mum and John have been going to Benidorm for over 10 years, twice or 3 times a year. They love it. As I said earlier John has been all over the world so sight-seeing is not high on his agenda, but 'getting the sun on his back' as he puts it definitely is. They've lots of friends out there too and they enjoy going back regularly and they'd rather have a cheaper holiday a few times a year than more expensive ones less frequently.

When Mum announced that she was taking me to Benidorm in June as a birthday present for my 40th I was ecstatic! My sister Sue had been a couple of times with Mum and John, Mum's friends Allan and Nigel and Neil, Sue's boyfriend and they'd all had a great time. I could never go as I couldn't afford it because of the kids. But now they were grown up. Marc was 18, Kate was 17 but didn't live at home now and although James was still at school and only 13 my neighbours and good friends Carole and Harry were going to look after him for the fortnight and make sure he had his meals and that Marc was taking proper care of him. It was all arranged I could go! Then a couple of weeks beforehand, Harry was poorly and Carole said she didn't want the strain of taking care of James to make Harry any worse and could I find someone else? I was devastated. There wasn't anyone else. Sue my sister was coming with us too so I called Mum to let her know. 'Oh no! It's *your* birthday' Mum wailed, 'we are so looking forward to you coming isn't there somebody else you can leave him with?' Mum asked. In the background down the telephone line, I could hear John shouting 'Bring him with us, Pat get him a flight, we're not leaving my Grandson with anyone, he's coming with us'. Oh how wonderful of John, that was such a relief, I would just need to get James a passport, and I hoped that it wasn't too late to get him one. He'd never been abroad before, so I got onto the passport office website to see if I could get one in time. I found out that I could, we'd need to pay a bit extra but we'd have it in time.

Mum booked an extra flight for James and all she needed from me was his passport number when it arrived but she could add that to the booking later. He was flying Easyjet from Luton with me and we'd arrive in Alicante twenty minutes before Mum, John and Sue who were flying Monarch from Manchester airport.

The days were ticking by and James' passport still hadn't arrived we were due to fly in 2 days time; I was getting worried and called the passport office directly. 'It's been dispatched Mrs Banks it'll be with you later today or tomorrow' the clerk assured me. And thank goodness the very next day it arrived. We were all set our bags were packed and my friend Steve was taking us to the airport the next morning.

I had printed off our flight reference details and we were just queuing at the check-in desk, when I glanced down at the tickets 'Oh no!' I yelled. Mum had booked James' flight in the name of James Banks! James has been known as Banks since he was 2 when we moved to Milton Keynes, but his real name and that on his passport was Hayes. They wouldn't let us board for our flight. I called Mum panic struck. 'Mum we can't fly' I howled. 'What's up now?' Mum shouted back it was a bad line, and the air traffic control must have been interfering with the signal I was getting. 'You've booked James' flight in the name of Banks, he's Hayes Mum and they won't let us board. 'Oh hell' Mum shrieked. 'Can you buy him a new flight?' she asked. 'I'll try and I'll call you back' I gasped. 'We're just about to go through security' the line cracked again, 'but call me back as soon as you know'.

I headed off to the information desk, James was pale, he was already worried about flying for the first time and had begged me to send him ahead on a boat so that he didn't have to get on a plane, but I told him that was ridiculous and would take weeks, he had to come with us on the plane. The chap on the information desk wasn't very helpful; the flight was fully booked so we couldn't buy a new ticket. Although he said we could change the name on the flights but it was an extra forty pounds but we could only do it with the original credit card that the flights had been booked with. Mum had bought the ticket and I tried to explain to him that she was in Manchester Airport and I didn't have her card details. I stepped away from the desk, worried about how much time we had, but called Mum back to explain. Luckily by now they were through security and were sitting in a bar in the departure lounge. 'She's always got some sort of drama' I could hear John in the background grumbling to Mum. 'Shut up John it's not her fault, I booked the flight in the wrong name' Mum retorted. 'Well she should have checked this out before now, everything is always last minute with you lot!' John was right; we were always having some sort of drama. Mum gave me her credit card details and I jotted them down and queued back up with other passengers to speak to the helpdesk chap again.

Fifteen minutes more of queuing and I'm back with the guy. He inputs all of Mum's credit card details only to tell us that these are not the ones she booked the original flight with, so I will have to call her again. Mum was flapping by this time and struggled to give me the details of a different credit card and I repeated the queuing process again and at last the flight was sorted, James could check in. Phew!

James and I got on the aeroplane. He then proceeded to immediately put himself to sleep. This is a technique James has perfected over the years since he was quite small. If ever he is afraid of anything, he just goes straight to sleep, I often wondered when he was little if he was actually fainting from fear, but it appeared not. We were delayed for about half an hour as some baggage has to be removed from the hold but eventually we were about to take off when James awoke. 'Are we there yet?' the famous question from all kids when travelling. 'No we've not taken off yet' I replied and the look of horror from James was quite frightening. 'Don't worry, you'll enjoy this bit, sit next to the window so you can see us take off, you're going to love it' I reassured him. James nervously swapped seats with me as the engines started up, he immediately fastened his seat buckle as we started to hurtle along the runway and grabbed my hand with an almost death like grip. Then the most amazing smile came from James. He's always been a bit of a speed freak and loves cars, and when we are on the motorway he's always trying to get me to put my foot down. He realised that a plane could travel much more quickly than my Mondeo on the M6 and was rather enjoying the experience. Then we were up in the air and James loved it. I knew he would.

A mere two and a half hours later and we were collecting our baggage from the carousel at Alicante airport. We could see the lovely June sunshine out of the windows and we were very excited. I switched on my mobile phone to see if Mum has landed yet and almost straight away a text came through saying 'Black Hawk Down'. This is Mum's usual signal that she's arrived safely at her destination. It's either that or 'The Eagle has landed'. So I immediately called her, and she informed me that they had a tail wind and picked up a bit of speed so got there at about the same time as us. We arranged to meet outside the airport near the coach park where the 'Resort Hopper' bus that Mum had booked would transfer us to our hotel.

When we got outside, Sue was there along with Mum and John. Mum seemed quite distressed and had something brown all down her holiday clothes, Sue was sniggering. What transpired was that Mum decided to put her cup of hot chocolate into her handbag whilst she carried things along. I don't really need to say any more but the fact was it was now all down the front of her top and the length of her trousers and her handbag was swimming with the stuff. John was shouting that he'd told her not to put it in her handbag, but Mum was blaming him all the same. I sighed and rolled my eyes at Sue, she gave me that knowing look. That was a good start to the holiday.

The coach trip to the hotel was none eventful apart from the fact we were the last to get dropped off, so a forty-five minute journey ended up taking well over two hours from leaving the airport to getting to our hotel. We were booked into an apart-hotel which housed many apartment type rooms with full catering and washing facilities as Mum and John prefer self catering than being tied to rigid meal-times in a hotel. We were next door to the Sol Pelicanos hotel where they film the TV series Benidorm with Johnny Vegas, otherwise known as Mark Pennington who actually lives quite near to my Mum and sister in Thatto Heath in St Helens and they know him quite well. We can use that pool too and it's quite surreal to see the set where they film the comedy sketches.

We had unpacked and John had been for the usual supplies of water, bread, butter and milk, so that we could make some lunch. John's case was packed with enough bacon for an army so we were having bacon butties and Sue had the frying pan and kettle on. Mum was now complaining that her mouth is hurting and instructed John to go to the chemist below our hotel for something for an ulcer which she thinks she's got under her dentures. 'God only knows what he'll come back with' Mum complains, 'They don't speak a word of English in that chemist; he'll probably end up with piles cream'. We all burst out laughing, we were definitely Brits abroad, Mum pretended to know a bit of Spanish and definitely had all the strange pronunciations off pat and I'd learned how to ask for two large beers as I was convinced that's all I needed to know in Benidorm. Sue had already hung out her Union Jack towel and a Welsh dragon towel from the balcony and James has his Liverpool football shirt on and Union Jack shorts, so we are the perfect stereotypical Brits.

Ten minutes later John was back 'I've got you Bon Jovi for that ulcer, they knew exactly what you needed in there' he announced. '*Bon Jovi?*' Mum enquires. 'Oh you mean Bonjella' she shrieks. Did you actually ask for Bon Jovi?' Mum is almost peeing herself with laughter as are both Sue and I. John confirmed that he asked for Bon Jovi and they gave him the correct stuff. John is famous for getting his words mixed up, but even in Spain they know what he's on about.

So we'd settled by the pool for the rest of the afternoon to soak up some rays. I was oddly feeling quite tired and didn't fancy going out in the evening, and I was surprised that Mum was banging on about visiting

Paul, her friend who owns the Terrace Bar which is a short taxi ride from where we were staying. 'Paul's got a quiz on tonight, we have to go, and he's expecting us' she said. 'Well I might stay in this evening, you go on without me' I reply. 'Oh no, you can't' she shrieked. 'He's expecting all of us'. 'OK' I said, 'I'll get ready and come along'. What I didn't know was that Mum had organised a surprise for me there. Sue knew exactly where the place was and agreed that when we were ready we'd go ahead. I wanted to walk to waken myself up a bit so Sue and James walked with me and Mum and John got a taxi over. It was only a short walk and we were there in about 10 minutes or so. When we arrived at this bar that I've never been to before in my life, I saw a gigantic poster in the window, and guess who was pictured on it? Me! Sue was laughing her head off, Mum had arranged this poster, 'Happy Birthday Siân 40 years of age' and mine and Sue's photographs were on it, Mum had sent it on ahead of us to Paul at the Terrace bar. I was really pleased if not in a state of shock for a few minutes. Paul's bar was fantastic. Paul and his staff took special care of us and as Mum and John had been going there for years they treated us like part of the family. Paul's food is exceptionally good and we returned on many occasions for his excellent roast dinners, the 'Best in Benidorm' as we often say.

Mum had got it all arranged, lots of places to visit and entertainment acts to watch. She mentioned 'Sticky Vicky' the local magic show, but it all sounded rather pornographic Sue stuck her nose in the air and I declined that suggestion. Some other friends of Mum's and ours Allan and Nigel would be out in Benidorm at the same time and we had arranged to meet up during the holiday. Paul from the Terrace Bar has also arranged bowling and a party of us were planning to do that the following week. Mum wanted to see the Westlife tribute act that was appearing along with the look-a-likes Rod Stewart and Tina Turner at Morgan's Tavern and we arranged to go there a few nights later.

I was stunned when we arrived a few nights later at Morgan's Tavern. It looks like a ship from Pirates of the Caribbean from the outside, but I realised when we got inside that it's where they film the bar and entertainment scenes in the comedy series 'Benidorm' on ITV. How spectacular. Mum knows where they film everything in Benidorm and she's been regularly 'tweeting' on Twitter with Derren Litten the series writer and I'm sure she's angling for a walk on as an extra in the show. She's even regularly listening to Benidorm's Excite FM radio show where her friend Mark Nolan broadcasts. It was only a couple of weeks ago when I walked into her front room to hear a dedication to Siân, Sue and Trashy Pat (Mum's line-dancing nickname) blaring from her laptop... I digress... so we were all having a wonderful time but Mum seemed a bit subdued this particular evening and although it's not unusual she did seem to be up and down to the ladies quite a lot. I assumed she must have Spanish tummy or her water works are playing up as usual and we continued with the evening watching Rod Stewart and then Tina Turner. We were just waiting to see Westlife which Mum had been going on about for almost a week by then. When she grabbed John by the arm and flew out of the place knocking shocked waiters and waitresses flying in her wake. Sue and I looked at each other blankly and I asked 'what's up with her?' 'She's been waiting for this for ages and now she's done a runner?' Sue shrugged and James came back from the bar with another tray of cocktails and we continued with our evening. We never really found out what was wrong with Mum that night and when we quizzed John about it she just yelled at him to shut up. But every time we mention Mum in

Morgan's Tavern she changes the subject and gives John a strange look.

The next evening we were off to a different bar, and Sue and I were knocking back the gin and tonics and Bacardi and cokes respectively. There was nothing spectacular going on this evening, just a Scouse comedian, a chap on a fiddle who I'm certain was one of the members of Westlife the previous evening and also behind the bar in Morgan's Tavern along with a drag act. We were all sat at the table enjoying the evening. 'I thought that was your voice Pat' all of a sudden we heard this camp shriek coming from behind a curtain, and out strode a very glamerous drag queen known locally as 'the Cock in a Frock'. I don't know his real name but I think Mum knew him from St Helens. Mum was concert secretary at the Thatto Heath Labour Club and regularly put acts on. 'Blimey, fancy meeting you here' shrieked Mum 'It's a bloody small world Pat'. He replied. John just raised his eyebrows and we settled down for a filthy night of humour, courtesy of the Cock in a Frock.

We all had a terrific time and in the end Mum, James, Sue and I left Allan and Nigel with John to carry on with their evening.... Back at the apartment we all decided to stay up and have a few more drinks while waiting for John to come home. There was a strange noise at the door and loads of sniggers. In came Nigel and Allan with a laughing John – they proceeded to tell us that John has got drunk and fallen out of the taxi. John staggers to the centre of the room and proceeded to announce 'I did not fall out of the taxi' he slurred 'my body got out, but my legs refused to leave!' We all, as usual, fell about laughing.

The next evening was more of the same, plenty of good food at Paul's Terrace Bar and then a few drinks. This evening we decided to go to the Stretford End.

This is a sports bar near to our hotel. John is an avid Everton fan, along with Sue and both James and I are mad for Liverpool so for the lot of us to be sitting in a Manchester United theme bar is a sight to behold. Anyway there was a football match on that John wanted to see so off we all went. The bar has a large outdoor section with massive plasma screens up on the walls so that the patrons can watch the Sky Sports channels, we were all in good spirits, James is asking for more Euros so that he can play pool with some other youngsters he's met. All of a sudden there was a massive cracking sound and the plastic garden seat that John was sitting in, went from under him, as he was on a slight incline he bashed his head against the wall behind him and went rolling down the path. Mum yelled out and was in a total panic, John seemed unconscious and James was desperately trying to help his Granddad up and although it was awful for John as usual Sue and I were in complete hysterics and not much help. We'd had lots to drink and seem to have no control when unfortunate things happen accidentally.

Well the long and the short of it was John had to be taken with an almost hysterical Mum to the local hospital for stitches as blood had started gushing from his head. He was fine in the end, but I don't think Mum fully recovered from the shock of it all, and they've recently removed all the plastic garden chairs from their garden and replaced them with solid wooden ones. By the time they got back to the hotel room, Sue and I were completely legless. I was ready for bed and was finding it hard to keep my eyes open; however Sue seemed to have a new lease for life. She was chatting loudly on her mobile to God knows who and wandering around spilling Bacardi everywhere, I was trying to get her to go to bed as James was pulling his face on the sofa and I knew that Mum and John would be back soon and John would want

286

some peace and quiet. Sue had recently been to see the doctor at home as she couldn't sleep very well and had been prescribed some tablets. These appeared to be clashing with the amount of alcohol we were drinking and sending her loopy as she was virtually incoherent as she jabbered on.

Eventually I made her go to bed and shortly afterwards John and Mum got back, I was glad to see that John was now fully recovered and we all settled down in bed.

I don't know how long after it was but we were all woken by this insane chatter, it was Sue again, streaking now naked through Mum and John's bedroom like 'wee willy winky' but without the nightgown. John and James didn't know where to look, Mum was shouting and I was almost at the point of chucking her off the balcony. Eventually she settled down, and I don't think she remembered a thing the next day. But suffice to say she laid off the booze for most of the rest of the holiday.

For our last night we were having a special treat and going to Benidorm Palace. This is like a Las Vegas style show, where semi naked girls in feathers parade around. There was to be a comedian on and also some 'brat pack' look alike crooners, Sammy Davis Junior, Frank Sinatra and Dean Martin. John particularly liked this kind of music so we were all going to have a great time. The evening consisted of a three-course-meal and entertainment, all for the reasonable price of fifty odd Euros each. Bargain. James kept visiting the bar as usual he was our waiter and as they didn't seem to care how old he was they served him with our cocktails and we certainly downed a good few of them.

When the comedian came on, who should it be but Ricky Tomlinson. Mum and John know him through their connections with the Labour party, and as we were sitting close to the front Ricky spotted my Mum with her pink hair and in his loud Scouse voice shouts 'It's Pat' and 'My arse' at the top of his voice on many occasions. Mum later met him out front and bought his signed autobiography, perhaps he'd like a copy of mine!

So that was my holiday and 40th birthday celebration, 2 weeks we won't forget in a hurry!

# Chapter 58

## 2006 – Blind Date

No it wasn't Cilla again! This year was one of those milestone birthdays, this time my 40th and it seemed to pass me by as they often do. I'm not complaining but I think your attitude to birthday's changes with your age. When you are younger you can't wait to be a teenager or become twenty one because these dates mark a change in your life, when you can drive, when you can officially drink and when you can vote. After that birthdays come and go and the years are marked by the significant birthdays of others, children and parents. When you reach retiring age it all becomes important again. Just think how many times do you hear old people say with pride? 'I'm 80 next year', it's like being a child again and birthdays matter.

I had a great time in Benidorm and I came back with a great tan and presents for Kate and Marc and when I got home Kate and her friend Leigh were just getting ready to go out to Milton Keynes city centre so they stopped for a chat as I unpacked. I could see that Kate was staring at me and after a while she said 'You look really nice Mum and much younger than 40. You need to get a new bloke'. Oh no, Kate's at it again, going on about me finding someone.

'I'm happy as I am Kate; you know what happened with Stuart' 'we're all better on our own'. I told her but it started me thinking.........

I was happy to be single and although I had no intention of dating I did understand how Kate felt. When James is out with his mates in the evening and Kate and Marc go out I think she feels sorry for me when I am left at home alone. But I'm happier than I've ever been and have lots of nice friends. I think this book will show why I'm happy now with a quiet life!

'We were talking to a really nice guy yesterday' Kate sheepishly admitted. 'He's really great and has a fantastic BMW Convertible' she went on.

I was dumbstruck. 'We told him all about you and that you were a 'yummy Mummy' and he wants to take you out.'

Now I was cross. My 17 year old daughter was arranging a blind date for me. 'No way, absolutely no chance' on the other hand I started to panic 'who is it? Do I know him, what have you been telling him?' I can't think who Kate knows, it must be someone much younger than me, how would she know anyone my age?

'It's Sarah's Dad' she eventually admits. 'Sarah's Dad? What about Sarah's Mum?' I shriek. 'Oh they're divorced, they've been divorced for years'. Kate assured me but Leigh is laughing. I had no idea who Sarah was let alone her Dad so I was none the wiser.

Kate sensed that she had made me curious 'He's really trendy Mum and he's only a year older than you. We've arranged it all he's going to pick you up at about nine o'clock tonight. Wait till you see his car, he must be loaded Mum, go on please meet him.'

I was speechless, which is rare for me, I was furious, but at the same time, I felt sorry for the poor sod that had been set up for a date with me. I don't know what came over me, but after knocking back quite a bit of the duty free I'd brought home, I agreed and as Kate said she'd seen him in the pub the night before but didn't have his number and it was all arranged anyway. I either had to go out to avoid him and leave Kate to explain when he arrived or just go out for the date and then let him down afterwards.

So I got ready and then waited upstairs so I could see him from the bedroom window. At least I would know what he looked like before we had to meet face to face. It would also give me time to escape out of the back door before Kate got to the front door, just in case he was too scary.

I'd never been so nervous and I have certainly never had a blind date before, but at least I was looking my best due to the holiday and tan. So I had a bit of liquid courage and with half of a bottle of wine inside me I felt more relaxed.

I watched the car arrive which I must say was gorgeous, a brand new convertible pale blue BMW with cream leather seats, he had got the roof down. Very impressive!

He was blond and looked quite nice from a distance, as he hopped out of the car. I started to go down the stairs thinking that this wasn't going to be too bad after all. He dashed down the steps to my house and there was a knock on the door. Kate went to answer it and I was standing half way up the stairs as he came in.

'*Oh no*!' I thought. I was on the stairs but nevertheless as I descended I realised that I was still towering over the midget. I'm 5'7' and close on 5'11' in my heels. He couldn't be much over 5 feet tall. His blond hair was dyed – badly, and was actually quite thin and yellow.

He resembled a miniature Peter Stringfellow and with his shirt hanging open to the waist they could be brothers. He had obviously been overdoing the sun-bed and his skin looked like sun dried tomatoes. The shirt buttons that were fastened were in the wrong order so his shirt looked like it was too small for him. To top it all he was actually wearing a gold medallion on a chain and it looked like his chest hair was a wig.

'Katie was right, you are a yummy Mummy' he leered.

'Nice to meet you' I lied through gritted teeth, glaring at Kate.

As we often say 'he was full of himself' and he obviously had huge amounts of completely misplaced self confidence along with the huge amounts of what I could remember from my Dad as 'High Karate' aftershave. As I left for our 'blind date' I turned to Kate, who is only a tiny 5'4' herself. 'Didn't you think about how short he is compared to me? I hissed.

'He didn't seem so short sat in the pub' She replied grinning wildly.

'Yes its hysterical Kate, thanks a lot!'

Needless to say after that one date, we didn't see each other again.

# Chapter 59

## 2006 – Robbie

It was about to be Sue's thirty-seventh birthday and although that's not a special birthday, I wanted to do something nice for her. Sue rang me one day in May saying she could get tickets for Robbie Williams' next concert which was going to be in Milton Keynes at the Bowl. I was excited nearly as much as Sue, but she was almost apoplectic when she told me that the last night of his concert was the 19th of September – her birthday! 'OK, get the tickets, and I'll pay and that can be your birthday present from me'. Sue was made up and although we had a while to wait, Sue was ecstatic when the tickets came through.

Eventually the day came, I booked the day off work so that we could make a whole day of it and Sue was driving down, we were in constant conversation as she pelted down the M6 in her little yellow Fiat Seicento. The next thing I knew she was calling me on the phone again 'Where are you now?' I asked all excited. 'I'm at Crew' she yelled down the phone, the noise from her car was deafening. 'I've got to turn back' she screamed. 'Why what's up? Is it the car?' I was panicking then, I knew how much she was looking forward to the concert and nothing would stop her from going, Robbie is her all time hero, she loves him. 'I've forgotten the tickets'. She was almost crying now. 'Don't worry we've plenty of time, it'll only put about an hour and a half on your journey, turn back'. We couldn't get in without the tickets so she had to turn around.

So about four hours later Sue had arrived, she must have had the engine on her one litre Fiat, screaming its head off all the way down, but she had made it and we were ready to go. We drove to the city centre; I'd arranged that we'd park at the Hockey Stadium in Steve the Head Chef's car-park space. I often worked there and we are good friends, and then we'd walk down to the Bowl on foot, it's only about half an hour's walk and it was a lovely day. We were armed with our Bacardi Breezers and it was a nice leisurely stroll.

When we got there we were really early and decided to browse around the merchandising stalls. Sue bought nearly everything on offer and I got a t-shirt. I'd never seen Sue so excited about anything in her life. We started to make our way through to the main arena to find a spot to sit. The Bowl is a massive outdoor arena where you sit on the grass. There is a stage where the bands set up and then all the audience is around in a massive bowl shaped circle on the embankment. Many famous bands have played there, including Queen, the real Bon Jovi, (not the mouth ulcer ointment) David Bowie, Oasis, Take That and even Michael Jackson!

We were all set for the concert. On first was Basement Jaxx. They were fabulous and they played all their famous songs. Next up was Orson, they were very good too. And finally the main event. The stage lights were flashing and there was a countdown of numbers from ten to one. The crowd was going wild; I'd never seen so many pink cowboy hats and fluffy rabbit ears in my life. As they all shouted three... two... one – I turned to look at Sue and she was actually shaking and crying. 'Don't cry I thought you'd love this' I screamed above the noise. 'I am I am' she yelled back. Then out came Robbie and Sue was screaming her head off, I like Robbie Williams but Sue was ecstatic' She sang her head off and danced her arse off the whole way through that concert and it was another of the happiest days of our lives. A day we'll never forget, thanks Robbie.

# Chapter 60

## 2006 – A blast from the past

Kate was still nagging me to find a man. 'I'm happy on my own Kate, don't go on. If you'd had my life you wouldn't be so eager to find anyone either' I told her in no uncertain terms.

'You should get on a dating website' she went on. 'I am not going on a dating site, all sorts of weirdo's are on those, freaks who can't find anyone the normal way' I shouted. 'I'm going to register you on Match.com she said, 'don't you dare, I'm not interested' I blasted her.

So as far as I was concerned that was it, end of conversation. I really am happy on my own and if I never meet another man I don't care, that is the truth. So when I started getting emails into my hotmail account with the subject of 'Your hot matches'. I realised Kate had in fact added me to the dating site Match.com. But I had no interest and just deleted them the emails. I didn't even bother to login to find out how to delete the account.

It was only one day when I was deleting the deluge of 'hot matches' that I accidentally clicked on one which opened it rather than deleting it. Staring back at me was a picture of a chap 'my hot match' who seemed familiar. After closer inspection it was Alan Bennett. The old friend from years ago, the one who I was pals with years before when I'd met my 3rd husband Mark. What was he doing on a dating website? I had heard he'd remarried a few years before and I'd seen him in Tesco with a new baby.

My curiosity was sparked so I found out from Kate how she'd registered me on the website and got the username and password off her that she'd used. Of course she'd not subscribed to the extortionate fees so after all that I couldn't make contact with Alan unless I signed up. Bloody hell! That was the most expensive email I had ever sent, it cost me sixty quid to sign up! Apparently you get a few months for that but all I wanted to do was send an email to an old friend. I couldn't believe that someone I actually knew was recommended as a possible date. Anyway I did it and sent him my mobile number.

A few hours later he sent me a text message and we exchanged a few texts and arranged to meet up. Alan was now living near the Galleon pub in Old Wolverton so we arranged to meet there. I remembered Alan being a bit of a drinker so I warned him not to be s**t faced when I got there. He laughed and promised me that he wouldn't. Strangely I was nervous but also excited.

Alan and I hit it off again straight away; he was just the same as before just about 10 years older. And that's how we got back together again. It was nothing serious, like before we were just dating, but Alan is good fun and I like his Mum and Dad and sister Jackie. They're all really nice.

# Chapter 61

## 2007 – It's over at last

Those sad years when I was with Jimmy, James's Dad, have always been with me. In some ways they have made me a better person. I'm kinder and more thoughtful; I try to help other people more, like I was helped when I needed it. But the fact that I took James away from his Dad and all his family has always nagged at the back of my mind. We'd been gone 12 years and we'd not spoken much about it over the years. James knew the truth but he'd had no interest in meeting his Dad or his other family.

So when I got a call one evening from Marc and Kate's Dad Paul, from the Isle of Man, I was quite startled at what he was telling me.

'Our Shaun rang to say, someone's been in touch with him to say Jimmy is dead' I was stunned. 'I'm not sure if it's true or not, whoever it is wants to speak to you, but I've told our Shaun not to give out your number'.

'No don't' I said panic rising in my voice. 'It might be a ploy to find out where I am'.

Hardly anyone from back home knows where I live. Mum always says 'down south' if anyone asks, she never says where I live and we've been very careful.

'Who was it who was asking do you know'. I enquired. 'Someone called Michelle, do you know her?' 'Yes' I replied. 'She was Jimmy's brother Eddie's wife' I went on 'I kept in touch with her for a while when I moved down here, but not spoken to her in over ten years.' That was the end of the conversation. I had no intention of finding out anymore. I didn't care. Or so I thought.

A week or so later, Paul phoned again, he said that this person had been in touch again, and could they just pass on a message to say that Jimmy was dead, they understood that I wouldn't want to get in touch but they wanted me to know.

After the call I sat down with James on the sofa. 'James, I've got something to tell you, and I don't know if it's going to upset you or not but I think you should know' I said. 'Your Dad, Jimmy, well he's died'

James just sat there with tears running down his face. 'Oh James, I didn't want to upset you, I wish I hadn't said anything now'. I said.

'I don't know why I'm crying Mum' he put his arms around me and sobbed. 'I never wanted to meet my Dad, but now I never can'. Oh what have I done I thought. Taking him away from his Dad, did I do the right thing?

A little while later James said that he was OK and he assured me he wasn't upset now, and it was just the initial shock.

But it was on my mind all the time now. I had to get in touch with Jimmy's family. The next weekend we were visiting my Mum, so I was going to find Jimmy's brother Eddie or his sister in law Michelle and find out exactly what had happened.

I didn't say anything to James but instead of driving straight to Mum's house we got off the motorway and I drove to the last address I'd had for Michelle, Eddie's ex-wife. I knocked on the door, but there was no answer. I had no idea where she was or even if she still lived there. She may have got back with Eddie for all I knew. So I drove the short distance to Eddie's last known address and went to the front door. Again there was no answer, but I knocked next door. I asked if Eddie Hayes still lived there. The neighbours said they'd lived there for the last eight years but no-one with the name of Hayes had lived there in the time they'd been there. James had refused to get out of the car at these two addresses and was getting more agitated. 'Please can we go to Nan's Mum, I don't want to meet them?'

'One more address, and I promise if there's no-one there, we'll leave it, I'll not bother looking anymore'. James didn't seem convinced but he agreed with me.

Just up the road was Jimmy's Dad's house, again I didn't know if he still lived there or not, it had been 12 years. I had no idea where Jimmy's sisters lived; I couldn't even remember their addresses.

Our last stop was to be at Jimmy's Dad's house. I parked up outside and urged James to come down to the front door with me. He reluctantly got out. 'I promise, if there's no-one here, we'll leave and not come back' I tried to reassure him. 'What if he goes mad at us?' He won't James your Granddad was nice and if he says anything I don't like we'll just leave, don't be scared.'

So I knocked on the door. James's Granddad opened it. 'James, it's Siân, this is your Grandson, James' I said. 'I knew you'd come' he said. 'Come on in'.

In we went, it was as though the past 12 years hadn't happened, they welcomed us with open arms, Helen was there, Jimmy's partner. They were so pleased to see us, and they explained everything that had happened.

Jimmy had died of a massive heart attack in the town centre. They had done a post mortem and he'd been buried the week before. Jimmy and Helen later took us to the grave in Whiston, it was all still new and the ground hadn't settled yet, all the flowers and wreaths were still there. It was quite sad, Jimmy was 45 and in the ground. James would never meet him.

Later that day, Jimmy told Maureen and Eddie – Jimmy's sister and brother that we were there and they invited us to Maureen's that evening so that James could meet all his family. When we got there, James was a bit overwhelmed. Jimmy had 3 sisters Jane, Maureen and Irene and a brother Eddie, they all had lots of children and even some of those had children of their own and everyone had turned up to meet James. It was all quite emotional. James had about 20 cousins, all his aunts and uncles and his other Nan Renee and his Granddad were all there. Eddie went on to tell us that he'd searched everywhere to find us, the police and social services wouldn't give them any information about us, he had been to my first ex-husband's parents house to see if he could track us down, but they had also moved. He told us he had almost given up and on the following Monday morning he had arranged to see his local MP in St Helens to see if he could help, he was desperate to find James. The funny thing is that if he had gone into his MPs office on that Monday, he'd have been face to face with my sister Sue who is the MPs Secretary. So he would have found us in the end. The last thing he'd said before I turned up to Jimmy's Dad's house was

'I'm never going to find him am I?' Then as if by magic we turned up.

Jimmy's Dad also told us that two years before, he and Helen were going to sell that house and move, but at the last minute they changed their mind. If he'd have moved I would never have found him.

I think James felt awkward everyone was staring at him; I guess they saw Jimmy in him. They had only just lost their Son and Brother and Uncle but now they had James, his only son. A little part of him was still with them. Over the coming weeks, I took James around to meet other relatives he'd not met before. He was quite shy but he hugged everyone, he even got to meet his Great-Nan Lucy just before she died, and had his picture taken with her, which he keeps in his room now.

Something good has come out of what was a very difficult time for us. I have my wonderful James and he now has his massive extended family. He seems particularly fond of his Granddad and they have a great rapport. I'm glad I took James up there that day it all turned out wonderfully in the end.

# Chapter 62

## 2007 – I want a power shower

I'd wanted a brand new bathroom for as long as I'd lived in this house. It was an ex-council house and still had the awful council standard bathroom suite. White bath; sink with no pedestal just stuck to the wall and a disgusting looking toilet with a cream plastic cistern. I hated it. We had an electric shower in the bath, but it hadn't worked for a long time and was a death trap it was funny that no one had ever been electrocuted in there as it has all be wired up incorrectly by my ex husband. The floor was a beige lino and the wall tiles which only went half way up the walls were an off greenish-white, with a kind of water embossed look to them. There was antique pine tongue and groove along the side of the bath, it was absolutely hideous. It was the one room in the house that you couldn't decorate or do anything to it which would make it look any better.

I bought my house from the Council in September 2006 and got a pretty decent discount off the purchase price as I'd lived there for over 10 years as a council tenant. I took out a bit extra money on the mortgage as I was determined to have a brand new bathroom. So I'd been to B&Q to have a look at their bathrooms – what a selection! I immediately decided that I wanted a shower cubicle and no bath, and I was going to splash out (very apt) on an all singing all dancing power shower fully equipped with body jets. Fabulous. The good thing about B&Q is that they set out the bathrooms in their spacious showroom-come-warehouse with ideas for decoration and such, and I decided on black and white tiles like a chess board effect all over the walls – great! So after spending over a thousand pounds and within a week or so it was nicely delivered to my house, we were all set I just needed a plumber to give me a quote and I would be on my way to my dream bathroom.

Well 3 quotes later all the plumbers wanted over £2000 to install it, I was gutted! In my excitement I'd also bought a toilet and new wash hand basin for the downstairs loo as well and all the tiles.

So there was nothing else for it the quotes were too expensive so I had to ask my Dad if he can help. He's not actually my Dad but John is my Mum's husband after the Dad and step Dad and is an ex Merchant Navy Engineer who seems to be able to fix anything, so he's a good bet on fitting a power shower. As usual John never says no and the date was agreed that they would come down and spend a few days. John estimated that the whole re-fit would take about four days and they arrived on the Thursday with plans to be done by Monday or Tuesday at the latest.

So I would be sleeping on the sofa and Mum and John would have my bed. We had prepared for their arrival and my eldest son Marc had taken a sledge hammer to the bathroom tiles and got them all off, and he was going to do the heavy lifting of the bath, sink and toilets to be removed while John did all the technical plumbing stuff. Sorted. So we begin on the big clear out. It took a full day to get everything out of the house but we were on track. I'd bought everything we needed or so I thought, but that wasn't the half, John needed plumbing parts, piping of various different sizes. Washers, insulation, auto shut off valves, connectors, u-bends and God knows what else. So about five hundred quid later we returned from B&Q with all the paraphernalia and that was just the first trip there.

I got ready to put the new floor down in the upstairs bathroom. Grey floor tiling. John told us we need a membrane to stop any leakages from the shower going into the downstairs bathroom. So off we went back to B&Q for thick black plastic to create the waterproof membrane.

The toilet that was previously in the upstairs bathroom was an old fashioned thing with a massive soil waste pipe, what I failed to realise was that new toilets have a much smaller diameter waste. So John had to modify the connection from the new toilet to the old soil waste, it took at least half a day of swearing and cursing and John looking more and more frustrated. The day at last came to an end and we were hardly any further along. Another night on the sofa, but not too bad so far.

We were up early the next day and back to it. One toilet was fitted and now John was running flexible piping up the wall in the bathroom between the plasterboard so it didn't show, into the loft across the ceiling into Marc's room where the pump would be situated on the floor of the airing cupboard next to the hot water tank. Lord only knows what he was doing up there all day but he was shouting to Marc and James who were periodically going up and down the ladder to the loft with various tools.

My loft isn't the attic type of loft where you can easily get around; it's basically a roof space big enough for a dwarf to stand up or a full sized person to crawl around. The space is lessened by the fact that there are 3 water tanks up there. Heaven only knows why. All of a sudden the upstairs lights went out.

'Are you OK up there John?' I shouted

'Who bloody wired this place up' came a muffled scouse voice from the loft?

'I doubt it's been touched since it was built John in 1974' I called back.

'Well it's in a right state' John shouted. 'Get me a torch'.

'What's he doing up there? Mum asked

'Dunno – he's been up there all day and the lights are going off and on now'.

There was still no sign of John for a few more hours but James was up and down the ladder with regular cups of tea.

At around 5pm there was an almighty crash and we all dashed upstairs to find John's leg hanging through the ceiling in Marc's room. James and Marc are doubled over stuffing pillows into their faces trying not to laugh.

'Oh hell John' Mum yells, 'come down from up there'

There were various expletives John must have picked up from his Navy days and eventually we pushed his foot back into the ceiling. All I could think of was Frank Spencer and I was finding it difficult to control myself from laughing but at the same time I was desperately sorry for John who was almost 70 and I was worried that this job seemed to be much bigger than I originally thought.

Many years ago in 1975 John was severely burned aboard his ship where he was an Engineer in the Merchant Navy, when the engine room exploded. If it hadn't been for his quick reactions and bravery when he ran through the flames to shut down the engines, all hands would have been lost at sea as they were 900 miles off Hawaii. The story actually made ITV's News at Ten as at the time it was the longest ever air-sea rescue and they had to refuel the helicopter mid air to save everyone. This is an extract from an eye witness report as John was rescued from the burning super-tanker.

> *'The two injured men were helped by a State Registered Nurse, Her first hand knowledge and trauma treatment played very much a large asset in the eventual recovery of both men. Just after the fire, John Ireland managed to exit the engine room via the boiler room, the crew and other officers were within the engine room area and it is presumed the Donkeyman was escorted by the crew. John actually walked along the flying bridge with assistance to the mid-ship accommodation, where John found the ships hospital, They had to cut off Johns overalls, his eye glasses had melted on his face and at this stage he went into severe shock and dehydration (Quote John looked like a chimney sweep)'*

Well chimney sweep was nothing to what emerged from my loft; it was a sight like I'd never seen in my life. John was totally black from head to foot; he'd spent most of the day crawling under the fibreglass loft insulation. He was covered in a rash from the fibreglass and his hair looked like he'd had an electric shock! Maybe that happened when the lights went out? John had suffered some pain in his life but I think the loft in my house had taken him to the brink. He looked at breaking point and we were only 2 days in. We now had no running water upstairs for bathing so John had to get in the sink in the kitchen to clean himself up. It should all seem much better the next day – I hoped.

The next few days went well and we made good progress, John had re-plastered and artexed Marc's bedroom ceiling, I had tiled the bathroom floor and the walls were black and white tiles like a chess board, John had built two new false walls to hide the piping and fit the light-up mirror and hide all the electrics.

John was still spending quite a lot of time in the loft and the lights continued to flash on and off but he was getting there.

'Seeing as you're doing quite a bit of electrics, do you think you could put a ceiling fan in the landing for me' I've had it about 6 years and never had it fitted' John raised his eyebrows and gave my Mum a filthy look that he thought I'd not seen but as the hero he is, he agreed. 'And while you're at it, could you put a light in the landing cupboard as we can't see in there?'

'Yes 'Shawn' – John sighed. (Even John got my name wrong!) Mum had to go back to St Helens for a meeting she couldn't get out of and to check on their house, this had only been estimated as a 4 day job.

So we now had a new light in the landing cupboard but when you switched it on the bathroom light went out. John in his frustration accidentally smashed the cover to the bathroom light fitting, and we made another trip to B&Q to get a new one. Eventually when we switched the landing light and fan on from the downstairs switch the bedroom lights stopped flickering and all was sorted. John came down from the loft and promised never to return up there. He'd shown James where the auto cut-off taps were to isolate the tank and the shower cubical.

We were about 10 days in now and things were taking shape, including my back which was a very funny shape after so many nights on the sofa. Mum had returned from St Helens expecting to pick John up and take him home but we were still not finished.

John had removed the downstairs toilet and sink and was working on getting the new one fitted which all happened quite quickly but would the cistern fill? Would it hell.

'The bloody plumbing is up the spout, there doesn't seem to be enough pressure to fill the cistern' John informed us. 'It seems to be filling from the header tank rather than the mains and there's not enough pressure'.

'But the old toilet filled up no problem' I assured him.

'Yes but these new fangled cisterns work on pressure'. So John adjusted the plumbing once again to make the toilet fill and hey presto it worked! Good old John.

Next we had to get the cubical fitted, at last poor John could get a shower. I had bought a very expensive 3 bar pump which was required to create the necessary pressure for the power shower. We were all set to go but no pump! Whatever we tried the pump wouldn't work. A thin trickle of water came out of the shower head, we were expecting a geyser from such powerful pump.

So John got the manual out that came with the pump. He'd been an engineer in the Navy so he knew a thing or two about pumps.

I insisted it was faulty and would have to go back to B&Q but John was adamant he could get it going. In the end it had him beaten so he called the support number in the manual. What transpired was that you had to ring the help number because that was all part of the warranty. The pump would never start on its own, until you cross wired it and jump started it into action. That way the manufacturers knew it had been started correctly and the warranty was then valid. Blimey it sounded like a generator was in that back bedroom. Only the Lord knew how Marc was going to sleep through that if anyone had a late night or early morning shower!

But it was working and John was first in. He appeared refreshed and gleaming. At last we could get ourselves clean.

Next to be fixed was the glass cover for the light fitting in the bathroom. John climbed the ladder to fit it and at the last moment stepped off onto the toilet seat – crack!

It was broken in half – it was like Muldoon's picnic. One thing fixed as another broke. So back to B&Q for a new toilet seat.

Well that was it, beautiful bathrooms upstairs and downstairs – the 17 days that nearly broke John Ireland. He packed his tools and headed to the car and we all waved him off. John's parting comment was…

'If you want anything else doing… don't bloody phone me!' He's a great Dad and I'll never forget those 17 days.

John having a well deserved lolly break

# Chapter 63

## 2008 – A trip to Paris

The last 12 years working for Penna have been great fun and very varied. I started off as a Secretary and my job title was Candidate Services Administrator, this involved typing up CVs for clients and general office duties along with manning the telephones and reception. I got a small but significant promotion with the launch of our Online services website where I was to be the 'helpdesk' person. This really catapulted me into a role within IT and my job changed slightly to become Application Support Co-ordinator.

My luck continued when my boss Cara left suddenly and it was left to me to manage the whole Application Support function for the UK business. Shortly afterwards the job also included supporting our European offices in Madrid, Stockholm and Paris although I didn't get the chance to visit as our IT Manager Mark visited on a yearly basis and it was decided that I wasn't needed. That was until we started with our Internet based web conferencing system and the European offices began to use our Consultancy Tracking System. At last I was invited to go to do the training and accompany Mark on his regular visits to these exotic places.

I was looking forward to visiting these offices as I already knew the staff and I had met them many times when they visited London for training. At last it was my turn to visit them. My first visit was going to be for two days in Paris, the flights and hotels were booked and I packed a little bag with all my essentials including my camera. I enjoy taking photographs and regularly update an online diary of photographs titled 'Where am I today?' It's mainly for my Mum showing all the places I get to go. Some are quite ordinary taken on a platform at a train station, others are more interesting with windmills, churches, the huge cranes Sampson and Goliath in Belfast docks and the beautiful murals painted on the gable end of houses in Londonderry so I was looking forward to getting some snaps of the Eifel Tower and L'arc de Triomphe to add to my collection.

It was October and the weather wasn't fantastic, we arrived in the evening at Charles de Gaul airport. Mark as usual was flying BA from Heathrow and I was meeting him in the airport from my Easyjet flight from Luton. We had synchronised flights so that we'd be arriving within half an hour of each other. I was amazed at how long it took to get to the terminal building once we had landed, it's a huge airport. We touched down at about 7pm in the evening and as we were taxi-ing to the terminal I had got my things together and was just sitting waiting while we went along, over a motorway bridge with traffic below, past more aircraft and what looked like hotels and shops and still we were taxi-ing. I looked at my watch it was now almost seven-twenty. I happened to be sitting right at the back of the plane and one of the flight attendants sitting just behind me cracked up laughing 'Where's he taxi-ing to? Back to Luton?' Everyone in earshot laughed. Five minutes later we were at the terminal building and we started to disembark. I quickly found Mark in the baggage hall as we were waiting for our luggage. We found a taxi and within twenty minutes we arrived at our hotel and checked in. The reception was lovely and I thought the standard was extremely high I glanced at Mark and we exchanged knowing looks that this seemed rather expensive. We usually stay in the usual business class hotels like the Holiday Inns but this seemed far more upmarket. The usual hotel Mark stays in had been fully booked so the Paris office had recommended this one. I left Mark and we headed to our rooms, I was keen to explore and see what my room was like.

I could hardly believe my eyes when I opened the bedroom door. This place must definitely have been a five star hotel, the walls didn't have wallpaper they had silk hanging on them it reminded me of the Frankfurt suite I had stayed in years before with Jim Marshall. This place was equally luxurious with black lacquered furniture and gold soft furnishings. The en suite was gorgeous too all marble in black and white. 'Wow!' I thought. I hoped we weren't going to be in trouble for staying here.

Mark and I arranged to meet in the reception and then go out for something to eat. When we met I remarked about the hotel. 'Blimey, this isn't the Premier Lodge in Manchester is it?'

'I was thinking that' Mark replied. They must be making a profit in the Paris office if they book visitors in here'. We both laughed and headed out to find a nice restaurant for dinner.

The next day was spent in the Paris office working and training. Mark was looking at the systems and making a few adjustments to the equipment and I was providing training and overviews of our web conferencing and database applications. Elisabeth arranged a nice buffet lunch for us in the office and it was all very chic and classy – no sandwiches in plastic boxes for them. I could get used to life in Paris.

Do you fancy coming for a walk around the city this evening so I can take some photographs?' I asked Mark.

'Yeah sure, I've done the whole tour thing before with my Suzie but I can get us a map, I've a good idea of where the sights are and it'll make a change from staring at the hotel walls. Where do you fancy going? Mark enquired.

'Well I was thinking as the hotel is just off the top of the Champs Elysees, we could start at the L'arc de Triomphe, and head over to the Eifel Tower, just so I have a few souvenir photos'.

'Great, we'll get some dinner while we're out'

So it was all arranged and after a quick change at the hotel we were out on the tourist trail. It was raining so I put on some good walking boots and my anorak and I even took my brolly with me, always prepared, that me.

I was a complete tourist and was snapping at everything, Mark found this quite funny but humoured me. Mark had picked up a map in the reception of the hotel, and along with the satnav on his phone (Mark has all the gadgets) he knew exactly where our route was going and we started just as it was going dusk at the L'arc de Triomphe. The rain then started and it was pouring when we arrived at the Eifel Tower. I'd been to Paris before with my friends Roy and Gill to see the Tour de France cyclists coming back up the Champs Elysee at the end of the Tour and I'd had my picture taken then with the Eifel Tower behind me and it reminded me of Blackpool Tower. But I'd not realised the sheer size of the thing until we got up close, it's colossal and very impressive. I have to admit it's even better than Blackpool Tower. To commemorate the French presidency of the EU it had been decorated with blue

315

lights and a circle of stars to represent the member states.

Every hour the lights sparkled on the Tower and it was amazingly beautiful. We took our photographs and then headed south down the river towards Notre Dame, taking pictures as we went. The rain was easing off a bit. Every now and again it actually stopped for a while. Although it was raining it wasn't too cold and we were chatting as we walked and I was taking pictures of everything so we didn't realise just how far we had gone. Paris is a lovely city, quite compact and at night the buildings are floodlit so there was a lot to see. We arrived near the Louvre and I was stunned to see the old buildings merged with the new glass pyramid. The pyramid is sunk in to the ground and you can look right down into the museum from the street level. The Louvre museum was closing but there was still a few things to see in the lobby and we could also look up into the pyramid and see the people above us looking down at us, it reminded me of a chapter in the Dan Brown book 'The da Vinci Code'.

We consulted Mark's map and carried on towards Notre Dame and I was keen to take pictures of that too. On we marched. Eventually we could see it. It was beautifully lit and the floodlights picked out all the architectural features that are often missed during the day so I got some smashing shots of it. Looking up at the huge gothic building the bells began to chime and all I could think of was the hunchback shouting 'Esmerelda, Esmerelda' from the bell tower. I have seen many versions of the Hunchback of Notre Dame but the 1923 film with Lon Chaney as Quasimodo is my favourite.

On we went... the map was in French and we thought we were heading in the right direction as we were aiming to circle back to the hotel. We'd been walking for about two and a half hours by now and my legs were starting to ache, thank goodness for the 'Cat' boots – sturdy walking gear recommended for sight-seeing. Mark is about 6 feet four inches tall, and it was taking me all my time to keep up with his strides, I felt like a little kid trying to keep up with her Dad.

We seemed to be circling round as planned but as we turned a corner I felt sure I had seen the street before but I trusted Mark's navigational skills. It all started going wrong when we ended up in what appeared to be a red light district, there were some very scantily clad 'ladies' loitering in doorways and I was reminded of my hunt for a cuckoo clock in Frankfurt. I wish my French was good enough to understand the comments they were making about us as we hurried past. I was starting to feel hungry, and we passed some street vendors selling hotdogs, the smell was fantastic, it seemed better than the stalls we have back home and I was tempted to suggest that we should stop and try one, but as we were going to find a restaurant I just walked past savouring the smell. Mark had become strangely quiet now as he studied his sat-nav, I'm not sure he had a signal. On we went. I noticed a sign for the Rue de Rivoli and Mark assured me that this would take us northwards the Champs Elysees and our hotel. We kept going and about an hour or so later we were back at the Louvre, we were indeed going in circles? I was finding it quite hard going now and Paris was still in full swing and people were beginning to fill the bars and restaurants. We'd been walking for over 3 and a half hours by now and I was flagging and in desperate need of a rest, something to eat and a drink but we still had a long way to go so the trek continued.

Eventually we came to the Place de la Concorde and we thought we were getting closer to the Champs

Elysees. If you've ever visited Paris, you will know that the Avenue des Champs-Elysees is a VERY long road. It was packed like Oxford Street in London on a Saturday and this made our walk even harder going, we were battling along in virtual silence now, the battery in my camera was almost dead and what started off as a nice little Parisian stroll now felt like walking from Land's End to John O'Groats! Eventually I could stand it no longer, I had to stop.

'Please Mark can we stop and get something to eat?' I begged. 'I thought you'd never ask' Mark panted back. 'The first restaurant we see let's go'. We had planned on a nice French restaurant, but the first thing we saw was a pizzeria. So long as they had red wine we didn't care. We almost fell through the door and the waiter saw the exhaustion on our faces and hurriedly showed us to a table.

I almost snatched the menu from the waiter as he seated us. Mark had a very odd expression on his face as he sat down. He later explained that his knees were shot and our four and a half hour marathon walk had been a bit too much for them.

'Deux grands verres de vin rouge' I blurted. That O'level French was very useful and the most important phrase of two large glasses of red wine, seemed to be etched on my memory. Mark instructed the waiter to leave the bottle and bring another!

'Good thinking Mark!' I readily agreed.

After a very tasty pizza and a few glasses of red wine we were almost ready to hit the road again, it was only about ten more minutes to our hotel and when we got there I had the best night's sleep I think I've ever had.

The next morning I met Mark at breakfast and I asked him how far he thought we'd walked. He agreed with me that we must have done six or even seven miles. It did seem like a long way but a good night's sleep and decent breakfast had set us up for another day at the office.

When we got back together again for another Parisian lunch Mark had a revelation for me.

'I traced the route we took last night on the Internet' he said. 'You won't believe how far we went'.

'How far?' I asked.

'Over 11 miles! And that's not counting the fact we were lost and going in circles for a while'

I was stunned. Not only because of the distance but the fact that I had actually managed it without medical help.

That was certainly a sight-seeing tour to remember. We went on to visit Madrid and Stockholm the following month, but Mark seemed to be caught up with more work than usual and we only took short walks around the cities. I wonder why that was?

# Chapter 64

## 2008 - Edinburgh to Manchester

Back down to earth with a bump, no reader, that wasn't EasyJet; the international trips were over and Mark and I were travelling around the British Quarterly Development Meetings (QDMs) where we introduce new technology to our Coaching teams. This is quite an enjoyable part of the job as the people we meet are very nice and always receptive to our presentations, plus the free lunches are good! IT can be quite a geeky subject and people are often either immediately turned off or quite indifferent. Mark's phrase, 'We like to come out of the office and talk to people about their issues, so that you don't see us as people who work in darkened rooms fiddling with cables' is quite an apt description of how people perceive the IT team.

Our next two destinations were Edinburgh and Manchester. Mark lives close to Heathrow and always somehow seems to manage to be able to chat up the travel company reps and either flies business class or first class train to all his destinations at half the price I ever travel in economy or standard class!

That aside I'd excelled in the travel arrangements this time. Mark had flown BA to Edinburgh to meet me, I had flown Easyjet from Luton as normal and our flights coincided and we arrived within 20 minutes of each other.

We had a fabulous day in Edinburgh a very successful meeting with lots of home-made cakes and sandwiches for lunch. We'd started to rate the meetings by the quality of the lunch provided and as my very good friend Lynne organises the meetings in Edinburgh and her Mum also makes some of the cakes, this is one of our top destinations.

We left around four o'clock for the airport and as our next destination was Manchester I was staying with Mum and Mark was staying at a nice hotel in Manchester which he insisted he would book himself after the last fiasco when I booked the hotel. We try our best to keep the cost down and book into a Premier Lodge or Holiday Inn type hotel. Cheap and cheerful but usually an acceptable standard and you know what to expect. The last time we'd stayed in a Premier Inn or Travel Lodge close to the Manchester office so I thought I had booked the same one again. My mistake I'd got the wrong one. The Travel Lodge seemed to be a *'hotel'* where the Greater Manchester City Council placed the homeless in bed and breakfast accommodation. The average age of the people in the bar was about 17. The beds were like you'd expect in a Youth Hostel and I had a thinnest pillow I had ever seen. Even the kettle in the room was screwed down so it couldn't be stolen. To make matters worse it seemed that the WWE Wrestling was being held in Manchester that night and kids were running around the place screaming their heads off all wearing merchandise from the event and behaving as though they were full of 'E' numbers. The following morning, breakfast wasn't available so we made a quick exit and headed for the nearest Starbucks. Mark's parting words were 'Not our usual standard Siân, I'll book next time'.

So on this occasion Mark had booked into Malmaison and I was staying at my Mum's. Mum and John were picking us up at the Airport and dropping Mark at his hotel before we took the short motorway journey to St Helens. I had planned to meet Mark the next morning at the Manchester office.

So back to Edinburgh airport and we walked through the departure gate and onto the security checks. I'd prepared and had all my electrical items, iPod, phone, camera, laptop out of the bag and I wasn't carrying any make-up to make sure we were not slowed down in security. We shuffled forward in the queue and as always I was convinced the guards were watching me. We eventually get to the x-ray machine and metal detector. The grumpy guard took one look at me and said 'Take your shoes off madam and walk through the detector' As usual the alarms went off and the butch looking female staff smiled as they ran their hands over me with a bit too much enthusiasm.

Mark was laughing hysterically 'There's always one Siân, and it's always you' He's right, it always is me. Eventually we got through and had a couple of relaxing G&T's in the airport bar while we waited for our flight. As we had booked our flights separately we were seated miles apart, I was in seat 6B and Mark was in seat 28A. We tried to change them but the check-in desk clerk told us the flight was full so we couldn't. Not to worry it was only a short flight from Edinburgh to Manchester.

The flight was called and as we walked to our gate I glanced out of the window. 'Mark is that a propeller aeroplane we are getting on?'

Mark took a look and shook his head. 'Jeez Siân, what have you booked, Dan Dare Airways?'

I noticed the colour was draining from his face. Mark is 6'4' and the plane looked rather small, I wondered if he could actually stand upright when we got aboard.

'I picked Flybe because they were cheap' I said defensively, 'the only other flight was via the Isle of Man and we had to change, this was only £2.40 each.' I thought I had made a great choice and saved the company a few bob in fares.

'No bloody wonder it's cheap' Mark said as he stared at the little aircraft.

We boarded the plane and I was right Mark couldn't stand upright; he had to stoop until he got to his seat further back in the plane. We sat on the tarmac for a few minutes waiting for everyone else to board; I was surprised when only 2 other passengers boarded as the clerk had earlier said it was fully booked. Shortly the propellers started and we were off. I glanced back down the aisle and Mark now seemed fine and was ordering red wine from the stewardess; he always seemed to have a way with flight attendants and now had 3 little bottles in front of him. As the stewardess passed by me she said 'Why don't you sit with your friend?' 'The girl on the check-in desk told us the flight was full and we couldn't sit together'. I replied. The stewardess fell about laughing 'These flights are hardly ever booked up, you've got the plane to yourselves, sit where you like, they're 'taking the mick' down there' and she tottered off in her heels.

I moved and sat next to Mark just as the propellers seemed to kick up a gear and the plane started to vibrate violently. He put a glass of red wine in front of me; I hoped it would settle my nerves. The flight was quite enjoyable in the end but the noise was deafening and we spent the hour shouting at each other just to hear ourselves. The noise and the vibration only added to the 'Biggles' atmosphere in the small plane and the 3 bottles of wine and the gin and tonics helped us see the funny side. We were just banking to prepare for our approach to Manchester Airport's

323

runway, when our glasses slid across the pull down trays. We grabbed them just in time and burst into laughter again. Mental note to oneself: Don't book flights on Flybe aeroplanes again.

The next day Mark and I were to give a technology presentation in the Manchester office so I was thrilled to take the opportunity of a night with Mum and Mark was happy to fend for himself in the hotel. As we were walking through the arrivals hall at Manchester Airport my phone rang. 'Which door are you coming out of?' It was Mum, she was there already waiting to pick up Mark and I from the airport and then drop Mark at his hotel.

I looked towards the exit doors to see if there was a sign but then I spotted Mum and John outside standing by the side of their Ford Focus.

'There they are Mark, that's my Mum and Dad'. As usual Mum flung her arms around me as if I had been trekking down the Amazon for the past five years; she then moved onto Mark and exuberantly introduced herself. Just like me Mark is keen on social networking and he is also keen on electronic gadgets, so Mum had added herself as a friend on Mark's Facebook page even though she didn't know him to ask his advice on the latest techie gadget. Whenever she sees something new is coming out, she immediately asks me about it and then tells me to check with Mark whether it's any good or not.

Mark had never met her before but he finds this quite sweet and indulges her. 'Oh I feel like I know you already Mark'. Mum goes on. John grabs our cases and asks about our flight, and I go into great detail about the noise and vibration on the propeller driven flight, John isn't the least bit surprised that it's a fiasco as he thinks most things I organise are. 'Did she leave her stuff on the plane?' John yells at Mark, she left all her bloody travellers cheques behind when we went to Ibiza'

Trust your parents to embarrass you!

We all piled into the car, Mark and I are consigned to the back like a couple of kids, while Mum and John argued about the satnav and got their seat belts tangled. The posh voice came from the TomTom satnav and we lurched forward.

Mum and John only live about half an hour away from the airport and know Manchester quite well. Mum had programmed the address of the hotel into the satnav but she only had the name of the street not the number. This lack of detail didn't seem to matter and it only took about ten minutes before the satnav told us that we were nearing our destination. That was when the trouble started. We appeared to be in the correct road but the satnav kept sending us down a back alley. Mum kept reversing back out and John was getting agitated. 'I don't know why you listen to that damn thing, it's always wrong'.

'Shut up John, everyone has satnav' snapped Mum, 'I bet you have satnav don't you Mark?' Mum could hardly see out of the back window with Mark and I blocking her view and she proceeded to mount the pavement.

'Watch that bloody bollard Pat' John screeched at Mum.

I just wanted to die with embarrassment. I was constantly apologising to Mark for their behaviour, Mark just laughed.

We continued to drive down the unfamiliar city streets getting deeper into the city and more and more lost. We passed what looked like an all night barbers with a few foreign looking men gathered outside. They looked a bit 'shifty' but we were completely lost so we decided to ask for directions, there were four of us so what could go wrong? They turned out to be nice bunch of guys and they gave us directions. Off we went again and guess what - we ended up back down the alley again.

'Pat, there's a map in the boot. Pull over and let me get it'. John was getting annoyed.

'Shut up John. This satnav will find the way, I'm sure we're nearby.' said Mum. The tension in the car was electric; I wasn't going to have a great evening after all this if we ever found the hotel and dropped off Mark.

Mark interrupted the chaos by announcing that he could see the hotel sign, we'd been past it about five times and no one had noticed. Mum screeched to a halt and Mark and I were almost catapulted into the front with her and John. Mark leapt out and Mum popped the boot open so he could get his case and laptop bag.

I turned to wave Mark off, only to see him racing across the carriageway. I think he thought it was safer to make that dash for it across a busy road than to spend any more time with my mad family in the Ford Focus!

# Chapter 66

## 2009 – Another flight!

We were launching a new website at work called Penna Sunrise. This was a major piece for work for the Development team as we had over eighteen thousand users of our old client site and it was getting a bit dated. Ian was our new Developer and he reminds me of a cross between Max out of the BBC soap Eastenders and Jenson Button, he's a keen snowboarder and seems to live the 'playboy' lifestyle. His graphic and design skills have really moved Penna forward with our online offering creating a funky new website which is the envy of our competitors. Ian designed this book's front cover for me and I'm over the moon with it.

George is our 'back-end' man. Not back-end as in pantomime horse but the technology part of a website rather than the user interface. He's a truly gifted Programmer, he works mostly 'under the hood' on the business layer and architecture of the site. George has a slight resemblance to Roger Federa and he actually asked me to write that into this book after I joked about his looks, he might not be too happy to see it in print. I don't think he plays much tennis but he's a Spurs fanatic his little girls call Spurs the cock-a-doodle team, after seeing the crest emblazoned on his football shirt. George has recently gone freelance and created my website www.sianbanks.com to help me promote this book and has done a fantastic job.

Next are Simon and Ekta, on this project they have formed a double act, working together on many parts of the site. Simon is affectionately known as Doc or more commonly 'The Evil Dr D' as he actually is a Doctor and in a previous life he worked in pharmaceuticals as a scientist. He's far too clever for us and if you're having a quiz team Simon has to be on it, as he knows everything. Needless to say when we enter any company quizzes, we usually win! Ekta is our glamorous lady Developer, who has a wicked sense of humour and laughs at everything, her only downfall is that if we're off for lunch or out for a drink after work, we are always waiting for Ekta she's always on the phone! We suspect she may be running a call centre in Mumbai.

Mariya is our student developer a lovely girl from Romania, we have to be careful not to say Mariya 'Can you pop over here to help with this' – as her surname is actually Popova!

Our glorious leader is Geoff, the Sunrise project had nearly been the death of him, he had been looking very pale towards the end and I'm sure he's lost weight. Geoff although 40ish has a very boyish face and could pass for someone in their twenties. I would love to have that misfortune but Geoff finds it exasperating, he also has a very striking resemblance to the actor James Spader.

At last we had gone live with the new site and we all wore Superman t-shirts which I provided as I love this team and they are all supermen and women and we drunk tequila sunrise cocktails to celebrate the new site with its new name.

I am the Application Support Manager and part of my role is to demonstrate the site to our career coaches who will be working with this site with their clients and provide their training.

(The Sunrise Dev Team – George, Ekta,
Geoff, Mariya, Ian, Simon and me)

So once again I was travelling around the country
to our various offices. Luton Airport had quickly
becoming my second home. The airport was getting
busier each time I arrived there. We were due to go
live with the site in June, just when the airport was
chocker block with holiday makers. I never left home
too early to get to Luton as it's only half an hour away
so I'm always there in time for flights. The road into
Luton has been improved quite a lot over recent years,
but this particular morning I was due to be flying to
Aberdeen and the road was completely grid locked at
6am in the morning. I'd left my car in the furthest
car park which is the long stay car park, as it was the
only one I could get near, and then I was stuck on a
bus load of holiday makers. The bus was stationary
and I kept checking my watch to see how long I had
to catch my flight.

As we were all stood there on the giant bendy bus, there was a shriek from halfway back. A man, who actually looked a bit worse for the drink, was clinging to a strap shouting. 'Let me off, let me off'. A few concerned passengers were calling to the driver. 'Let him off, he wants to get off'. The driver yelled back. 'No-one get's off this bus!' Everyone was now complaining about being stuck in the traffic. 'We're going to miss our flights'. Someone shouted. The driver yelled again. 'No-one get's off this bus!' 'It's Health & Safety Regulations!' There were a number of people walking with their cases alongside the bus, and they seemed to be getting ahead of us because we were only crawling along.

The pale man shouted again. 'I've got to get off!' But the driver was sticking to his guns, no-one was getting off his bus. Then another passenger yelled at the top of his voice. 'He's gonna be sick!' That shifted the driver, the doors flew open and someone shoved the man and his case onto the pavement, at last he was off into the fresh air. All the passengers quickly realised that there appeared to be nothing wrong with the man at all and he had quite a spring in his step as he dashed for the airport terminal which was now in sight. I checked my watch again, I'd been on this bus for a good half hour now and I was getting slightly agitated as EasyJet planes won't wait and you have to be through the check-in half hour before your flight. At last we were moving. Luckily I'd checked in online, so all I needed to do was get through security. That would be no mean feat in June with all the other holiday makers particularly on a Friday which is the busiest day.

The bus screeched to a halt and the door were flung open, I grabbed my case and made a dash for it. As usual I hadn't thought ahead and I was wearing heels. And not only heels but the worse type, the ones that slip off the back of your foot with every step. I was dragging my small case on wheels and running as best as I could in unsuitable footwear towards the revolving doors to the airport terminal.

As I dashed through my heel got caught in the carpet of the revolving door and I hurtled full length across the floor as a multitude of passengers trampled past me. I was now bright red in the face and I'd hurt my knee, no-one helped me but I leapt to my feet and made another dash for the escalator to take me to the security lounge.

I was puffing and panting and making a mental note that I need to lose weight and get in shape as I arrived to a heaving throng of jolly holiday makers all queuing in an up and down snake of a line which must have hundreds of people in it. It was going to take me ages; I glanced again at my watch. The flight would actually leaves in 30 minutes! I was never going to make it. Thankfully the queue was moving quite quickly. I'd got my shoes off, my coat off, iPod, camera, and mobile phone out and in the tray in preparation, along with my laptop which had to be scanned separately. I was relieved not to set off the alarm which usually happens when I go through an airport scanner. I was through! I dashed to the departure board to see which gate my flight was leaving from. 'Oh No! It was leaving from gate 1. And it actually said FINAL CALL in huge red letters. Gate one is about a twenty minute walk from the departure lounge, I was going to have to run.

Right I needed to get organised, I removed my coat again, pushed the trolley handle in on my case before picking it up and I kicked off my shoes. I was now in bear feet and I sprinted with every ounce of energy I had to the gate.

Picture the scene. I'm not of athletic build whatsoever and I'm certainly not light on my feet. So I was thundering along like a herd of buffalo down the corridor. People were ambling along with their children dragging trolleys and I was yelling 'Out of the way! Out of the way!' at the top of my voice as I galloped my way along like an elephant. I was struggling now to keep going and it seemed so far, I was at gate 5 by then, so four more gates and I'd be there. I almost knocked over an elderly couple as I charged along like a demented rhino.

I was extremely short of breath, and was blood red in the face as I came to a stop at the EasyJet desk. The girl looked startled as I flung my boarding card at her, puffing and panting trying to ask if the flight was still there. 'Yes, we're waiting' she stammered back.

I now had to follow her down a flight of stairs to the tarmac, where she pointed to the plane. I picked up all my stuff and galloped off again. The flight attendant was frantically waving to me and my legs were like jelly as I leapt up the stairs two at a time to the plane. Another attendant snatched my case from me and I was pushed into my seat on the front row, desperately trying to squeeze in between the two very large business men already seated. The plane was silent as every eye was on me for delaying the flight; I could hardly breathe as I sat down. The door immediately slammed shut and a stern voice came over the tannoy saying that now *all* passengers (ME) were on board we would be leaving momentarily.

The plane lurched forward and within seconds we were taxi-ing to the runway. How I made that flight without having a heart attack I'll never know!

(The super Dev Team – Me, Ian, Mariya,
Geoff, Kath, George & Ekta)

# Chapter 67

## 2009 – The Benidorm swingers

2009 was a big year for my sister. It was her 40$^{th}$ birthday and I had been trying to think of something memorable that I could give her as she was always very thoughtful with the family birthdays and always managed to think of something special. And then one night I was half asleep and I suddenly thought of the ideal memorable present, it was so obvious. I would take Sue to Spain with me for a long weekend. The more I thought about it the more convinced I was that a nice girly weekend would be a lot of fun for the both of us and it would be something to remember. The next day I booked the flights and told Sue, she was over the moon. I normally go to Benidorm every year with my Mum and Dad and son James but due to work commitments I had missed it this summer. So this weekend with Sue would make up for me missing my usual holiday, I would have to pack my usual 2 week's worth of fun into a long weekend.

At last the time for our holiday came. We stepped off the plane in Alicante into the hot sunshine and we started getting into the holiday mood. Our spirits had already been lifted by the many gin's and glasses of wine we'd already consumed in the airport and on the plane but now with the glorious weather we were raring to go. We boarded the bus for Benidorm and arrived about an hour later very hot and very sweaty as the air conditioning on the bus had broken down. There was nothing else for it; we would have to go to a bar for drink. Luckily the bus stop is quite near to the Terrace Bar which is owned by Paul a friend of ours so in we went. It was lunch time and he insisted we should have lunch with him before we went onto the hotel just down the road.

We really love Benidorm and as we've both been many times we know our way around the town. We are both addicted to the TV show 'Benidorm' staring Jonny Vegas, as we often recognise many of the places where they shoot the scenes, in fact the pool scenes are filmed at our usual hotel.

It was a great start to the holiday, lots of cooling lager at less than a Euro a pint and a good lunch with old friends. We were very merry as we staggered off to check in to our hotel.

Check in was like being met by old friends and we were soon heading for the pool with plenty more drinks. We spent the afternoon talking, dozing and eyeing up the local talent. Like all hotel swimming pools there was a mixture of holiday makers and locals. Some of the locals are employed in the hotel but many are friends of the manager who sneak into use the pool and chat up the holiday makers. We could tell how long the holiday makers had been there by the amount of 'tan' on their semi naked bodies, some were already peeling but others were still pastey white. As old hands at this game we had used the local tanning salon before flying out so we fitted in and to be honest we looked 'drop dead gorgeous' and were attracting some admiring glances from the guys around the pool. The sun was beginning to set so we headed back to our room via the local supermarket, The Dial Prix, to load up with supplies for our room. At less than 2 Euro's a bottle we stocked up with plenty of white and rose wine but we were keen to have a healthy holiday so we bought an apple each and some crisps. We continued drinking in the room as we changed before hitting the town. We had been drinking since about 5am and apart from lunch at Pauls we hadn't had much to eat so we were beginning to feel a little fragile.

The next day neither of us could remember much about the evening but we were sure we had a good time. I seem to remember Sue falling in the sea and me wading in to save her. Sue claims I wasn't helping at all but trying to push her under, I find that hard to believe but it's all a bit of a dream so who knows.

As we were feeling a little tender we went out to the local Geordie Bar for some breakfast before taking our first drink of the day. If the young ones on hen and stag parties can do this for 2 weeks, we were sure we could keep it up for 4 days.

After a much needed hearty breakfast we decided we needed souvenirs; after all it was Sue's 40th, so we walked into the town. For anyone who's been to Benidorm you'll know there's no shortage of overpriced and tacky trinkets, donkeys and memorabilia. We spent an hour wandering around the shops fending off the shopkeepers who kept telling about their bargains. And then we both saw it at the same time, it was a bright pink t-shirt with a printed logo saying 'I'm not 40 – I'm 22 with 18 years of experience' it would suit Sue perfectly so she had found her memento of her 40th holiday.

Our mission accomplished we gave up on shopping and headed back to the hotel pool. It was still boiling hot and we spent a quiet day relaxing just chatting and sunbathing with our legs dangling in the water, perhaps we're not as wild as we like to think we are. Then all of a sudden there was the thundering noise of someone running and all of a sudden I was launched directly into the freezing pool, right into the deep end, thank goodness I can swim! There was a gang of lads on a stag weekend messing around the pool so as I was swimming to the surface I assumed that it must be one of them larking about.  As I surfaced there's a grinning maniac on the side of the pool next to Sue with his equally mad wife screaming with laughter and pointing at me in the water. Well we don't mind a bit of fun and there was no harm done apart from the fact that my hair was now plastered to my head and I was shivering as the pool was freezing, like all Spanish hotel pools. Anyway we got chatting to them and found out that he was a Geordie and she's Scottish and although he said he was 59 and she's 39, they both looked like they're in their 50s not that it mattered, they seemed very nice and in fact remind us of the two swingers Donald and Jacqueline in the Benidorm programme, especially as that character is also Scottish.

We spent the afternoon with them by the pool and we had a good time talking about our families and backgrounds.  We explained that we were sisters and that it was Sue's 40th birthday that very day. They were amazed because we looked so different. I'm a rather buxom voluptuous girl of about 5'7' and I have jet black hair. Sue is the complete opposite; she is tiny, about a size 8 dress with long blonde hair and only 5'3' tall. Although we have the same Mum and Dad when we were kids I used to tell Sue that she was adopted, I used to tease her, Sue would cry and she seemed to believe me until Mum found out and told her I was lying.

Anyway we seemed to get on so well with this odd couple that we decided to go out as a foursome in the evening. We were on floor twelve and they were on floor ten so we decided that we would go down to their room when we are ready at about 7ish. We had downed another bottle and a half of wine while we were getting ready and this along with the beers we'd had in the afternoon meant that we were already in a great mood for going out to celebrate Sue's actual birthday.

We decided we were ready, it would be impossible to look any more gorgeous than we did. I leant over the balcony and yelled, 'Charlooooootttttt!' at the top of my voice and there she appeared looking up to me.

'Are you ready' she asked

'Sure are' I replied, 'we'll come down now'

And off we went. All day they had been complaining to us that Spanish Vodka and Bacardi tasted funny and had we noticed. We just agreed and said it not too bad if you use proper coke, but we couldn't say we'd noticed any difference. Their room was identical to ours and we were soon sitting on the balcony discussing where we're going for the evening. We know quite a few bars and I kept going on about seeing Sticky Vicky who everyone else seems to have seen, including my retired parents and my son, but I'd not. Vicky Leyton is in her 70s and she's been doing her act in Benidorm for years, she's otherwise known as Sticky Vicky and she is a very famous act, anyone who's been to Benidorm will now be sniggering. If you've never been I can only describe Sticky Vicky as an adult magic show. She performs completely naked and all I can say is it's not a rabbit she pulls out of a hat. But she does pull various objects out of a very unusual place!

Jimmy was a rather large chap very friendly well a bit too friendly, but there seemed to be no harm in him, after all we were there with his wife and they had a family back home and all seem quite down to earth. He was thrusting drinks at us, mine was vodka and coke and Sue's was Bacardi and coke and I think Charlotte had Vodka too. We all sat around chatting for about half an hour and all seemed fine, except that on second thoughts we agreed with them that the Vodka and Bacardi did taste a bit strange. Between you and me it tasted like rocket fuel, God knows how many measures he'd put in the glasses but it was certainly blowing my head off.

And unbelievably that's where the story ends... our minds are blank, neither Sue nor I have any recollection of the rest of the evening apart from a few hazy moments. I recall being violently sick over a wall and Sue remembers sitting in a very shiny chrome bar but that's all we can remember.

We woke up the next morning to discover we were both in the same room but we had no recollection of getting there or any real memory of the evening before apart from arriving at Jimmy and Charlotte's room.

So it would seem that we had Rohypnol and cokes all round, we thought the drinks tasted funny. We didn't see the swingers again until the Monday and they filled in a few of the gaps, apparently we arrived at the Jokers Bar (that's the chrome Sue remembers) and had a drink each. I then said I needed to go outside for some fresh air as I wasn't feeling too good, that's apparently when I was vomiting over the wall. It then seems that we wandered off in separate directions. Some of this stacks up, but going home separately doesn't, as only one of us had a key and I doubt if Sue would have been able to find her way back to the hotel on her own. But it would seem that no harm was done, we both felt ok and as nothing untoward seemed to have happened to either of us we put it down to being completely legless.

It was only a few days later when Sue was regaling the story to Norman and his wife some friends back in St Helens when Norman said, 'Was his name Jimmy and her name something like Claire?' Sue was astonished and said 'She was called Charlotte' and then Norman said 'That's her. They were in Turkey last year and the same thing happened to us...'

So it was a holiday to remember even if we can't remember the details – they really were like 'Jacqueline and Donald' the characters from 'Benidorm'.

*(Sue's 40ᵗʰ)*

# Chapter 68

## 2009 - Penna partay

Well my book is almost finished I've been writing it a couple of months now and the last thing I expected as Christmas 2009 is approaching that there will be any more chapters to add to the book. It was the Penna London Christmas party on the south side of the Thames at Tower Bridge. We'd had an excellent time as usual and the free bar was very busy. They are a great group of people to work with and I'm lucky that I also enjoy socialising with them. My best mate at work is Kath, she is our gorgeous Sharepoint Developer. She lives up on the moors just outside Manchester and we share fantastic conversations about my gay dogs and her beautiful horse Snip. We're both Northern lasses and share the same humour. Snip is a thoroughbred horse and Kath's pride and joy, however she's extremely, shall we say 'highly strung' and Kath spends most weekends like a rodeo cowgirl galloping at full throttle across the moors, or while Snip is rearing up like Champion the Wonder Horse, clinging on for dear life, so there's always a good story to share on a Monday after our team meeting where Kath and I have a good post weekend catch up.

We both headed off from the party to find a taxi we were very drunk and very happy as we arrived back at our hotel. We were staying at the Tower Guoman sharing a twin room up on the ninth floor. It was a lovely executive twin room with all mod cons and decorated in cream and yellow stripes and when we got back we chatted for a while before we went off to sleep.

I don't know how long I had been asleep before I was woken by Kath violently shaking the hell out of me and a siren screaming its head off. I tried to get my eyes working and finally focussed on Kath with what looked like half of the smoke detector in her hand she seemed to be trying to dismantle the rest.

'What's going on... what time is it?' I groaned.

Kath was panicking 'I don't know but this smoke alarm is going off, I can't stop it'

'Well what have you done to set it off' I asked, adopting my long suffering parent voice.

'Nothing, it wasn't me, the damn thing just woke me up' Kath went on.

'Oh please stop it, my head is banging, we're gonna get in trouble' I yelled back over the din of the alarm.

I staggered out of my bed and climbed up on to the bed to get a look at the alarm, surely all we had to do was pull out the battery. But this was no ordinary smoke alarm, it was all wired in and there were no batteries to pull out. Eventually I gave up and left it screaming and stumbled back into bed pulling my pillow over my head. I don't remember any more or what Kath did.

The next morning we woke up to find bits of the smoke alarm littered around the room so we collected them together and hid them at the bottom of the waste basket before going down for a lovely full English breakfast. We had forgotten all about the alarm when we packed up our things and went down to check out.

'Did you enjoy your stay at the Tower ladies?' the hotel receptionist asked.

'Yes lovely thank you' both Kath and I chanted together.

'Sorry about the fire alarm going off in the night, we apologise for the disturbance and you having to be evacuated' she told us.

'Evacuated?' Kath and I glanced at each other.

'Yes we had to evacuate the hotel, there were over twelve hundred guests in the assembly points, we are sorry because it was so cold last night'.

'We didn't come out, was there a fire?' I asked beginning to realise what had happened.

'No, there wasn't a fire, it was just set off accidentally by a guest breaking the glass but you should have come down to reception' the receptionist smiled.

'Oh no, we thought it was a faulty smoke alarm in our room..'

Luckily for us the receptionist just laughed and we made a hasty departure from the hotel. There's always a drama where I am... you've probably noticed.

# Chapter 69

## 2010 – Breakdown

You may be thinking after all these years and such a collection of stories the title of this chapter is where I actually have a nervous breakdown. I've often wondered what triggers a breakdown as my life has certainly had plenty of events that could have driven me to the Jeremy Kyle show, but thankfully so far so good.

This particular morning I was working from home as usual, I really enjoy working from home, some days I work all day in my pyjamas and I'm ashamed to say some times I don't even brush my hair. No one is visiting and I'm not going anywhere so why bother? Perish the thought of what some of my colleagues would think when we're in our online web conferences when I'm sitting there in my dressing gown, but I'm sure I'm not the only person working from home who does this.

This winter had been a particularly cold one and we've had a lot of snow in Buckinghamshire so this particular day I'm dressed in bright pink pyjamas, fluffy pink and white dressing gown and pink slippers. As usual James was running late for college where he's training to be a mechanic. He usually gets the train from our local station at Wolverton, just two stops to Bletchley where his college is next to the train station, it's only about an eight minute journey. On a Tuesday it's just a half day at college and he's due to be in at one fifteen, but as he had missed his train, I had told him I would drive him there during my lunch break and he could get the train home, all was agreed.

So rather than rush to get dressed I threw a giant fleece over my dressing gown, shoved on my son's Swedish style woolly bob hat adorned with plaited ear flaps and a pair of Uggs, I grabbed my phone and purse and dashed out to the car before any neighbours saw me.

I hadn't been driving much during the last couple of weeks as there has been so much snow, but the roads were pretty clear now even though it was still bitterly cold. We got to the college in about fifteen minutes and I laughed at my reflection in the rear view mirror as I looked back to see James waving to me. What a state I looked in this get up, James must be embarrassed, thank goodness for the tinted windows.

I was just going past the football stadium in Bletchley and was about to get onto the A5 north to go back home when there was an almighty clunk from under the back of the car and the engine sounded like it was screaming. I pulled hastily into a bus stop just ahead and shut the engine down. 'What on earth was that?' I thought to myself, I looked at the petrol gauge (this is my only mechanical knowledge), which was registering half full, so it was nothing to do with fuel, no other warning lights were on, except for the flashing airbag light which has been on constantly since I bought the car.

What it actually felt like was that the clutch cable had gone. I wasn't too worried as a few months before, the clutch cable went on my sister's little fiat, and I managed to drive that home for her in second gear all I needed to do was bump it into gear and I would be off. So I tried, now this seemed to be something completely different as when I put it in gear and let the clutch out there was that almighty screaming sound again and the car only inched forward. I tried again and appeared to only be rolling towards the traffic lights, perhaps I'd make it.

No such luck the car ground to a halt and now I was wedged half on the road and half in the snow on the side verge. There was nothing for it, this car wasn't going anywhere. So with my hazard lights flashing I sat there thinking.

I was very sorry to say that there was actually no-one who could help me. Although James is training to be a mechanic, he doesn't have a tow truck or the skills to get me going at the moment. Anyone I know with a car who could perhaps tow me with a rope was in work themselves and my cheeky comment to the RAC man recruiting outside Tesco's the other day of 'No ta mate I'm in the D..A..D I'll phone him if I need help' was ringing in my ears; as Dad lives 160 miles away in St Helens and I couldn't possibly call him to tow me home.

Luckily I had my phone on me, and what I needed was a breakdown truck to get me home, I'd sort out getting whatever needed fixing later, but I needed to get home, after all I had only nipped out on my lunch break, I was supposed to be working! So as usual the only people who could help me were Mum and John. So I immediately called.

'Oh John, it's you, I've broken down in Bletchley God only knows what's wrong with the car but I need a tow truck, can Mum look one up on the internet and give me a telephone number please?' I pleaded down the phone.

It's your eldest, she's broken down in Bletchley, here get hold of this phone, she needs a recovery truck' John yelled at Mum.

Mum came on the line 'What's up love?' she asked.

I repeated the whole story and tried to cut to the chase that she needed to Google car recovery Milton Keynes and give me some numbers. Mum's very adept with the internet and immediately got me 2 numbers so we ended the call and I got onto phoning them.

The first number was unobtainable and the second was a fax machine which screeched down the line, in my haste I'd panicked Mum and she'd read out incorrect numbers. So I got back on and relayed all this back to her.

'Just phone the RAC and tell them you're not a member or the AA or Green Flag, we're in Green Flag we get it free with our Advantage Gold Account with NatWest'. Mum rambled on not realising I was half blocking the road at traffic lights and time was of the essence.

'Yes, yes Mum, could you just go back to Google and find me some recovery numbers again though, I don't think the RAC will help' I pleaded with her.

'She can't phone the RAC, she's not a member, I keep telling her to join'. I could hear John shouting at the top if his voice. 'She spends all that bloody money on Sky in every room, she should have breakdown cover' he ranted on.

I know he's right my priorities never seem correct and I made another mental note to cancel Sky Sports. What would my son Marc say?

Mum was getting a bit frantic and insisted I call the RAC to see if they would pick me up so I took the number. I was sat there after pressing 1 for this and 2 for that then listening for over 8 minutes to the recorded voice which kept telling me that due to the inclement weather all their operators were helping someone else and they hoped not to keep me waiting too long. It dawned on me that instead of ringing Mum and Dad and upsetting them I should have rung one of those 118 numbers that find you exactly what you want. Immediately I was singing '118 24 7... give them a call... its directory heaven.'

I hung up on the RAC and gave the Yellow Pages a call 118 247. And as advertised immediately they gave me the number of three breakdown recovery organisations in Milton Keynes plus they text me the numbers. I had got a pen and paper in the car and I got back on to Mum to tell her I was sorted.

'Oh what a good idea I never thought of you ringing them, and both Mum and I were now singing the Directory Heaven song. All seemed fine.

So I called the first number, Barry answered 'Sorry love we're snowed under' I pardoned his pun, it hadn't occurred to me that every breakdown truck along with the RAC, AA and Mum's beloved Green Flag would be busy due to the vast amounts of snow and ice. 'Call this number' Barry went on, 'His name is Andy and tell him Barry told you to call'. So as instructed by the very helpful Barry, I then called Andy.

Andy was also very helpful and said he'd be with me in 30 to 45 minutes. 'Oh what a relief'. I thanked Andy profusely and hung up. The engine would still run on the car and the seats are heated so thankfully I was plenty warm enough as it was well below freezing outside, so I was going to be fine until Andy and his breakdown truck arrived.

I put the radio on and prepared to sit and wait. While I was sitting there I could do a bit of work as my phone is a PDA and I can access my emails so that would pass the time. It also occurred to me that my boss would wonder where I was if he tried to get hold of me, so I called him. Geoff is very understanding and I knew he'd be sympathetic and probably wouldn't be surprised by the fact that I have yet another minor catastrophe in my life. Geoff's phone went to voicemail so I left him a message explaining what had happened. I took a couple of calls from colleagues one being from Mark our IT Support Manager, who is also privy to my catastrophic lifestyle but he wished me luck and advised me not to get too cold while I was waiting.

Oh Hell! I then realised that I was in my pyjamas and dressing gown with the most ridiculous hat on. Oh well, there was nothing I could do about it and the breakdown driver wouldn't know me, so who cares!

My mind started to wander and I remembered that my sister Sue and I had seen a family of what could only be described as oven ready turkeys on the side of the M6 the day after Boxing Day. A family of five had obviously broken down on the motorway and were safely out of their car which was on the hard shoulder; they had climbed up the grass embankment for safety and were wrapped in gold coloured emergency foil survival blankets. Sue and I had a good laugh at these poor souls, but thinking on now, they looked far more appropriately dressed than I was in this silly hat and dressing gown. Well there was nothing I could do about my attire; I'd just have to front it out.

Well time had been ticking on and I looked up to see a recovery truck flying past with the driver waving enthusiastically to me. I saw that as a signal that he would be dropping the car off that was on the back of his truck and he'd coming back to get me. With that I immediately called Mum to stop her from worrying. Ten minutes later the very nice man Andy was pulling up in front of my car. I stepped out of the car and he raised his eyebrows but tactfully didn't say anything about my appearance he just asked me what had happened to the car. I explained and he suggested after trying to get it into gear that it appeared to be the drive shaft or the clutch. Mum had already suggested that, which I completely ignored at the time as I assumed her vehicle mechanics knowledge would be nil just like mine, but she was right of course. The clutch or drive shaft it was, whatever that is? I assisted Andy in pushing what seemed to be the heaviest car in the world off the snow covered verge and onto the flat of the road, in the most unsuitable footwear known to man after slippers – Ugg boots. I'd have got more grip in flip flops and Andy was spending more time assisting me after falling over half a dozen times than he spent getting the car on the back of his tow truck.

At last I climbed into his cab with my phone and purse and off we went, thank the Lord! As we were heading up the A5 I noticed that Andy was glancing to me every now and again. I was dressed ridiculously so could expect little else but when I looked at him properly I realised that I knew him! Could this get any worse I thought to myself. 'I know you don't I?' I asked. 'Didn't you used to be the landlord of the Galleon in Wolverton Mill?' 'Yeah, you're Alan's girlfriend aren't you?' I was extremely embarrassed then. 'Yes, that's right, Alan is managing a pub of his own in Camden now, The Fiddler's Elbow' I tried to diffuse my embarrassment by waffling on about another subject.

I didn't have enough money on me to pay for the tow truck so Andy pulled into the local petrol station where there was a cash point, everyone was looking at me as I got out of the cab in my pyjamas and dressing gown and dashed to the cash machine. Well we made it back to my house and I handed over his forty pounds. We exchanged a glance and he gave me his card. He was kind enough not to mention my attire.

# Chapter 70

## …. and finally… MK Dons the Away Booth

Not satisfied with being a single Mum with 3 grown up children, the owner of two dogs and a demanding full time career, but I also have a second job which I first started with MK Dons when they were at the old Hockey Stadium in Central Milton Keynes.

I worked behind the bar in the conferencing suite with my French colleague Stephane, but sometimes Stephane and I would work in the Sports bar, where the beer frothed out of the pumps so ferociously we had almost decided to start wearing Wellington boots whilst serving beer.

The Hockey Stadium was always a temporary home and the MK Dons moved to a brand new state of the art stadium in Bletchley, to the south of Milton Keynes so that brought an end to having soggy shoes behind the bar every Saturday afternoon.

Stephane and I were originally agency staff and when the football club moved locations we continued to work for the agency at our new site. Stephane was eventually employed full time by MK Dons but I remained as agency staff as I had my full time job and only wanted to work the odd shift when it suited me.

The agency continued with its contract and I worked at the new bar in the corporate hospitality suite. One evening they were short of staff in the ticket office and

Mark, the General Manager, asked if I wouldn't mind working in there for the evening. I didn't mind at all and was looking forward to doing something different for a change. It was a good evening and I met my new friend John who was a regular in the away ticket booth, he had started selling 'away tickets' at the first ever 'Dons' game at the old Hockey Stadium when MK Dons were originally Wimbledon FC. We had a good laugh and I hoped we'd be working together again another time.

The following week I received a phone call from Gayle, the ticket office manager, saying that the agency had lost the contract because they'd sent a lot of foreign staff and most of them couldn't speak English. Gayle offered me a job working in the away booth with my new friend John. I was really pleased; I think John must have put in a good word and so the following Saturday I was back selling tickets. As a life-long Liverpool fan I've always been interested in football and now I could watch it regularly and get paid for the privilege. All I had to hope for now is that either MK Dons would be promoted to the premier league or they'd draw Liverpool in the FA Cup. Happy days!

The away booth is a funny little place located near to the entrance gate for the away fans; it comprises a couple of rooms, one with two cash windows and a back room for storage or counting money. It doesn't have any direct access to the main stadium so we have to use an outside door when we leave with the takings. John and I are stationed at two cash windows very much like a post office counter. We have been at the new stadium for three years and we still have a bare concrete floor which is very cold underfoot so we wear boots to keep our feet warm. There's a small heater but we've resorted to bringing in additional fan heaters just to keep from freezing to death. Some of the ceiling tiles are missing due to a leak, which we watched develop over a few weeks. It first just looked like a small brown stain, as if someone had been working in the ceiling space and perhaps knocked over a cup of coffee or tea. The following weeks the stain got bigger and bigger and the smell in there was awful. Eventually on day we came in for an evening match and the ceiling was bulging and looked like it was going to burst, so we called for maintenance again and it was arranged that someone would fix it. The following week when we returned we could see exactly what had been leaking, it was a soil waste coming from an upstairs toilet, thank goodness that ceiling hadn't come through on us, as it seemed to have been full of effluent – we now knew what the awful smell was and we still have missing ceiling tiles!

The internal lighting is fine for afternoon games but when we sell tickets for evening games we are unable to see out of the booth and customers suddenly appear in front of us from the blackness. It feels like being in a zoo but from the animal's view of the world. We are on show for the passing fans and we often see them pointing and laughing.  The counter has two stainless steel trays that fill with water when it rains and the internal worktop is just a little too wide for Johns little arms to reach the money tray. John and I have to speak through little microphones as do the fans when purchasing their tickets. Considering the Club Sponsors at the time of construction were Marshall Amplification, you'd imagine a good sound system would be in place but sadly no. John's voice comes through his speaker sounding like a robot and I spend most of the evening shouting at the fans as I can hardly hear them and they can't hear me due to the wind whistling through the microphone and the constant feedback if we turn it up too high.

We also have to put up with the bird mess that is splattered on the outside window ledge and against the windows. In fact recently an unfortunate Leighton

353

Orient fan was s\*\*t on from a great height whilst purchasing his ticket due to the roosting overhead. This latest season we've had Cathy a little Irish lady come cleaning the ledge and cash tray so that we and the fans don't have to pass money and change through the bird poo or water and get it all over our hands. We can never understand a word of what she says, mainly due to her strong accent but also the interference of the sound system so we just nod in the right places as she is scrubbing the window ledge and windows.

The fans are a strange group of individuals and although it's not fair to generalise there are a number of distinct types that visit our booth.

We have the typical football thug who normally arrives a few minutes before kick-off and then complains because there is a queue. When he arrives at the window the strong smell of alcohol tells us that he has just left the pub. At this point they are either offensive making personal comments or they are past caring and throw money into the tray shouting 'ghee us a ticket'.

We also have the telepathic customers who just stand there assuming that you know what they want because they have looked at you. There is an even more frustrating variant that doesn't even look at you but still assumes you know exactly what they want.

Then we have the 'show off' customers who think the act of buying tickets is an opportunity to impress their friends by being very witty and making the assistant (us) look stupid. We can normally turn this one around by making them repeat their request by pretending not to be able t hear them – this makes them confused and normally their friends jump in to help, it's great fun. One particularly rude customer referred to John and I as 'the beauty and the beast' and John with his quick thinking humour retorted 'If he calls you a beast again don't serve him Siân'.

And then we have the historian who tells us all about Wimbledon and how the club should have stayed in London, as I understand it that wasn't an option. They drone on and on and we sometime hold up a hand to stop them and say 'Do you want a ticket or not? There is a queue you know' – that normally shuts them up.

There are also a small number of fans that really shouldn't be allowed out on their own and they can be very frustrating as all they want to do is talk while we are trying to sell tickets.

But to be fair most of the fans are very nice people who are polite and clearly state what they want, give us the right money and even say thank you.

As we sit in our goldfish bowl we spend quite a lot of time 'fan watching' and we often know they type of fan to expect based on the club we are playing. South coast teams like Torquay have lots of senior citizens other places have fans with six fingers on each hand and a few dwarves, but it all adds to the hilarity.

We have some regular callers too. Jimmy the cop is a favourite and he always wants some of our fruit pastilles. He used to have a female colleague who seemed to have a bit of a thing for me, but after a while I started hiding in the back room and when John shouted that the coast was clear I'd return to my post. She must have put in for a transfer as we've not seen her for ages, perhaps I broke her heart. Next to visit is Andy from Marketing, he's always smiling, pleasant and friendly and enquires how many tickets we've sold and if we are OK for change.

It's also quite good fun watching the car park staff direct traffic with their Gestapo type authority, they often bang on our window demanding we move our own cars six inches to the left or right and now they also have to contend with McDonalds drive through traffic following the opening of the new branch opposite the stadium, it's all very confusing for them.

Why did I write this you may be asking? Well over the years when something has happened or a conversation has started on a particular subject, I seem to have the awful habit of saying 'You know what? Something like that happened to me.....'. My friends have often said 'You should write a book Siân, how could all this happen to one person?'

Well one day at Stadium MK John and I sat in our little booth when something happened, maybe a customer made a remark or we talked about something and my one liner came out again. 'Wait till I tell you what happened when...'. But on this particular day when John said the words that many have said in the past 'You should write a book'. I replied 'Not you too, I don't think I could make it into a book It's only funny when I tell people and it's not all been funny'. 'I could help you.' John replied. 'I've helped write books before, granted they're about slaughter houses but I know how to put the structure together'.

'Are you serious? I asked him. Again my mind started to wander. 'Oh you could be my ghost writer.' I laughed. 'I'd be like the character from that television programme Little Britain, who is like Barbara Cartland wearing a pink negligee and I'd dictate to you. 'Chapter 28... The End'.

We both burst out laughing and then went into detail of how John could bring a Chaise longue into the booth and I'd bring a screen, I'd throw a stocking enticingly over the top and would dictate to John as he sold tickets for MK Dons at the same time.

That's where the plan was hatched to write this book. In the away booth at MK Dons!

# Epilogue

So that's how it started, John talked me into it and we've had many an 'editorial meeting', along with his wife Ellen laughing over the content. There's always a drama where I am... you've probably noticed.

(My lovely family – left to right, Me,
Kate, James and Marc at the famous
'Concrete Cows' in Milton Keynes)

I hope you enjoyed my stories, I only wanted a quiet life but as you can see I've been falling from one calamity into another, but I have a lovely family around me which keeps me going. Let's see what the next thirty years brings.

THE END

# About the Author

Siân Banks is divorced and lives in Buckinghamshire with her 3 grown up children and 2 dogs. Born in Holyhead, Anglesey in 1966, and raised by her mother and grandparents in Merseyside.

Siân now works in London for an HR Consultancy in the IT department managing the support of the company websites and applications.

This is a collection of funny stories based on true events that have occurred since Siân left school in 1982, there is also a darker side where she was a victim of domestic violence and abuse and what she did to change her life and that of her children. It continues in good humour until the present day, that being 2010 and has been written for Siân's family and friends.

18195607R00220

Printed in Great Britain
by Amazon